Deaf Students and the School-to-Work Transition

Deaf Students and the School-to-Work Transition

by

Thomas E. Allen, Ph.D.
Brenda W. Rawlings, B.A.
Arthur N. Schildroth, M.A.

Center for Assessment
and Demographic Studies
Gallaudet University

with invited contributors

·PAUL·H·
BROOKES
PUBLISHING Co Baltimore • London • Toronto • Sydney

Paul H. Brookes Publishing Co.
Post Office Box 10624
Baltimore, Maryland 21285-0624

Copyright © 1989 by Paul H. Brookes Publishing Co., Inc.
All rights reserved.

Typeset by Brushwood Graphics, Inc., Baltimore, Maryland.
Manufactured in the United States of America by
Thomson-Shore, Inc., Dexter, Michigan.

Library of Congress Cataloging in Publication Data
Allen, Thomas Eugene.
    Deaf students and the school-to-work transition / by Thomas E.
Allen, Brenda W. Rawlings, Arthur N. Schildroth ; with invited
contributors.
        p.   cm.
    Bibliography: p.
    Includes index.
    ISBN 1-55766-020-4
    1. Deaf—Employment—United States.   2. High school
graduates—Employment—United States.   3. College graduates—
Employment—United States.   4. Vocational guidance—United
States.   I. Rawlings, Brenda W.   II. Schildroth, Arthur N.,
1927–   .   III. Title.
HV2504.5.U6A38   1989
331.5′9—dc19   89-871
                                                                CIP

Contents

Contributors

Thomas E. Allen
Center for Assessment and
  Demographic Studies
Gallaudet Research Institute
Gallaudet University
Washington, DC 20002

Patricia Stoney Brown
Vice-President, American Society for
  Deaf Children
1000 Broward Road
Jacksonville, FL 32218

Marita M. Danek
Professor of Counseling and Director
  of Rehabilitation Counseling
  (Deafness) Program
104 Fowler Hall
Gallaudet University
Washington, DC 20002

Delwyn L. Harnisch
Associate Professor of Educational
  Psychology
Secondary Transition Research
  Institute
University of Illinois at Urbana-
  Champaign
51 Gerty Drive
Champaign, IL 61820

William P. McCrone
Professor of Counseling
Fowler Hall
Gallaudet University
Washington, DC 20002

Jacqueline Z. Mendelsohn
Board Member
American Society for Deaf Children
4120 Leland Street
Chevy Chase, MD 20815

Brenda W. Rawlings
Center for Assessment and
  Demographic Studies
Gallaudet Research Institute
Gallaudet University
Washington, DC 20002

Arthur N. Schildroth
Center for Assessment and
  Demographic Studies
Gallaudet Research Institute
Gallaudet University
Washington, DC 20002

Carol Bloomquist Traxler
Center for Assessment and
  Demographic Studies
Gallaudet Research Institute
Gallaudet University
Washington, DC 20002

Gloria Wright
Arkansas Division of Rehabilitation
  Services
7th and Main
Doneghey Plaza, North
Little Rock, AR 72203

Foreword

In 1983, the U.S. Department of Education, Office of Special Education and Rehabilitative Services (OSERS), launched a national initiative to provide interventions that would facilitate the transition from public school to work for youth with handicaps. Transition was defined as

> an outcome-oriented process encompassing a broad array of services and experiences which lead to employment. Transition is a period that includes high school, the point of graduation, additional post-secondary education or adult services, and the initial years in employment. Transition is a bridge between the security and structure offered by the school and the opportunities and risks of adult life.[1]

Variations on this basic conception have been developed to articulate the specific nature of transition from school to work and to wider community life. The transitional period is a demanding phase that requires the cooperation of numerous service providers, including special education, vocational education, and vocational rehabilitation, as well as labor, employers, and the family.

Competitive employment has been viewed as the most desirable outcome of the transition process, coupled with the capacity to live independently, socialize, and engage in community life. Some professionals have argued that the primary focus on competitive employment is misdirected and that the primary objective should be independent living, irrespective of employment status. Regardless, competitive employment remains the critical objective of the transition initiative implemented by the federal government.

The transition initiative gained legitimacy and support when Congress authorized funding to support transitional services for youth with handicaps with the Education of the Handicapped Act Amendments of 1983, PL 98-199, Section 626. Section 626, entitled "Secondary Education and Transitional Services for Handicapped Youth," was to strengthen and coordinate education, training, and related services to assist in the transition process and to stimulate the development and improvement of programs in secondary special education. This initiative included expanded provisions for transitional services, removal of work disincentives in Social Security laws, employer incentives in the form of job-targeted tax credits, counseling and vocational education services, and the removal of unfair wage practices with the Fair Labor Standards Act. In all, the attainment of competitive employment for individuals with disabilities, including

---

[1]Will, M. (1984, March–April). Bridges from school to working life. *Programs for the Handicapped*, (2), 105.

youth exiting public education, became the key objective of the federal disabilities policies.

The emergence of transition to work can be seen as a historical development consistent with the values underlying current federal education policy. The main purpose of education as a social institution is the integration of the next generation into societal structures. The very existence of the society is dependent upon the ability of its education system to *integrate* the young into its sociocultural structure. Schools accomplish this through the processes of cultural, political, and economic stabilization. In a postindustrial society as complex as that of the United States, integration is virtually impossible without formal schooling.

Historically, particular groups have been denied equal access to the education system. This denial has meant that ethnic and racial minorities, and individuals with handicaps (for the most part) have not been integrated into the mainstream of American society. The federal transition initiative is part of an evolving effort aimed at guaranteeing formal education to those citizens with handicaps to ensure their full participation in society.

However, in a society dominated by the pursuit of material wealth, the most important criterion for successful integration is the ability to gain and retain competitive employment. Without it, one is left at the fringes of society. In a capitalistic society, making the successful transition from school to work is essential for the achievement of full community membership.

Viewed in this context, the transition initiative was the logical next step in the historical development of federal special education policy. The first step was to ensure that all children with handicaps were given equal education opportunities, and the next was to ensure their access to employment. However, in a free-market economy, strongly resistant to government intervention, ensuring equal employment opportunities is a more complex undertaking because it has two dimensions: individual and social. The individual dimension focuses upon the preparation of the individual for employment, including the process of economic socialization conducted by the schools and adult service providers. The primary focus of the transition initiative has been on this dimension, acting as a reform movement in special education, vocational education, and vocational rehabilitation to better prepare youth with handicaps for employment.

The second, and possibly more important, dimension is the social, which encompasses the social structures that govern the labor market. The employment initiative of the 99th Congress was designed to have an impact on this dimension by removing work disincentives and by creating incentives in the labor market to increase the employment of individuals with handicaps.

As educators, our professional concern centers primarily on the individual and on providing better services to prepare students for employment and independent living. As citizens and policy analysts, our concern shifts to the social dimension, to advocate for a more equitable distribution of social goods and resources.

The transition period has become a primary point of concern because it leads to individual attainment of economic self-sufficiency and social acclimation. Focusing our efforts, as a nation, on transition from school to work will affect the lives of youth with handicaps who, like all youth, view the postschool years as a time when individual pursuits are fulfilled by becoming a contributing member of our society.

Delwyn L. Harnisch, Ph.D.
Institute for Research on Human Development
University of Illinois at Urbana-Champaign

Preface

For 20 years the Center for Assessment and Demographic Studies at Gallaudet University's Research Institute has collected information on the demographic and educational characteristics of hearing impaired children. The center's Annual Survey of Hearing Impaired Children and Youth has been the chief instrument for this data collection activity and has been the basis for most of the other work conducted by the center: studies on the achievement of deaf children, including the establishing of norms for the Stanford Achievement Test; examinations of the communication methods used by deaf students and their teachers; descriptions of the postsecondary opportunities open to these students; special state studies monitoring their placement and educational progress; and collaboration with other researchers and agencies using the Annual Survey as a sampling framework for their own work. Much of the 20-year history of the Annual Survey has been summarized in a book published in 1986, *Deaf Children in America* (Schildroth & Karchmer).

Perhaps no project of the center has been more challenging than the present study of the transition of deaf students from high school into their postsecondary careers. This transition is, as most passages in human lives, usually a time of stress and uncertainty, a period of intense anticipation and pervading doubt. For researchers trying to understand the transition of young adults into the larger community, it is a complex issue. Who can say when transition begins or when it ends? Does it even have a beginning or an end? How does one describe and analyze all the interactions of all the persons and agencies and groups involved in transition and then offer some insight into this process? Anyone who has collected survey information, as in the case of this book and its survey methodology, knows the temptation to oversimplify, to slant the picture from a particular point of view because the realities "out there" are so interconnected and so puzzling.

The transition of deaf high school students is, if that is possible, even more complex. Their transitions are the transitions of all men and women, hearing and deaf. However, they are permeated by the special quality of the deaf experience. Deaf persons—those born deaf or deafened at an early age—have developed a community of their own, a community with its own language and its own culture. They often experience a transition into their postsecondary careers and into the community of hearing workers and supervisors that is unlike the school-to-career transitions of hearing persons, a transition that involves the central issue of communication, of how one receives and interprets the world.

An insight into this unique transition experience of deaf students is what the chapters of this book aim to provide. Chapter 1 reviews history and legislation related to the transition issue in general and to the transition of deaf youth in particular; the authors discuss the mandate for transition services and try to separate the myths about this process from the reality. Chapter 2, written by two parents of deaf students, has no "myth"; it documents the "reality" of transition as experienced in their families. Chapter 3, written by the president of the American Deafness and Rehabilitation Association, reviews the issue of transition of deaf youth from the perspective of the rehabilitation profession; though not a response to the parents' chapter, it takes up some of the issues raised there and throws a somewhat different light on those issues.

Chapters 4, 5, 6, and 7 explore the information collected in two surveys, the focus of which was the transition of deaf high school students. Chapter 4 reviews technical aspects of the two surveys—reasons for the study, study methodology, development of survey forms, and characteristics of the study sample. Because demographic information on these students was collected over a 2-year period in the Annual Survey, it was possible to study differences between the students who left the schools and those who stayed. These patterns of "leaving" and "staying" are examined in Chapter 5.

The first survey, sent to the school counselors of deaf students, inquired about specific areas of vocational training of their students, about tracking of students and the cooperation of outside agencies in vocational training, and about the employment of these students while still in school. Results from this survey are examined in Chapter 6. A second survey asked deaf students themselves about their employment—kinds of jobs they obtained, hours worked per week, their pay—and about their experiences with rehabilitation agencies. The results of this survey are described in Chapter 7.

Assessment and the uses of testing for placement and tracking purposes is a major issue in the education and transition of deaf students: what tests are used with deaf students, how reliable these tests are, who interprets the results. Chapter 8 takes up this sensitive area, analyzing results from the counselor survey and reviewing individual achievement, vocational, and social-emotional tests used frequently with deaf students. Chapter 9 discusses results from a third survey conducted by the center, a survey of high school programs enrolling deaf students about their relationship to state rehabilitation agencies and the services provided to deaf students by these agencies.

A final chapter, Chapter 10, weaves together some of the many separate strands found in this book and attempts to create from these strands a coherent pattern of the transition of deaf students. Other patterns will result from other studies. (A follow-up study to the student survey described here has been completed; sent to the same students and to their parents 1 year later, the survey's results had not yet been published by the time of this writing.) No one pattern can "explain" this transition process for deaf students or provide "answers" to the problems uncovered in the complex relationships involved in this transition. It is hoped that the clarity and coherence of all the patterns will influence present and future policy decisions made in regard to the transition of deaf youth.

REFERENCES

Schildroth, A., & Karchmer, M. (Eds.). (1986). *Deaf Children in America*. San Diego: College-Hill Press.

Acknowledgments

This book represents the work of many individuals who contributed to the preparation of the manuscript, supported the research, and provided the information that forms the core of the book. Every staff member of the Center for Assessment and Demographic Studies (CADS) contributed to the numerous activities related to the Annual Survey of Hearing Impaired Children and Youth and the Study of Deaf Students in Transition from School to Work. Two staff members of the center deserve special credit for their work in this study. Sue Hotto combined her skills in editing and graphing with her word-processing expertise, and then managed also to organize the final, interminable "pulling it all together." Hank Young typed and edited and retyped and re-edited manuscripts and tables; he also made popcorn for everyone on the bad days when we were not "pulling it together."

Special recognition also goes to Dorothea Bateman, Kathleen Berault, Linda Fields, Kay Lam, Gail Ries, and Mary Carole Starke, who coordinated the mailing of over 24,000 survey forms and the data processing and analyses of the responses. Geir Hindar, a doctoral intern at CADS, contributed extensive literature reviews and valuable assistance in the conceptual stages of the project.

The Gallaudet Research Institute (GRI), under the previous leadership of Raymond J. Trybus and more recently that of Michael A. Karchmer, provided the financial support and encouragement that enabled CADS to devote its energies to this important project. Robert C. Johnson of GRI contributed his time and skills in editing manuscripts. Thanks are also due to I. King Jordan, president of Gallaudet, and other Gallaudet administrators who recognize the importance of national statistical data on deaf individuals.

Most important, we recognize the time and effort provided by thousands of deaf students, their teachers, counselors, and school administrators who reviewed the survey forms, completed them for the study, and coordinated the data collection at the schools. The high level of response to the study and the thoughtful comments offered by many of the survey respondents point up the fact that the subject of transition from school to postsecondary careers in the community is a topic of great importance to all those involved in deaf education and rehabilitation.

The Mandate for Transition Services

Myth or Reality?

Marita M. Danek
and William P. McCrone

Employment is a major goal of the educational and rehabilitative services bridging the transition from high school to adult life in the community. There are both optimistic and pessimistic views of the employment opportunities that will become available to deaf persons in the last decade of the 20th century.

Recent events in the United States have enhanced the employment prospects of persons born deaf or deafened at an early age, whose general work history in the past has often been one of chronic unemployment or serious underemployment. These events include a general recognition of the rights of persons with disabilities fostered by federal legislation. Public Law 93-112, the Rehabilitation Act of 1973, and its subsequent amendments, required state rehabilitation agencies to focus efforts on severely disabled persons who often need multiple services over extended periods of time. Public Law 94-142, the Education for All Handicapped Children Act of 1975, mandated a "free appropriate public education" to all handicapped children. Numerous other legislative enactments, at both the federal and state levels, have enhanced public awareness of government's responsibility to assist persons with disabilities in receiving suitable career training and other transitional services, and also to eliminate discrimination against these individuals in finding and keeping jobs.

In addition to the federal and state legislation, there is a generally encouraging picture regarding the national economy. Unemployment has been kept at a relatively low level, and Bureau of Labor statistics project growth in service work, technology, the professions, sales, and management (Johnston & Packer, 1987). A low birth rate has contributed to a shortage of workers in certain occupational fields. This, in turn, has prompted employers in these job areas to increase salaries, to offer various types of incentives and benefits to keep their experienced employees, and to provide on-the-job training for entry-level workers. Such a favorable economic climate, though not without its skeptics, creates opportunities for persons traditionally underrepresented or underpaid in the workplace—women, ethnic minorities, and disabled individuals.

Other events closer to the deaf community have influenced this positive outlook toward employment of deaf persons. The Commission on Education of the Deaf, established by Congress in 1986 to assess the quality of education of deaf children and adults in the United States, made a series of recommendations in its final report in 1988 that, if adequately implemented, would broaden educational and employment opportunities for these individuals. The significant increase in the number of special postsecondary programs for deaf students—growing from less than 30 in 1970 to over 150 in 1987—will undoubtedly also contribute to the higher skill levels of deaf workers, enabling them to compete more successfully in their careers and to achieve greater job satisfaction.

Perhaps more difficult to assess in terms of their influence have been the events at Gallaudet University during the spring of 1988, when a determined group of deaf students, faculty, staff, and alumni at the school were successful in their efforts to overturn the decision of the university's board of trustees appointing a hearing person to the Gallaudet presidency and to obtain the appointment of a deaf president. These well-publicized events established the capability and leadership qualities of deaf persons, and served as a further step toward erasing stereotypes of deaf persons held by many within the larger hearing community.

There is, of course, a negative side to this generally optimistic picture. Primarily, there exists a communication barrier, which is an obstacle to full integration of deaf persons into a workplace largely inhabited and supervised by hearing individuals. Progress has been made through the use of interpreters and captioning services and through a variety of technological advances—hearing aids, telecommunications and alerting devices, computers, and so forth—but these have neither eliminated all communication difficulties, nor eradicated fears and prejudices in some members of the hearing community whose contact with deaf persons has been either nonexistent or minimal.

A second major obstacle to employment for many young deaf workers is that of limited English language proficiency. In the very areas noted above having the greatest potential for growth (e.g., the professions, technology), use of the language of the hearing majority is, realistically, difficult to circumvent. Studies over the past 30 years have shown an average English reading level of third to fourth grade for deaf students graduating from high school. This delay in English language development may well prove to be the most formidable obstacle to both initial employment and advancement.

Several other more general problems cloud the employment outlook for deaf workers. There are the interpretation and implementation disputes concerning federal legislation. There is the uneasy relationship between special education and rehabilitation (described in Chapter 9 of this book). There is also a question of the value of vocational education for students working in a field of rapidly changing technology and being forced to make career changes several times in their lives. What kinds of vocational or prevocational education will assist these workers in adapting to new work environments? What kinds of assistance will deaf high school students need from the school and rehabilitation agencies to prepare them to work in such environments? Answers to these questions are still being sought.

A critical element for deaf students in their preparation for and entry into the world of work is the transition process. For all disabled students this process involves a collaboration between the school and the social and rehabilitation agencies serving them. For deaf students especially, it is only through close cooperation among various individuals (i.e., the student, the family, and the employer) and these service agencies that a successful transition can be accomplished.

The remainder of this chapter provides a more precise definition of transition, traces public policy and legislative initiatives affecting the transition process, and discusses how these initiatives relate to deaf youth and the systems responsible for serving them.

WHAT IS TRANSITION?

While the concept of transition is not new, the label that describes the process, recent federal emphasis on the transition of youth with disabilities, and legislation and appropriations that make transition programs possible are. Briefly stated, the transition process responds to the question, "After high school, what?" The answer to that question poses varying degrees of difficulty for all American high school students. Freedom to choose a vocation and life-style is fundamental to a democratic society. This freedom provides theoretically unlimited possibilities but also many pitfalls. One may choose a vocation for which one is unsuited, in which there are no jobs, or in which existing jobs are becoming scarce.

The difficulties of the average American high school student in selecting an appropriate vocation are multiplied many times over for students with disabilities. The U.S. Commission on Civil Rights (1983) has reported that unemployment rates for persons with disabilities are higher than for persons without disabilities. One study (Rusch & Phelps, 1987) estimates that approximately 67% of all persons with disabilities are unemployed.

Estimates of employment rates among disabled youth vary widely, depending on the disability type, gender, presence of a secondary disability, locality, how employment is defined, and other factors (e.g., full- or part-time work, competitive versus sheltered workshop employment). In a study of former special education students (predominantly learning disabled or mentally retarded) in Vermont who exited high school between 1979 and 1983, 55% were found to be currently employed (Hasazi, Gordon, & Roe, 1985). A Colorado study of recent graduates of special education programs reported that only 32% were employed fulltime and that their wages were much lower than average (Mithaug, Horiuchi, & Fanning, 1985). Nationwide estimates are that of the 2.5 million youth with disabilities who have left school since 1970, only 23% are in college or fully employed and 40% are earning wages at or near the poverty level (Project PERT Operations Manual, 1985).

Since 1977, the number of students with disabilities in public education programs has increased 17.6% (U.S. Department of Education/ OSERS, 1986). The number of 18- to 21-year-olds receiving special education services has increased much more dramatically during this period— by 88.3% (Halloran, Thomas, Snauwaert, & DeStefano, 1987). As more and more students with disabilities have access to appropriate educational programs and stay in them for longer periods of time, the question of "After high school, what?" becomes more pressing. To exit school and move successfully into adult life and to achieve employment and participate fully in the life of a community, this basically constitutes the transition from dependence to independence (Cartwright, Cartwright, & Ward, 1984). This transition occurs during late adolescence when the youth with a disability must master a succession of developmental tasks, some of which are delayed, while simultaneously dealing with disability-related issues (Szymanski & Danek, 1985). For increasing numbers of students with disabilities, particularly severe disabilities, planning for the movement to independence requires services and coordination from an array of service providers.

As noted by Harnisch in the foreword to this book, the transition concept has been strongly promoted by Madeleine Will (1984a, 1984b, 1985), in her role as Assistant Secretary of the Office of Special Education and Rehabilitative Services (OSERS), U.S. Department of Education. Will has emphasized the multiplicity of services required by young disabled persons in the transition from school to work and has pressed for cooperation among the various individuals and agencies attempting to meet these needs.

A pragmatic, working definition of transition has been suggested by Wehman, Kregel and Barcus (1985), one that provides a basis for a further discussion of transition:

Vocational transition is a carefully planned process, which may be initiated either by school personnel or adult service providers, to establish and implement a plan for either employment or additional vocational training of a handicapped student who will graduate or leave school in three to five years; such a process must involve special educators, vocational educators, parents and/or the student, an adult service system representative, and possibly an employer. (p. 26)

Transition Components

The transition process involves several components: 1) personal factors, including the individual's characteristics and his or her perception of transition; and 2) environmental factors, including the individual's social support system and the service delivery system. The model of transition articulated by the Office of Special Education and Rehabilitative Services (Will, 1984b) focuses on environmental components, as does an expanded model presented by Halpern (1985). Although personal factors are extremely critical to the transition process, a discussion of these are presented later in the chapter as the focus turns to deaf youth.

The Will model (1984b) uses the high school as the foundation from which transition services emanate. Employment is the outcome, and three kinds of "bridges" to employment are conceptualized: 1) no special services, 2) time-limited specialized services, and 3) ongoing specialized services. The Halpern (1985) model defines the transition outcome more broadly as "living successfully in the community" (p. 480). In the Halpern model, employment is only one aspect of community adjustment. The quality of the residential environment and that of the interpersonal network are equally important.

Family Support System

The family exerts influence on three dimensions of work adjustment: work personality, work competencies, and work goals (Szymanski, Hershenson, & Power, 1988). Although parent participation in transition planning is considered essential, the actual level of parental involvement frequently is less than optimal. For example, parents of older students actually participate less in individualized education program (IEP) conferences than do parents of younger children (Lynch & Stein, 1982). This occurs despite the fact that older students frequently need parental support and involvement to participate in adult services, employment, and community living (Johnson, Bruininks, & Thurlow, 1987).

Family involvement and support have recently been deemed of sufficient importance to be mandated by federal legislation. PL 99-457, enacted in October, 1987, requires an individualized family service program (IFSP). Rehabilitation legislation permits services to families of disabled persons, and workshops on parent-employer partnerships are becoming increasingly important in identifying practical strategies to help youth succeed in the transition to work (National Information Center for Children and Youth with Handicaps [NICHCY], 1987). Regardless of the level of transition services required, the process cannot be successful unless families and agencies systematically plan for it with an individualized transition program (ITP) that is developed at least by the time the youth is age 16.

Who "Owns" Transition?

Although at first glance such a question seems unnecessarily territorial, a review of transition-related legislation and policy initiatives indicates philosophical and pragmatic "tugs" on transition programs within the service delivery system and across disability and consumer groups. It is only by examining these more general tugs that one can clarify the transition concept as it applies to deaf youth.

To a large extent, transition is "owned" by the special education and developmental disability communities. As an entitlement program, it is special education that serves all students with disabilities: An entitlement program *must* serve all who apply. Entitlement programs are automatically available without specific criteria for inclusion beyond basic qualifications (e.g., age, disability status) (Wheeler, 1987). Since the passage of PL 94-142, the Education for All Handicapped Children Act of 1975, all youngsters with disabilities must receive a "free appropriate public education" in the "least restrictive environment." The developmental disability community has spearheaded the philosophical underpinnings of transition, beginning with the normalization and deinstitutionalization movements of the 1960s. These philosophical underpinnings have joined forces with the cost-effectiveness and employment emphases of the 1980s, culminating in the 1983 President's Employment Initiative for Persons with Developmental Disabilities and the 1984 amendments to the Developmental Disabilities Act (PL 98-527) emphasizing employment-related activities (Whitehead, 1986).

Other service delivery systems, particularly "eligibility" systems, which include most adult service systems, work with selected subgroups that exit the school system. The selection criteria for eligibility programs may include: disability type and severity, age, functional limitations, potential for success (as defined by the program), or any combination of these criteria. "Tugs" and "pushes" occur when unintentional conflicts between programs occur, employment disincentives are legislated, or mandated initiatives work at cross-purposes.

In summary, then, current thinking stresses that, to provide effective transition services, systems must look beyond the boundaries of age-limited needs of disabled persons or the time-limited nature of their services and define areas of *inter*agency responsibilities so that the lifetime needs of disabled persons are met.

A brief review of disability and transition legislation illustrates the complexity of the service delivery system.

TRANSITION LEGISLATION AND PUBLIC POLICY

In Table 1.1, selected transition and transition-related legislation and public policy initiatives are summarized. Most of this legislation and policy authorizes rehabilitation, special education, vocational education, Social Security, and developmental disability programs that target employment, access to employment, or the removal of work disincentives as outcomes.

Rehabilitation Legislation

The state-federal rehabilitation system is an eligibility program that provides vocationally oriented services to adults with disabilities who meet certain eligibility criteria. The program spends over $1 billion per year putting handicapped people to work (McCrone, 1983; McCrone & Arthur, 1981). Rehabilitation-related legislation pre-dates all other federal disability legislation. Indeed, the federal government first authorized rehabilitation services in 1920 in response to the need to retrain disabled World War I veterans and industrially injured workers for more suitable employment. Over the years, every new piece of legislation expanded the program; additional disability groups, services, programs, and outcomes were authorized and ever-increasing funds were appropriated.

Rehabilitation has always been a time-limited service that attempts to achieve employment outcomes for the maximum possible number of disabled persons. However, individuals for whom an employment outcome was doubtful or who were too severely disabled or who had motivational or behavioral problems that might interfere with work performance were frequently declared ineligible in the early days of rehabilitation. The recent emphasis on services to severely disabled persons; increasing consumer involvement; and the importance of transition, supported employment, and related concepts in rehabilitation have lessened the preeminence of eligibility issues in rehabilitation.

In many ways, what has happened in recent decades in public education parallels what happened in the state-federal rehabilitation program. Both have been influenced by broader societal movements. "Normalization," a term coined by Wolfensberger (1972), implies participation for disabled persons in the mainstream of society to the greatest degree possible. "Mainstreaming" subsequently has been used to refer to the educational placement of children with disabilities in the least restrictive environment

Table 1.1. Selected transition and transition-related legislation and public policies

Year	Rehabilitation	Education	Other
1943	*PL 78-113: Vocational Rehabilitation Act Amendments* · Emotionally disturbed and mentally retarded individuals are made eligible for rehabilitation services		
1954	*PL 83-565: Vocational Rehabilitation Act Amendments* · Facility and workshop development funds		
1965	*PL 89-333: Vocational Rehabilitation Act Amendments* · Rehabilitation center funding · Extended evaluation services for severely disabled individuals (up to 18 months)		*Social Security Act Amendments* · Social Security funds used to cover cost of vocational rehabilitation services for Social Security Disability Insurance (SSDI) recipients
1972			*PL 92-603: Social Security Act Amendments* · Supplementary Security Income (SSI) program pays support to persons who are not covered by the Social Security program and who have extremely limited assets
1973	*PL 93-112: Rehabilitation Act of 1973* · Emphasized services to severely disabled persons · "Civil rights" for disabled persons · Mandatory client inclusion in rehabilitation planning through the individualized written rehabilitation plan (IWRP)		

1975 PL 94-142: Education for All Handicapped Children Act
· Free, appropriate education in the least restrictive environment for all handicapped children ages 5 to 21

1976 PL 94-482: Vocational Education Act Amendments
· 10% set-aside funding for disabled students
PL 94-103: Developmental Disabilities Assistance and Bill of Rights Act (DDA)
· Care and training of developmentally disabled citizens in the least restrictive setting

1978 PL 95-602: Rehabilitation, Comprehensive Services and Developmental Disabilities Amendments
· Independent living rehabilitation program for severely disabled persons without work potential
· Title V replaced the categorical definition of developmental disability with a functional one

1983 PL 98-199: Education of the Handicapped Act Amendments
· Funding and support for secondary education and transitional services for disabled students, ages 12–22
President's Employment Initiative for Persons with Developmental Disabilities
· Employment-related activities

continued

Table 1.1. *(continued)*

Year	Rehabilitation	Education	Other
1984	*PL 98-221: Rehabilitation Act Amendments* · Discretionary programs for transition-ing severely disabled individuals	*Department of Education, Office of Special Education and Rehabilitative Services Transition Initiative* · Cooperative supported employment projects with the Administration of Developmental Disabilities	*PL 98-524: Carl D. Perkins Vocational Education Act* · Assessment, support services, and counseling and transition services for disabled students · Programs to be offered in least restric-tive environment · 10% set aside to be used for addi-tional staff, services, and so forth, not provided to other individuals in voca-tional education *PL 98-527: Developmental Disabilities Act Amendments* · Established supported employment as a priority for state planning councils funded under that act · Redefined developmental disability consistent with PL 95-602
1986	*PL 99-506: Rehabilitation Act Amendments* · Supported employment services		*PL 92-603: Tax Reform Act* · Extended permanently a tax deduc-tion of up to $35,000 for businesses for the removal of architectural and trans-portation barriers · Work-related exemptions for disabled employees
1987		*PL 99-457* · All states must provide services for handicapped children from birth · Services include diagnostic screen-ing, early education programs, special equipment, transportation, and financial and legal services for families	*PL 99-643: Employment Opportunities for Disabled Americans Act* · Continued cash payments and/or Medicaid coverage to Supplemental Se-curity Income (SSI) recipients who work

(LRE) most appropriate to each child's needs. The 1975 Education for All Handicapped Children Act (PL 94-142) was in the planning stages as the Rehabilitation Act of 1973 (PL 93-112) was enacted. As previously stated, PL 94-142 required that public schools provide free and appropriate public education for children with disabilities (ages 5–21) and that these children be educated with nonhandicapped students to the maximum extent possible. Again, as with rehabilitation legislation, education legislation subsequently expanded the intention of the original legislation with transitioning emphases (PL 98-199) and vocational education participation (PL 94-482, PL 98-524).

Related Legislation

Related legislation, as noted in Table 1.1, attempts to remove work disincentives (PL 92-603, the Tax Reform Act of 1986, and PL 99-643), targets specific disability groups for transitioning (PL 94-103, PL 98-527), and provides services for transitioning severely disabled persons (PL 99-506).

The history of legislation and public policy in transitioning is interwoven across disciplines, programs, government agencies, and support services. Many of these initiatives are complementary, although the complexity of the system may be difficult to navigate (Szymanski & Danek, 1985), or may work at cross-purposes with employment outcomes (e.g., income security through Supplementary Security Income and related benefits may outweigh the insecurity of a job) (Conley, 1985; Johnson et al., 1987). A complete analysis of the systems is beyond the scope of this chapter. However, the summary in Table 1.1 should assist the reader in interpreting the data provided in this book in relation to the transition of deaf youth.

TRANSITION OF DEAF YOUTH: ISSUES PAST AND PRESENT

The mainstreaming and transitioning initiatives over the past decade mandated by PL 94-142 and PL 98-199 and other legislation have received their greatest definition, support, and promotion from disability advocates outside the deafness arena. For example, much of the impetus for mainstreaming came from advocates for retarded individuals excluded from public education. Such exclusion was ruled illegal in *Mills v. Board of Education of the District of Columbia* (1972) and the *Pennsylvania Association for Retarded Citizens (PARC) v. Commonwealth of Pennsylvania* (1972) legal suits (Moores & Kluwin, 1986).

Historically, deaf children in the United States have been predominantly educated in day or residential programs for deaf students, although there has been a trend toward the integration of deaf children in public school settings since World War II (Moores & Kluwin, 1986). This trend has accelerated considerably since the passage of PL 94-142 in 1975. Although mainstreaming is now a reality for many deaf children, it remains controversial for several reasons, including the special communication and learning needs of deaf children and the lack of adequate support services for these children in local school systems.

Just as the mainstreaming initiative was not developed to meet the educational or socialization needs of deaf youth, neither was the transitioning initiative promoted for them. Mainstreaming and transitioning are inextricably linked, with mainstreaming the conceptual antecedent of transitioning. It is logical to maximize educational benefits for disabled youth first and then ask *for what* one is educating. What are the employment and independent living outcomes for these students? Will they be able to make the transition from school to work?

About the same time that mainstreaming and transitioning were being promoted, advocates for students with learning disabilities, mental retardation, and other mental or emotional conditions were engaged in further advocacy and legislative initiatives. In the mid-1970s, "developmental disabilities" was coined to describe severe mental or physical conditions that have the potential to impede development. The Developmental Disabilities Assistance and Bill of Rights Act (PL 94-103) of 1976 defined developmental disabilities to include autism, cerebral palsy, epilepsy, mental retardation, and other conditions closely related to mental retardation, that originate prior to age 18, that have continued or can be expected to continue indefinitely, and that constitute a substantial handicap to such persons' ability to function normally in society. Later legislation, PL 95-527 and PL 95-602, shifted from a "categorical" to a "functional" definition: The identification of specific disabilities was removed, the age limit was changed from 18 to 22, and functional limitations were required to occur in three or more specified areas. The full definition of developmental disability in PL 95-527 is as follows:

- A chronic disability attributable to a mental or physical impairment or both
- Manifest before the age of 22
- Likely to continue indefinitely
- Resulting in substantial limitation in three or more of the following areas of life activity: 1) self-care, 2) receptive and expressive language, 3) learning, 4) mobility, 5) self-direction, 6) capacity for independent living, or 7) economic self-sufficiency
- Reflecting the need for a combination and sequence of special, inter-

disciplinary, or generic care, treatment, or other services that are of lifelong or of extended duration

Deafness as a Developmental Disability

Is profound prelingual deafness a developmental disability? According to the definition of PL 95-527, many deaf youth would be considered developmentally disabled in that they have communication, educational, and language deficits, and frequently they cannot function independently in society without substantial assistance.

However, the PL 95-527 definition can be interpreted in different ways. For example, early prelingual deafness, *without early and appropriate intervention,* can certainly leave the individual severely compromised in many of life's major tasks, including vocational competence and the capacity to participate fully in society (Stoddard-Pflueger, 1977). Conversely, it can be argued that appropriate educational intervention should provide the foundation for most deaf students to compete successfully in the job market, even if they require periodic support in maintaining a job (Whitehead & Marrone, 1986). Certainly one would expect such benefits to be maximized since the passage of PL 94-142.

Obviously then, the question of whether deafness is a developmental disability is not easily answered. Answering it requires the ability to quantify the effect of a less than optimal environment upon individuals who lack consistent input from one of the major senses. Although an optimal environment would theoretically prevent the emergence of vocational, social, or educational limitations, such an environment rarely, if ever, occurs in real life. Certainly, many deaf youth meet the criteria most recently established for developmental disabilities in PL 95-527.

The exclusion of deaf children from the developmental disability category appears to be an oversight rather than a deliberate choice. The politics of disability are such that each disability group and its advocates must, of necessity, compete with others for limited resources. Developmental disability advocates have little incentive to stretch the boundaries of which disabilities are truly "developmental" disabilities; federal and state priorities and appropriations can only be stretched so far. Deafness advocates most frequently wish to maintain the autonomy of early onset deafness as different from, and requiring different appropriations and initiatives from, the general category of developmental disability. However, the planning and implementation of employment-related activities are currently receiving extensive federal-state attention and support through the Administration on Developmental Disabilities (ADD), which has major responsibility for overseeing state Developmental Disabilities Councils and for establishing supported employment demonstration projects. That early onset deafness is not typically considered a developmental disability is unfortunate insofar as deaf youth and adults are excluded from well-supported, highly visible programs currently at the forefront of the transition movement.

Developmental Issues of Deaf Youth

The developmental deficits of deaf youth have been described extensively in the professional literature. Because early onset deafness curtails many opportunities for informal, incidental learning, the potential exists for difficulties in social adjustment, academic achievement, and vocational competence (Christiansen, 1982; Meadow, 1980; Meadow & Trybus, 1979; Moores, 1986; Passmore, 1983; Schein, 1987; Schein & Delk, 1974; Schlesinger & Meadow, 1972).

Social Competence

Over 90% of all deaf children are born into families where both parents have normal hearing (Rawlings & Jensema, 1977; Schein & Delk, 1974). The overwhelming communication barrier imposed upon the deaf child in a hearing world means that deaf children are frequently socially isolated, even within their own families, and have a limited opportunity to interact with an ever-widening variety of individuals. Therefore, without compensatory interventions (above and beyond that afforded by the usual family interactions) and without adequate parent-child communication, the social development of deaf children within the broader hearing world may lag or be uneven (Greenberg, 1980; Greenberg, 1983; Schlesinger & Meadow, 1972).

This is a complex issue and one that cannot be exhaustively explored in this chapter. It appears reasonable to assume both cognitive and affective components to this perceived social lag in deaf youth. Cognitively, deaf children often cannot easily learn social skills, values, and norms within the hearing world due to lack of auditory input and deficits in educational and linguistic competency (Liben, 1978). Affectively, social interaction within this world can be limited. Thus, there are both qualitative and quantitative differences in the deaf child's social experiences at home, at school, and in everyday interactions with the hearing environment (Culhane & Williams, 1982; Liben, 1978).

Academic Competence

Deaf youth generally have lower levels of academic achievement, as measured by standardized tests. The Stanford Achievement Test has been used extensively in nationwide studies conducted by the Center for Assessment and Demographic Studies at Gallaudet University (Allen & Karchmer, 1981; Karchmer, Milone & Wolk, 1979; Trybus & Karchmer,

1977). In 1983, mean reading comprehension scores for deaf students taking the Stanford were at about the third grade level (Allen, 1986). Mathematics computation scores leveled off at around the sixth to seventh grade level by the time the deaf students were 18 years old (Allen, 1986).

Vocational Competence

Vocational achievement is inevitably influenced by educational and social competence (Christiansen, 1982; Passmore, 1983; Schein, 1987; Vernon, 1970). In *The Deaf Population of the United States,* Schein and Delk (1974) noted a disproportionate representation of deaf persons in many job categories when compared with the hearing population. Deaf persons were less frequently found in professional, technical, and managerial positions and in clerical, sales, and service industries. Conversely, they were overrepresented as craftsmen and in manufacturing industries. Later studies indicate labor-force participation for deaf adults appears to be decreasing, possibly due to changing economic factors and a shift from manufacturing to a service-oriented economy (Christiansen, 1982). Empirical data have been sparse over the past 10 years, but observational and anecdotal impressions are that labor force participation has continued to decrease, particularly for younger and minority deaf workers. Work disincentives such as Supplemental Security Income are sometimes cited as a factor in the unemployment of deaf youth. There is, undoubtedly, a multiplicity of factors presently operating that have both a positive and negative impact on future employment prospects for deaf youth.

Historical Approaches to Transition with Deaf Students

Although deafness professionals are not currently at the forefront of transitioning initiatives, there exists a long history of collaborative efforts to assist deaf youth to enter appropriate occupations. Historically, professionals in deafness rehabilitation and education have had closer relationships and more coordination of services than is true for most other disability groups. The low-incidence nature of early onset deafness and the scarcity of professionals who could communicate with and understand deaf people served to forge a common bond among state residential school teachers and administrators, rehabilitation counselors and administrators, and other deafness service providers. Their commitment to working with deaf people, rather than to a particular service setting, was the unifying bond. In earlier times educators might become rehabilitation counselors, administrators of special projects, or researchers for a demonstration grant in deafness. They had more in common with each other than with other special educators or rehabilitation generalists.

The educational system for deaf people was a highly structured, somewhat closed one with control in the hands of educators trained in deafness, many of whom had deep roots in the deaf community. Educators in state residential schools, and to a lesser degree those in day schools, adopted an "in loco parentis" approach to the deaf child's development, assuming responsibility not only for the educational but also for the social, economic, and vocational adjustment of their graduates. Rehabilitation professionals were usually not as highly trained, particularly in deafness rehabilitation; however, many had extensive informal exposure to deaf persons in their families or communities.

Early Rehabilitation Agency–School Relationships

In 1948, Hoag published a comprehensive summary of cooperative relationships between public residential schools and state rehabilitation agencies. Hoag, an educator at the New York School for the Deaf, conducted this study as his master's thesis upon the recommendation of Boyce Williams of the federal Office of Vocational Rehabilitation. In justifying his concern over cooperation between schools and rehabilitation agencies, Hoag struck a prophetic note: "The post-school assistance provided by the rehabilitation service bridges very well the gap from termination of school to complete vocational adjustment" (1948, p. 8).

Forty-one state agencies responded to his survey questionnaire, which examined the extent of working agreements between schools and agencies. Of those who responded, only 6 reported having written agreements; 31 had verbal agreements. Of the 64 schools that responded to the questionnaire in Hoag's study, 42 indicated that either written or verbal agreements had been made. He also cited studies from the 1930s (Martens, 1936; Walker, 1935), indicating that a significant number of deaf persons who received residential school vocational training did not enter or remain in the occupation for which they had been trained. All this evidence supported the establishment of an early relationship with rehabilitation.

Some unique arrangements were reported. North Carolina had a three-way agreement between the North Carolina School for the Deaf, the North Carolina Division of Vocational Rehabilitation, and the Bureau of Labor for the Deaf of the North Carolina State Department of Labor. Louisiana reported that a special rehabilitation counselor had an office at the residential school to "help develop a specific vocational objective for the older students (16 and up) in the last few years of their formal education" (Hoag, 1948, p. 19).

At the same time, some interesting attitudes were also revealed. One school administrator wrote of rehabilitation:

> This I do not believe in! I have made it a point not to inform students that the vocational rehabilitation agency will furnish so many wonderful services.

> Students must feel self-reliant . . . I do not feel that the deaf need as much help in rehabilitation as they need in habilitation—their work towards their life's work, which is the job of the school. (Hoag, 1948, p. 24)

Another respondent noted:

> We feel that the [rehabilitation] agency should work with the adult deaf who have been unable to establish themselves due to no school, or due to poor or inadequate schooling. It is the job of the school to train boys and girls under twenty-one. The two do not overlap much. (Hoag, 1948, p. 22)

One finding highlighted in the conclusion to Hoag's (1948) study was the fact that those respondent states having rehabilitation specialists in deafness—16 states at that time—had the most cooperation and the highest level of satisfaction with their cooperative efforts. This is reminiscent of the study of general special education students conducted almost 40 years later (Harold Russell Associates, Inc., 1985) in which transition programs with rehabilitation counselors as part of the team were most successful.

Other conclusions from the Hoag (1948) study include the following:

1. Specialized counselors in deafness are crucial to the development of effective rehabilitation programs.
2. The number and frequency of referrals from schools to rehabilitation agencies correspond positively with the existence of cooperative agreements between the two.
3. Cooperative arrangements for "adult education" (e.g., vocational training for older deaf adults) and the use of audiometric facilities at residential schools should be considered.

Meetings and Workshops in the Fifties

The first formal meeting of professionals in deafness that included deaf consumers occurred in 1957 at the Institute on Personal, Social, and Vocational Adjustment to Total Deafness held at the New York School for the Deaf in White Plains (Adler, 1974). A major emphasis at that meeting was on multiply disabled deaf persons and youth. Subsequently, the Maryland School for the Deaf in 1959 sponsored a national workshop to develop "Guidelines for the Establishment of Rehabilitation Facilities for the Deaf" (1961). The emphasis, again, was on the needs of severely and multihandicapped deaf persons (e.g., deaf-blind, deaf–mentally retarded). These guidelines formed the basis for subsequent research projects and demonstration programs in deafness in the 1960s.

Sixties Emphases

The 1960s, a period of expanded funding, saw many workshops on deafness, sponsored by the Vocational Rehabilitation Administration. In

1966, 18 years after the Hoag survey (1948), a workshop on rehabilitation casework standards for the deaf noted that, "too many counselors fail to understand the need to establish and maintain contacts with residential and other schools for the deaf in their areas" (Falberg, 1966, p. 48). This same workshop emphasized that the rehabilitation counselor should "contact the client as early as possible . . . the planning should start in the school situation" (Falberg, 1966, p. 48). A cooperative program between the schools and rehabilitation agencies was recommended that emphasized early involvement with parents and early contact with students to assist with educational planning and to provide counseling and guidance services.

The Las Cruces Conference

The National Conference for Coordinating Rehabilitation and Education Services for the Deaf, held in Las Cruces, New Mexico, in 1967, is still considered pivotal for its recommendations for effective working relationships. The conference called together over 200 leaders in the fields of education and rehabilitation and in deaf organizations. It was the first time such a conference was funded jointly by the United States Department of Education and the Rehabilitation Services Administration. The Las Cruces conference struck an optimistic note, buttressed perhaps by the largesse of federal financing in the 1960s and the vision of unlimited expansion that characterized that era in America's history.

One can only marvel at how current the following issues raised by this conference still seem: 1) the lack of social, academic, and vocational readiness of deaf youth to assume work roles upon graduation from a state residential school; 2) the lack of community-based resources for deaf youth served by rehabilitation agencies: few adult education and on-the-job training opportunities or postsecondary programs; and 3) stereotyping of deaf youth for certain jobs and premature tracking of deaf students into particular trades in schools.

The conference also displayed concern over the lack of demographic information on the dispersion of deaf people, deaf youth with secondary disabilities who were receiving services from neither schools nor rehabilitation agencies, parental over-protection, lack of interpreter services, and low public interest in deafness.

The conference offered the following recommendations:

1. *Rehabilitation services*   Rehabilitation counselors should be made available in residential schools, either assigned to the schools directly or made available through state offices. They should become involved earlier, participate in the evaluation and planning process, and be able to communicate. Caseload size and "closure" pressure should be reduced; they work against more-difficult-to-serve clients.

2. *Interagency coordination* Since deafness services cut across bureaucratic lines, the coordination and integration of these services are particularly important.
3. *Education* Deaf students should be permitted job exploration rather than job selection and training.
4. *Community services* Regional training centers are needed as well as greater utilization of sheltered workshops. Accessibility to community services should be increased through interpreter training.

Accomplishments of the 1950s and 1960s

The Vocational Rehabilitation Amendments of 1954 (PL 83-565) authorized new categories of services through: 1) research and demonstration grants, 2) extension and improvement grants, and 3) rehabilitation facility improvement (Wright, 1980). Between 1955 and 1965, over 90 research projects in deafness were authorized under this legislation.

Those were the halcyon days of rehabilitation, often referred to as the "Golden Era of Rehabilitation" (Rusalem, 1976); annual funding for the federal-state rehabilitation program quadrupled between 1954 and 1965 (Rubin & Roessler, 1987). As noted previously, the 1965 Vocational Rehabilitation Act Amendments (PL 89-333) provided further expansion of rehabilitation and promised services to deaf persons through special provisions for "hard-to-rehabilitate cases": 1) extended evaluation to determine rehabilitation potential, 2) expanded funding for facilities, and 3) new funding of experimental and innovative projects.

With this type of attention, the number of deaf persons rehabilitated under the federal-state system increased rapidly. Between 1945 and 1966, for example, 32,148 deaf persons were reported as rehabilitated by state agencies. However, fully one third of those persons were rehabilitated in the 5-year period between 1961 and 1966.

Seventies Issues

During the 1970s, similar themes were echoed periodically for coordination of services among rehabilitation agencies, residential schools, and other systems serving deaf youth.

The Tarrytown Conference of 1971

A small group of deafness rehabilitation professionals met in Tarrytown, New York, in 1971 to identify problems, needs, and recommendations in the field. Several issues relevant to transition were cited: community facilities (counseling and referral centers, comprehensive rehabilitation centers), which continued after short term federally sponsored demonstration funding expired; information dissemination about these facilities; and regional job training programs for deaf people.

The 1972 National Conference

In 1972, the Council of State Administrators for Vocational Rehabilitation (CSAVR) and the Arkansas Rehabilitation Research and Training Center sponsored the National Conference on Rehabilitation Services for the Deaf. This was hailed as the first time a committee on services for deaf people had met under the auspices of CSAVR.

A major issue in the early 1970s for educators, one that dominated the conference, was the acceptance of "total communication" as a legitimate communication modality for teachers in residential schools. Total communication was defined as the simultaneous use of all modes of communication—sign language, gesture, fingerspelling, oral speech, lipreading, and so forth (Mindel & Vernon, 1971).

Residential schools had long struggled with the "manual versus oral" controversy (Moores, 1986), and fresh research in the sixties was supportive of the total communication approach to instruction. Interestingly, communication modality was never an issue within rehabilitation agencies. Most prelingually deaf adults used some variant of sign language to communicate, and rehabilitation counselors were basically pragmatic about communication: whatever method was necessary to communicate with their clients, they used, if possible.

At the 1972 conference, several speakers alluded to difficulties in finding support for services and personnel specialized in deafness within many rehabilitation agencies. Other issues included the dearth of resources for multiply disabled deaf youth (particularly the "low achievers"). There was some discussion of possible legislation authorizing federally funded comprehensive regional centers for deaf youth. Cooperative relationships between residential schools, rehabilitation agencies, and state vocational education divisions were emphasized.

A strong recommendation was made at the 1972 conference for the establishment of state or regional planning groups to develop priorities for deafness rehabilitation programs. Membership in these groups was to be cross-disciplinary; including educators, consumers, university training personnel, and interpreters.

Current Issues in the Transition of Deaf Youth

In retrospect, what is perhaps most striking about the past 40 years of workshops, meetings, and conferences of the various professionals serving deaf youth is the lack of continuity. Every conference and workshop seems to echo the same themes, issues, and recommendations as if they have suddenly surfaced unexpectedly. A continuous long-term strategy is conspicuously absent.

So, on balance, where do we stand regarding the issue of transition and deaf youth? Are we any further ahead conceptually and practically than we were when Hoag conducted his survey in 1948?

Educational Issues

PL 94-142 and PL 98-199, although not intended to address the problems inherent in deaf education, have certainly changed the way deaf youth are being educated and prepared to assume a work role. During the 1984–1985 academic year, over 35% of all deaf youth (age 12 through 20) were being educated in a mainstream setting (Schildroth, 1987). The mainstream environments varied from integrated instruction with hearing students to special classes within a regular school.

When these youth leave either regular/local or special schools, there are approximately 150 postsecondary programs available that provide varying kinds of accommodations and support services for deaf students (Rawlings, Karchmer, & DeCaro, 1988). Interpreters, counselors, notetakers, and various kinds of assistive devices (rare or nonexistent even 20 years ago) are not uncommon now. There are also over 300 rehabilitation facilities nationwide, ranging from sheltered workshops to comprehensive rehabilitation centers, that provide the spectrum of vocationally oriented training specifically for these youth. It would appear that deaf youth currently have unprecedented accessibility to educational programming.

But a closer inspection raises discomforting questions. Is appropriate educational programming available in mainstream settings—particularly when educational personnel are unfamiliar with deafness, with the assessment of deaf students' capabilities, and with the development of reasonable instructional strategies for deaf youth? Is the "bridge" from school to work, postsecondary training, or rehabilitation facility constructed any better than it was 40 years ago when only a handful of specialized personnel and resources existed? Does the sheer complexity of the systems involved and the vast array of options available impose a responsibility on parents and professionals that is difficult to fulfill?

The choice of an appropriate educational placement is a difficult one, complicated by the low-incidence nature of deafness and the very special educational needs of deaf children (Moores & Kluwin, 1986). The potential for misplacement exists in every situation. And an inappropriate or inadequate educational foundation makes successful transitioning all the more difficult.

Rehabilitation Issues

The federal-state rehabilitation system currently has the potential to serve deaf youth in their transition years. Since 1975, guidelines for services to deaf rehabilitation clients have existed in the form of a "Model State Plan for Rehabilitation of Deaf Clients" (Schein, 1975). Although approved *in concept* by most states, the adoption and implementation of a reasonable and workable plan for each state are not yet a reality.

Almost all states currently have designated State Coordinators in Deafness (SCDs) and Rehabilitation Counselor Specialists in Deafness (RCDs). However, the recruitment, retention, and qualifications of such specialists remain problematic. In 1985, over 68% of rehabilitation experts nationwide reported a shortage of RCDs in their geographic area (Danek, 1987). Some state agencies are hiring rehabilitation counselors who lack the preservice education and communication skills to work effectively with deaf people. Some agencies are serving multi-handicapped deaf people in smaller numbers than population statistics indicate should be served (Danek & Lawrence, 1981). Also, a recent study of deaf rehabilitation clients in New York State found that 28% of the deaf clients accepted were not placed in jobs (Mathay & Joyce, 1986).

Other problems exist. Case finding is complicated by the diversity of educational settings, making cooperative arrangements between the area RCD and school personnel time-consuming and difficult. In addition, lack of clarity exists about *when* to begin to serve transitioning deaf youth and which system (school or rehabilitation) takes the initiative in the transition process. The rehabilitation system has been involved in transition to varying degrees since the 1940s. Legislation in the 1970s gave schools extended responsibility, and rehabilitation agencies subsequently assumed a less significant role (Szymanski & Danek, 1985). Still, there seems to be a less aggressive case-finding stance among many state rehabilitation agencies than the situation would warrant.

Public policy initiatives that depend on the vagaries of political expedience and funding make long-term rehabilitation planning capricious. For example, the pre- and postservice training of RCDs is contingent upon cyclical funding and training grants that do not exceed 3 years. Many successful demonstration projects in deafness were funded by the Rehabilitation Services Administration (RSA); when funding ran out, these projects were unable to obtain permanent long-term funding. The highly touted Commission on Education of the Deaf report (COED, 1988) noted that "RSA's expectation that the states would continue the programs without federal support was erroneous" (p. 69). Finally, periodic emphases on various selected disabilities have given rise to a cynical view among rehabilitation old-timers of a "disability of the month" syndrome. This year deafness or deaf-blindness may be "in"; next year it may be "out."

Within the field of deafness itself, competition exists for scarce resources—funding and personnel. As a result, a patchwork of resources and programs has emerged nationwide that is more reflective of local, county, and state initiatives and the energy of local leaders in deafness than it is of a comprehensive response to the unmet service needs of deaf youth and adults.

The National Association of the Deaf (NAD) legislative priorities in rehabilitation published in 1986 (Olson, 1986) noted a need to establish regional training centers for deaf people, with a system of satellite centers in each region. Echoing a similar theme, the COED report (1988) recommended one comprehensive rehabilitation center in each federal region for deaf adults and noted that there are no large federally funded comprehensive rehabilitation centers to serve the needs of lower functioning deaf adults.

The theme of transitioning deaf youth was addressed most recently by W. Calvin Melton (1987), president of the Council of State Administrators of Vocational Rehabilitation. He offered the following remarks to the 1987 Conference of Educational Administrators Serving the Deaf:

> Rehabilitation and education have a common interest and concern in contributing what we can in the area of lifelong learning and employment of hearing-impaired individuals. We have a shared responsibility to identify the needs of those we are charged to serve and, through a cooperative planning effort, provide services that lead to education, independent living, employment, and a better quality of life. (Melton, 1987, p. 315)

Environmental Issues

The following legislative, economic, and attitudinal factors are having an impact today and, most certainly, will influence the ability of today's deaf youth to achieve meaningful and productive lives:

- Legislative mandates, as discussed earlier in this chapter, including the Rehabilitation Act of 1973 and its amendments; the Education for All Handicapped Children Act and its 1983 amendments; the Carl D. Perkins Vocational Education Act of 1984; and the Employment Opportunities for Disabled Americans Act (PL 99-643)
- Public policy initiatives such as supported employment (now also legislated), the Transition of Youth with Disabilities Priority (Office of Special Education and Rehabilitative Services, U.S. Department of Education), and the Employment Initiative from the Administration on Developmental Disabilities (Wheeler, 1987)
- Continued decline of U.S. manufacturing and the growth of new jobs in service industries—as noted previously, these new jobs will demand much higher skill levels, particularly in the ability to read, follow directions, and compute (Johnston & Packer, 1987)
- Technological advances that provide accessibility for deaf adults— telecommunications technology, TV decoders, alerting systems, signaling devices, and other assistive devices

- Disability awareness in the media and among the general public resulting in the reduction of pejorative language ("deaf-mutes," "deaf and dumb") and negative stereotyping of deaf persons and their abilities—for example, popular support for a deaf president at Gallaudet, as a result of student and faculty demonstrations in March, 1988, brought deafness and deafness-related issues into the media spotlight

Family Issues

By the time a deaf child becomes an adolescent, the family of that child will have been involved with a wide range of professionals from medical and educational systems. Parental contact with professionals is not always easy or conflict-free, particularly because there are strong and frequently opposing professional positions about the "best" way to educate the deaf child.

Family involvement in educational decisions affecting the deaf child has been formalized by recent legislative and federal program initiatives (Szymanski et al., 1988). The importance of family involvement in career planning and transition has also come to be recognized (Beckett, Chitwood, & Hayden, 1985; Kokaska & Brolin, 1985).

Historically, families turned over many of the career-counseling and career-planning activities to residential schools, which, as noted previously, assumed a complete "in loco parentis" stance with regard to their deaf students' educational and vocational plans. The traditional role of the residential school in the vocational planning process for deaf youth has now been reduced. Parents now can, and must, become more involved in the planning, implementing, and monitoring of vocational and career activities prior to and during the transition process.

Becoming involved is not an easy task, particularly for the parents of deaf children and adolescents. These parents must understand several complicated service and benefit systems, some of which compete or work at cross purposes (Conley, 1985; Kiernan & Stark, 1986). The transition process itself, or the anticipation of it, may trigger a reactivation of adjustment issues related to the child's hearing loss (Mendelsohn & Mendelsohn, 1986). Also, professionals may be predisposed to perceive families as meddlesome or difficult. Power (1986) noted that 88% of rehabilitation professionals in a surveyed sample believed that families could impede clients' success in training or supported employment.

In 1987, the National Association of the Deaf Ad Hoc Committee on Education made several recommendations regarding family and community education ("Need for family," 1987). Those relevant to transition include the following:

- Each state should designate an individual, agency, or school responsible for centralized provision of information and training to families with deaf members.
- Professionals serving families with deaf members need highly specialized training in their discipline, in family issues, and in deafness.
- There are many deaf children who are not fully participating members of their families due to lack of communication and other barriers to integration. Therefore, families should receive assistance that will allow their deaf children to become full participants in the family unit.

The participation of family members in the education and rehabilitation process is perhaps the most crucial variable in the transition equation. To the extent that the families of deaf youth can provide unbiased support, encouragement, and uncritical involvement in the transition process, the process will be that much more successful.

FINAL REMARKS

In summary, this chapter has reviewed multiple issues involved in the transition process in general and, specifically, that process as it applies to deaf youth. Although similar themes have been echoed historically (at least from the 1940s), there appears to be no time like the present to capitalize upon many of the legislative, public policy, and systems initiatives of recent years—it is time to make transitioning a *reality*.

REFERENCES

Adler, E. (1974). Trends in delivering rehabilitation services to severely handicapped deaf persons. *Journal of Rehabilitation of the Deaf, 8*(1), 23–28.

Allen, T. (1986). Patterns of academic achievement among hearing impaired students: 1974 and 1983. In A. Schildroth & M. Karchmer (Eds.), *Deaf children in America* (pp. 161–206). San Diego: College-Hill Press.

Allen, T., & Karchmer, M. (1981). Influences on academic achievement of hearing impaired students born during the 1963–1965 rubella epidemic. *Directions, 2*, 40-54.

Beckett, C., Chitwood, S., & Hayden, D. (1985). The parent role in the transition from school to work. In S. Moon, P. Goodall, & P. Wehman (Eds.), *Critical issues related to supported competitive employment: Proceedings from the first RRTC symposium on employment for citizens who are mentally retarded* (pp. 129–140). Richmond: Virginia Commonwealth University, Rehabilitation Research and Training Center.

Cartwright, G., Cartwright, C., & Ward, M. (1984). *Educating special learners.* Belmont, CA: Wadsworth.

Christiansen, J.B. (1982). The socioeconomic status of the deaf population: A review of the literature. In J.B. Christiansen & J. Egelston-Dodd (Eds.), *Socioeconomic status of the deaf population* (pp. 1–59). Washington, DC: Gallaudet College.

Commission on Education of the Deaf. (1988). *Toward equality: Education of the deaf.* Washington, DC: U.S. Government Printing Office.

Conley, R.W. (1985). Public policies obstructing transition from school to independence. In L. Perlman & G. Austin (Eds.), *The transition to work and independence for youth with disabilities* (A Report of the Tenth Mary E. Switzer Memorial Seminar, May, 1986). Alexandria, VA: National Rehabilitation Association.

Culhane, B., & Williams, C. (1982). A review of the role of education in socialization. In B. Culhane & C. Williams (Eds.), *Working Papers #2: Social aspects of educating deaf persons* (pp. 1–32). Washington, DC: Gallaudet College.

Danek, M. (1987). Personnel shortages in deafness. *American Rehabilitation, 13*(3), 8–14.

Danek, M., & Lawrence, R.E. (1981). The multiply disabled hearing-impaired client: Implications for rehabilitation practice. *Journal of Rehabilitation of the Deaf, 15*(3), 1–9.

Falberg, R. (1966). Commentary on case study. In S. Quigley (Ed.), *The vocational rehabilitation of deaf people* (pp. 44–53). Washington, DC: U.S. Department of Health, Education, and Welfare.

Greenberg, M.T. (1980). Hearing families with deaf children: Stress and functioning as related to communication method. *American Annals of the Deaf, 125,* 1063–1071.

Greenberg, M. (1983). Family stress and child competence: The effects of early intervention for families with deaf infants. *American Annals of the Deaf, 128,* 407-417.

Guidelines for the establishment of rehabilitation facilities for the deaf. (1961). *American Annals of the Deaf, 106,* 341–364.

Halloran, W., Thomas, M.A., Snauwaert, D., & DeStefano, L. (1987). Imminent considerations in transition service delivery. *Interchange, 7*(3), 1.

Halpern, A.S. (1985). Transition: A look at the foundations. *Exceptional Children, 51,* 479–486.

Harold Russell Associates, Inc. (1985). *Consensus seminar proceedings and recommendations: Report on development of staff rules for supported and transitional employment services* (Contract no. 300-85-0094). Washington, DC: DHHS, Administration on Developmental Disabilities.

Hasazi, S.B., Gordon, L.R., & Roe, C.A. (1985). Factors associated with the employment status of handicapped youth exiting high school for 1979 to 1983. *Exceptional Children, 51,* 455–469.

Hoag, R.L. (1948). *A study of the cooperative relationships between the schools for the deaf and the rehabilitation agencies.* Unpublished master's thesis, Gallaudet College, Washington, DC.

Johnson, D.R., Bruininks, R.H., & Thurlow, M.L. (1987). Meeting the challenge of transition service planning through improved interagency cooperation. *Exceptional Children, 53,* 522–530.

Johnston, W.B., & Packer, A.E. (1987). *Workforce 2000: Work and workers for the twenty-first century.* Indianapolis, IN: Hudson Institute.

Karchmer, M., Milone, M., & Wolk, S. (1979). Educational significance of hearing loss at three levels of severity. *American Annals of the Deaf, 124,* 97–109.

Kiernan, W.E., & Stark, J.A. (1986). Employment options for adults with developmental disabilities: A conceptual model. *Remedial and Special Education, 7(6),* 7–110.

Kokaska, C., & Brolin, D. (1985). *Career education for handicapped individuals.* Columbus, OH: Charles E. Merrill.

Liben, L.S. (Ed.). (1978). *Deaf children: Developmental perspectives.* New York: Academic Press.

Lynch, E.W., & Stein, R. (1982). Perspectives on parent participation in special education. *Exceptional Education Quarterly, 3*(2), 56–63.

Martens, E.H. (1936). *The deaf and the hard of hearing* (Bulletin 1936, No. 13). Washington, DC: Government Printing Office.

Mathay, G.A., & Joyce, E.F. (1986). A study of closed cases: Implications for the administration of deafness rehabilitation services. *Journal of Rehabilitation of the Deaf, 20*(1), 5–13.

McCrone, W.P. (1983). Alice in rehabland. *Perspectives for Teachers of the Hearing Impaired, 2* (4), 9–11.

McCrone, W.P., & Arthur, R.A. (1981). The deaf applicant: Considerations for personnel managers. *Personnel Administrators, 26*(6), 65–69.

Meadow, K.P. (1980). *Deafness and child development.* Berkeley: University of California Press.

Meadow, K.P., & Trybus, R. (1979). Behavior and emotional problems of deaf children: An overview. In L. Bradford & W. Hardy (Eds.), *Hearing and hearing impairment.* New York: Grune & Stratton.

Melton, W.C. (1987). Trends and directions in vocational rehabilitation and their influence upon the education of deaf people. *American Annals of the Deaf, 132,* 315–316.

Mendelsohn, J., & Mendelsohn, B. (1986). Families in the transition process: Important partners. In L. Perlman & G. Austin (Eds.), *The transition to work and independence for youth with disabilities* (A Report of the Tenth Mary E. Switzer Memorial Seminar, May, 1986) (pp. 93–102). Alexandria, VA: National Rehabilitation Association.

Mills v. Board of Education, 348 F Supp 866 (DDC 1972).

Mindel, E.D., & Vernon, M. (1971). *They grow in silence: The deaf child and his family.* Silver Spring, MD: National Association of the Deaf.

Mithaug, D.E., Horiuchi, C.N., & Fanning, P.N. (1985). A report on the Colorado statewide follow-up survey of special education students. *Exceptional Children,* 51, 397–404.

Moores, D. (1986). *Educating the deaf: Psychology, principles, and practices* (3rd ed.). Boston: Houghton Mifflin.

Moores, D., & Kluwin, T. (1986). Issues in school placement. In A. Schildroth & M. Karchmer (Eds.), *Deaf children in America* (pp. 105–123). San Diego: College-Hill Press.

National Information Center for Children and Youth with Handicaps. (1987, March). Parent-employer partnerships: Developing employment opportunities for youth with disabilities. In *Report of a National Conference.* Alexandria, VA: Author.

Need for family educators and counselors in deafness. (1987, June). *NAD Broadcaster,* p. 1.

Olson, G. (1986, November/December). Nad's legislative priorities in rehabilitation. The NAD Broadcaster, *10*(8), 5.

Passmore, D.L. (1983). Employment of deaf people. In D. Watson, G. Anderson, N. Ford, P. Marut, & S. Ouellette (Eds.), *Job placement of hearing impaired persons: Research and practice* (pp. 5–16). Little Rock, AR: Rehabilitation Research and Training Center on Deafness/Hearing Impairment.

Pennsylvania Association for Retarded Citizens (PARC) v. Commonwealth of Pennsylvania, 334 F Supp 1257 (Ed. Pa 1971).

Power, P. (1986). Families, illness and disability. *Journal of Applied Rehabilitation Counseling, 17*(2), 41–44.

Project PERT Operations Manual. (1985). *Postsecondary education/ rehabilitation transition for the mildly mentally retarded and the learning disabled.* Unpublished manuscript, Woodrow Wilson Rehabilitation Center, Fishersville, VA.

Rawlings, B., & Jensema, C. (1977). *Two studies of the families of hearing impaired children* (Series R, No. 5). Washington, DC: Gallaudet College, Office of Demographic Studies.

Rawlings, B., Karchmer, M., & DeCaro, J. (1988). *College and career programs for deaf students.* Washington, DC: Gallaudet University.

Rubin, S., & Roessler, R. (1987). *Foundations of the vocational rehabilitation process* (3rd ed.). Austin, TX: PRO-ED.

Rusalem, H. (1976). A personalized social history of vocational rehabilitation in America. In H. Rusalem & D. Malikin (Eds.), *Contemporary vocational rehabilitation* (pp. 29–45). New York: New York University Press.

Rusch, F.R., & Phelps, L.A. (1987). Secondary special education and transition from school to work: A national priority. *Exceptional Children, 53,* 487–492.

Schein, J.D. (Ed.). (1975). *Model state plan for vocational rehabilitation of deaf clients.* New York: New York University Deafness Research and Training Center.

Schein, J.D. (Ed.). (1980). *Model state plan for vocational rehabilitation of deaf clients: Second revision* (2nd ed.). New York: New York University Deafness Research and Training Center.

Schein, J. (1987). Hearing impaired people in the workplace. *Shhh,* 8–12.

Schein, J.D., & Delk, M.T. (1974). *The deaf population of the United States.* Silver Spring, MD: National Association of the Deaf.

Schildroth, A.N. (1987). Two profiles of deaf adolescents: Special schools and the mainstream. In G.B. Anderson & D. Watson (Eds.), *Innovations in the habilitation and rehabilitation of deaf adolescents* (pp. 31–38). Little Rock, AR: National Deaf Adolescent Conference.

Schlesinger, H.S., & Meadow, K.P. (1972). *Sound and sign: Childhood deafness and mental health.* Berkeley: University of California Press.

Stoddard-Pfleuger, S. (1977). *Emerging issues in rehabilitation.* Washington, DC: Institute for Research Utilization.

Szymanski, E.M., & Danek, M.M. (1985). School-to-work transition for students with disabilities: Historical, current and conceptual issues. *Rehabilitation Counseling Bulletin, 29,* 81–89.

Szymanski, E., Hershenson, D., & Power, P. (1988). Enabling the family in supporting transition from school to work. In P. Power, A. Dell Orto, & M. Gibbons (Eds.), *Family interventions throughout chronic illness and disability* (pp. 216–233). New York: Springer.

Trybus, R., & Karchmer, M. (1977). School achievement scores of hearing impaired children: National data on achievement status and growth patterns. *American Annals of the Deaf, Directory of Programs and Services, 122,* 62–69.

U.S. Commission on Civil Rights. (1983). *Accommodating the spectrum of individual abilities* (Clearinghouse Publication #81). Washington, DC: Author.

U.S. Department of Education/OSERS. (1986). *Eighth annual report to Congress and the implementation of the Education of the Handicapped Act.* Washington, DC: U.S. Government Printing Office.

Vernon, M. (1970). Potential, achievement, and rehabilitation in the deaf population. *Rehabilitation Literature, 31,* 258–267.

Vernon, M., & Hyatt, C. (1981). How rehabilitation can better serve deaf clients: The problems and some solutions. *Journal of Rehabilitation, 79,* 60–62.

Walker, I. (1935). The federal survey of the deaf and the hard of hearing. Part I. Preliminary data. *American Annals of the Deaf, 80,* 116–125.

Wehman, P., Kregel, J., & Barcus, J.M. (1985). From school to work: A vocational transition model for handicapped students. *Exceptional Children, 52*(1), 25–37.

Wheeler, J. (1987). Why transition is needed. In J. Wheeler (Ed.), *Transitioning persons with moderate and severe disabilities from school to adulthood: What makes it work* (pp. 3–10). Stout: University of Wisconsin–Stout, Materials Development Center.

Whitehead, C.W. (1986). The sheltered workshop dilemma: Reform or replacement. *Remedial and special education, 7*(6), 18–24.

Whitehead, C.W., & Marrone, J. (1986). Time limited evaluation and training. In W.E. Kiernan & J.A. Stark (Eds.), *Pathways to employment for adults with developmental disabilities* (pp. 163–176). Baltimore: Paul H. Brookes Publishing Co.

Will, M. (1984a). *Bridges from school to working life: Programs for the handicapped.* Washington, DC: The Office of Special Education and Rehabilitative Services, Office of Information and Resources for the Handicapped.

Will, M. (1984b). *OSERS programming for the transition of youth with disabilities: Bridges from school to working life.* Washington, DC: U.S. Department of Education, Office of Special Education and Rehabilitative Services.

Will, M. (1985). Transition: Linking disabled youth to a productive youth. *OSERS News in Print, 1*(1), 1.

Wolfensberger, W. (1972). *The principle of normalization in human services.* Downsview, Toronto, Canada: York University Campus National Institute on Mental Retardation.

Wright, G.N. (1980). *Total rehabilitation.* Boston: Little, Brown.

Parents' Perspectives on the Transition Process

2

Jacqueline Z. Mendelsohn
and Patricia Stoney Brown

Each of the two women who contributed manuscripts for this chapter, Jacqueline Z. Mendelsohn and Patricia Stoney Brown, is a parent of a deaf youth. Ms. Mendelsohn is the former executive director of the International Association of Parents of Deaf Children (IAPD), now the American Society for Deaf Children; Ms. Brown is a former president, and current vice president, of the same organization. Obviously they are a "nonrandom" sample of parents. However, through their involvement with national organizations and their experiences with their own children—recent high school graduates currently experiencing transition to the world of work— they offer a broad perspective on the issues addressed by this book.

For their contributions, the editors requested that the parents provide some background on their deaf children pertaining to etiology and diagnosis and to describe their children's transition experiences. On the one hand, Joshua Mendelsohn and Stephanie Brown are individuals with very different experiences and backgrounds. They differ with respect to sex, ethnic background, etiology, age at onset of deafness, and educational experience. On the other hand, there are also many commonalities. Both are deaf children who were born into hearing families. Both have older hearing siblings. Both have parents who supported and actively advocated for their needs. And, most important, they share the experience of deafness. This single commonality has resulted in several themes that have recurred in their lives as they have moved from childhood into adulthood.

In Chapter 1, Danek and McCrone note that family participation and support are the most important factors in the complex transition process. Furthermore, it is mandated by law that parents be involved in the planning process for transition. Therefore, a book about transition that does not consider the parents' perspective would be incomplete. Subsequent chapters of this volume focus on summary statistical data, and, while statements from individual parents are no substitute for scientifically collected "hard" data, this chapter should complement the data presentation and lead to a broader understanding of transition issues facing deaf youth.

Although the two authors of this chapter are a nonrandom sample of parents with deaf sons or daughters, they are "random" in the sense that the authors of this book did not select them because of their views on certain critical issues in the education of deaf students (e.g., communication methodology or views on vocational rehabilitation). Indeed, the editors were not aware of the experiences of these parents regarding these issues before they were selected to write this chapter. It has been the policy of the Center for Assessment and Demographic Studies from its inception not to take preconceived positions in the field of education of deaf students but to make every effort to allow the data collected by the Center to guide its analyses and recommendations. The views expressed in this chapter reflect the experiences of two thoughtful and concerned parents deeply involved in the education of deaf youth. Deaf students and their families, and the educators and counselors serving them, must decide how well these accounts illuminate the transition experiences of their own lives and careers.

JOSHUA

by Jacqueline Z. Mendelsohn

I am the parent of one son who has just graduated from college and one who has finished his first year in college. I look back on the past 15 years since my youngest son was diagnosed as profoundly deaf with wonder, sadness, some anger, and a great deal of pride.

Joshua was diagnosed as profoundly deaf when he was 3 years old. Joshua, my husband, my son Aaron, and I were living in California at the time. We had experienced 3 years of having our questions brushed aside, having professionals diagnose Joshua as aphasic, anxious, slow, and the son of a hysterical mother. Fifteen years later, as a profoundly deaf young adult, Josh has become an independent, confident college student with his own goals for the future.

The journey from an undiagnosed toddler to a college student began as a seemingly endless, danger-wrought experience for us, as we only knew about raising a hearing child, only knew about the hearing world, and had only fear about the unknown world of deafness.

After 3 years of searching for answers to our questions about this child who didn't respond, who was extremely active, who constantly needed attention, and who caused great concerns about our parenting abilities, we finally got a diagnosis. Josh was so different from his older brother Aaron, who had always been well behaved. Aaron stayed in the playpen; Josh demanded constant attention. Aaron played by himself for hours with cars and trucks; Josh wanted me around constantly. Aaron listened; Josh threw temper tantrums. We had thought, through our positive experiences with Aaron, that we were good parents; Josh made us wonder about our skills. He was not predictable, he was not compliant, he never listened, and he certainly did not obey our requests.

Upon diagnosis, after 3 years of misdiagnoses, we became part of a parent-research program. Within 3 days after Josh's diagnosis we met our first group of parents and were able to talk about our experiences and listen to other parents' experiences of raising deaf children. The parent support and contact was a turning point for me. I could share my fears and my pain, and other people understood because they had experienced the same fears and pain. And because they had more experience, they could give me hope about this new experience of having a child who was not what we had expected—a hearing child. That same evening, 3 days after diagnosis, the Mental Health Services for the Deaf (now the Center on Deafness) taught us our first songs in sign language—"Twinkle, Twinkle Little Star" and "Bridge Over Troubled Water"; they taught us survival signs—juice, cookie, yes, no, mommy, daddy; and we met our home tutor and the psychiatrist who headed the program. We were showered with caring, with signs, with information, and with support. Deafness was presented positively—a challenge—and with high expectations.

The deaf adults I met, from whom I learned, and with whom I socialized, increased my view of deafness as an adjunct to my child, a factor of life that needed special attention, special education, and special communication. I did not learn to view deafness as a "negative handicap." I believe that the attitude of the people I met and from whom I learned colored my views of deafness and fostered positive expectations of myself and my son's abilities. Sign language was presented as language, not vocabulary, and we learned from demonstration, modeling, and many conversations with deaf and hearing people. I found myself well armed and well informed and feeling able to meet the challenges of deafness in spite of the emotional blow and readjustments that deafness brought to our family.

Elementary School

Three months after diagnosis, we moved from San Francisco to Anchorage, Alaska. We had already explored the program there before Josh was diagnosed, "just in case." (We suspected deafness long before it was confirmed.) We knew the program was in a public school, utilizing a new concept known at that time as *integration*, later as *mainstreaming*. There was no residential program, no school for the deaf, and I knew they used an innovative system called Signing Exact English (SEE). The program was very new, having just begun the year before in 1971. By the second grade, Josh was mainstreamed with an interpreter into a hearing classroom.

My husband's and my first experience with the program began with special requests. We had been so well taught, so well informed, so well cared for that we felt comfortable making requests for Josh's program that were not part of the program at that time (e.g., language development and creativity, and the establishment of parent groups). As parents trained in mental health, we felt it was as important for us to have parent-to-parent support as it was for Josh to have a good support program. Alaska was raw frontier; the Alaska State Program for the Deaf was new, and, for the most part, enthusiastic and receptive to new ideas. Josh was the first young child using sign language who was mainstreamed—first part time and then full time. As parents of a young deaf child, we turned to professionals for advice and to parents for support. An "outside expert" was brought in to evaluate the program and make recommendations. Because the program was so new, many of the personnel were receptive to different ideas. They used these ideas to formulate an excellent program. The intensity with which I became involved with ensuring excellence in the school program alleviated the feelings of isolation and strain precipitated by the experience of having a child different from other children, of not having models of other parents with deaf children, or of not having enough deaf adults from whom to learn.

In writing this chapter, I sorted through my emotions about raising Josh and found that parent-professional relationships became crucial to the transitions that have occurred throughout Josh's life. For example, I had had very negative experiences with audiologists before and at the time of Josh's diagnosis, which I realize colored my future relationships with other audiologists. I believe many parents who have had negative experiences with professionals maintain that attitude toward them and expect the worst from them. These negative experiences and attitudes can affect the transition of deaf youth from adolescence to adulthood because of the continuation of the difficult relationships between parents and professionals and then, often, between professionals and students.

Throughout Josh's school years we remained vigilant, intervening at times when we felt that educational services or interpreter services needed attention. We learned what we were entitled to as parents by establishing positive relationships with other experienced parents, with deaf people, with parent organizations, and with professionals in the field. Because of our background and training, my husband and I had an easier time establishing a peer relationship with professionals rather than being viewed as "just parents." The ability to relate with the professionals in the educational process was beneficial both to us and to Josh.

Experiences of isolation were always a focus, both ours and Josh's. As the only deaf child in hearing classes, Josh experienced being different. As he got older, parallel play gave way to gossip, wrestling, locker-room talk, and preadolescent stirrings. Relationships with hearing peers changed from being easy and nonverbal to strained and nonrelating. As he grew from early childhood to adolescence we had to help Josh bridge the gap because support services were less available.

When Josh was 11 years old, we moved from Alaska to Maryland and the process of coordinating Josh's special needs with the academic program and support services continued. We and Josh looked at all the programs available in Maryland and Washington, D.C., and Josh decided to attend the centralized public school program in Montgomery County, Maryland, rather than the state school or the school on the Gallaudet campus. This decision was made with us, but not by us. His choice was carefully thought out, taking into account both his academic and his social needs.

Adolescence and High School

In adolescence Josh's needs became social as well as academic. The issues focused around his ability to use public transportation independently, to take driving lessons, to go out with friends, to use a telecommunication device for the deaf (TDD), to watch captioned movies and television programs, to think of the future, and to stretch all boundaries—both at home and at school. Throughout these growing years the services involving parents lessened, and I no longer felt the need to have an intimate knowledge of Josh's program. If I had questions or problems, I began to ask Josh. It became time for Josh to be aware of his own needs, to become knowledgeable about the rights he had as an individual who was deaf, and to know where he needed to go for services.

Independent living skills are not part of the curriculum or related services provided by Public Law 94-142. I felt it was my responsibility to provide Josh with this knowledge because he was not getting it from the school program. I knew that Josh needed much more than competency in English to survive and thrive in a world where he is a minority.

This was also a period of time for Josh to make the emotional adjustment to the awareness of deafness, of the differences between hearing and deaf people and hearing and deaf society. As the parent, I needed to adjust my views away from looking only at the present to looking to the future—to Josh's life as a deaf adult, independent from his family. I learned from other parents about realistic expectations, about false information, about misguided goals. Our experiences were not as negative as others because Josh thrived in the academic environment; we knew that he would be able to go to college, and that his need for a place in society could be postponed for a few years. And the knowledge was also there that he, as an adult, would be armed with academic skills on a level with hearing peers, which would give him an advantage.

First Job

When Josh was 15, we began talking to him about getting a job after school. His brother had started working at 14 and we felt it was appropriate for Josh to begin to have his own financial resources. For the first time, Josh demonstrated insecurity. He argued against work because, "No one would understand me. I can't get a job because I'm deaf. I don't want a job!" We had huge discussions and arguments about his abilities; after all, he was sophomore class president, he was active with hearing students, he was (we thought) comfortable around adults and communicating with them. And then came the realization that, for the first time, Josh was scared. He was frightened that, as a deaf person, he would not be able to function with other people. I do not believe that he ever doubted his ability to do work. I believe that his fear was, from his beginning awareness of adolescence, that not all hearing people would understand him, nor would they be as tolerant as his peer group.

With luck and some research, the perfect job fell into his lap, one that involved a government agency and computers. The agency hired four high school students each year and wanted to include a disabled student. Hearing about Josh's skill on the computer, they called and asked him to come in for an interview. I went with him to interpret—we should have hired an interpreter to go with him instead of his mother—but once they began to communicate via the computer, they didn't need an interpreter any more. Josh worked at this agency three times a week and all summer for 2 years and continues to come home to his job during Christmas and summer vacations. The job offered him the opportunity to mix with people who had no knowledge of deafness or experience with deaf people. The job gave him the opportunity to figure out transportation, set up a budget, find time for homework and school shows—in short, how to juggle all the aspects of his life along with his desire to earn money. He quickly became enthusiastic about the job because he loved advancing his computer skills and he loved getting a salary. He began to budget carefully what he earned and what he spent, finding to his dismay how much he actually did spend. He became popular at work because of his curiosity and excitement at the challenge of a new project. He learned to overcome his fear of people who were not familiar with deafness and to help others overcome their fear of him. The job, his earning power, and the challenge the program provided gave him a sense of independence and of what could be. The balancing between school and peers and job gave him the opportunity to prepare for his future, to experience what life involves.

College

The senior year of high school was the time of beginning to look to the future, of making decisions about life after the 12th grade, of life in a college or university. The process of choosing a college was a difficult one. Josh had always attended public schools in a mainstream program and had always been in honors classes made up of almost all hearing classmates. His deaf friends seemed to be social rather than academic peers. As he grew into adolescence, he became more identified as a deaf person, with special pride in his involvement with organizations, issues, and events that were geared toward deaf people. He prided himself in being the "organizer" among his deaf friends, deciding on weekend activities, car pools, bus routes, and ski trips as well as occasional study groups.

Choosing a college became an identity issue—whether to go to an "all deaf college"; a college with an "all deaf" population on a hearing campus; a mainstreamed program within a large state university; or, completely on the other end of the spectrum, a major university with international prestige, high academics, and the admiration and recognition of the college educated—but no, or a minimal number of, deaf students. A college-bound youth is always faced with making decisions that affect his or her identity—academics, social opportunities, prestige, size, location. A deaf youth must also take into consideration the reality of being deaf, of needing special communication support, of being different, of being left out on a "hearing" campus, of losing out on national prestige on a "deaf" campus.

As might be expected Josh applied to an "all deaf" program; but having been in a mainstreamed program all his life, he decided that he did not want to be in a totally deaf community, even though his social life was, and is, centered around his deaf peers and activities.

Josh chose between two other programs to which he had applied and had been accepted. One was my husband's and my alma mater, a "top ten" university with 10 deaf students amidst 28,000 hearing students; the other was a state university with much less stringent entrance requirements with 200 deaf students amidst 28,000 hearing students. Josh visited both campuses, even though he had decided to go to our alma mater. However, after visiting this major university, Josh came out ashen—10 deaf students attending this university were not enough for him. In his eyes they were lacking a satisfactory social life, and he felt that social relationships were a crucial part of college life. He then went to visit the other campus with 200 deaf students and 28,000 hearing students. He loved the classes, the environment, the deaf center where all the deaf students gather, and, especially, the large number of deaf students. That college became his first choice and is where he is at this time.

To help Josh with making the decision about college and to remove our biases, we and Josh agreed that he should go to a counselor with whom he could brainstorm the pros and cons of each choice. He saw a social worker who was not connected with a college campus but who was familiar with signing, deafness, adolescents, and young adults. He and Josh met without my husband's and my emotions clouding the issues, and the result was that Josh clarified his feelings about his deafness and his identity and his priorities. Again, the decision was his; we had input, but he had to make the decision.

So, Josh now lives 3,000 miles away from home. He makes his own decisions about classes, about meals, about his girlfriend, about earning and spending his money. He decides when and if to study, what to eat, and when and if to come back to the dorm at night. He is becoming his own person, making his own decisions that affect his self-esteem and confidence.

Josh has gotten a job on campus in order to become partially independent from us. He thinks about his major and what he wants to do in life during and after college, but he doesn't think *too* much about the future, and he has no specific plans.

As Josh enters manhood, still seen through our eyes as a boy/man, we as parents have as many adjustments to make as he does. The reality of having a deaf adult in the family is a different feeling from having a deaf child in the family. There is no more pretending good communication, there is no more tickling and throwing the child up in the air instead of communicating, there is no more ignoring puzzled looks across the dinner table when the conversation is not interpreted or not everyone is signing. All the "should haves" and "ought to haves" come back to haunt us. Should we have sent him to a residential school? Should we have used American Sign Language instead of SEE with him? Should we have encouraged more speech? Will he marry a deaf woman and never come home again to his hearing family? Have we raised a healthy, independent, self-assured individual who can conquer life as it comes, who can make decisions that will be enriching rather than bitter and combative?

He is my son, my youngest, my last to leave home, and in many ways the most painful from whom to separate because of my involvement with him as a deaf child. Just as he must now venture out into life as his own person, a young adult who is also deaf, so must I now let go of my identity as the mother of a deaf child and venture out on my own, making decisions that don't necessarily involve considerations for deaf children or adults. It's a strange new world for both of us—he must find his own interpreters; I no longer need to remain vigilant to ensure that everyone is signing.

He has chosen to be in a world with both hearing and deaf persons—where he is a leader among his peers and an equal among those who are not afraid to communicate with someone who communicates in a different mode. He remains my son, my youngest, my special child—that will never change —but his life and mine now encompass so much more. The challenges are now his, not mine and his. I can only watch from afar in wonder at his strengths and confidence.

STEPHANIE

by Patricia Stoney Brown

Visiting Disney World's Magic Kingdom once again reminds me of our first visit to Disneyland 21 years ago, a little over a year after my daughter Stephanie had been diagnosed as profoundly deaf. Stephanie, who was 3 then, her 5-year-old hearing sister Terre, and I were on an outing with other families involved in a "summer experience" at California's John Tracy Clinic. We'd been learning the oral communication approach, so, as we walked around the amusement park, we parents tried frantically to maintain eye contact with our deaf children and talk to them in a way we hoped would make our speech understandable and enhance the children's enjoyment.

Our next visit to Disney World came 9 years later, shortly after our family was introduced to American Sign Language. Moving at a much slower pace, Stephanie, Terre, and I tried to recall and use the few signs we had learned. Our signing was clumsy, but Stephanie's experience, nevertheless, seemed genuinely enhanced by this new approach to communication.

Three years later, traveling to Disney World with a group of hearing impaired students, 15-year-old Stephanie whirled around the amusement park, signing so rapidly she made me dizzy. She assumed the role of tour guide for her best friend, and I had little to do but tag along and try to answer a few questions about new attractions.

Earlier today, 24-year-old Stephanie suddenly announced she had seen enough of Disney's Magic Kingdom. She would spend the afternoon alone at EPCOT Center, then meet us later at 6:30 P.M. It seems that each visit to Disney World has revealed more and more independence on Stephanie's part. My role as facilitator and supervisor has diminished each time. Stephanie is taking charge of her life.

The Hearing Loss

Stephanie lost her hearing after a 4- to 6-week undiagnosed illness. At the age of 14 months, she had been admitted to a hospital with a fever of "unknown origin" while we were on vacation in Florida. Our family is sure Stephanie was able to hear prior to her illness because she had been responding to sounds and had developed some vocabulary, such as "bye-bye," "bottle," and "go."

Within hours after her release from the hospital, I noticed she was *not* responding to sounds. I contacted her pediatrician at once. He reminded me how ill Stephanie had been and hinted I was an overly anxious mother who should stop worrying and "bring her back when she really gets sick." A subsequent visit to an ear, nose, and throat specialist led to the diagnosis of Stephanie's apparent deafness as "psychological." Deeply frustrated, I developed a fierce determination to find out what was wrong with Stephanie and what I should do about it.

Months later, Stephanie was at last diagnosed by an otologist as being profoundly deaf. It was difficult to tell precisely what had caused the loss, but the otologist explained that the shape of her audiogram resembled that of a hearing loss caused by high fever, drugs, rubella, or mumps. Indeed, Stephanie had contracted mumps by the time she left the hospital, but the otologist also suspected the preceding fever and the drugs administered during her hospitalization. A few months after this diagnosis, we were relieved to learn that there was no obvious, irreversible damage apart from the hearing loss.

Early Education

Stephanie's formal, but fragmented, educational experiences began at that John Tracy Clinic "Summer Experience for Families." Before attending this program, I had taken the clinic's correspondence course. Prior to that, I had taken Stephanie to a number of "speech and language" lessons at centers in the Virgin Islands. Two speech therapists there offered me the clearest and most concise information about deafness I had yet received. Nevertheless, my overall ignorance about deafness and, more specifically, about the needs of deaf children, made it impossible for me to relate this somewhat abstract information to my pressing concerns as a parent and to the pressing needs of my deaf child. (I did not then realize that one of my and Stephanie's greatest needs was to meet some successful deaf adults who could give us a clearer picture of what might be possible for her.)

During the next few years, back at our residence in the Virgin Islands, we enrolled Stephanie in any class or program we felt might benefit her. Usually, however, we ended up withdrawing her because the Virgin

Islands simply had no education programs specifically designed for deaf children. Finally, completely frustrated with this haphazard approach, a few other concerned parents and I submitted a proposal to the Virgin Islands legislature and the U.S. Department of Education. The proposal, which was funded, enabled me to start a class for deaf children between the ages of 3 and 12.

Using my background in elementary education and my parent training from the John Tracy Clinic, I started an oral program for a total of nine deaf students with emphasis on language development. Stephanie's elementary schooling, thereafter, was varied geographically, but was consistently oral, in line with my Tracy Clinic training. From my special classes in the Virgin Islands she went on to oral elementary programs in New York, North Carolina, and Florida.

From an Oral to a Total Communication Philosophy

When Stephanie was 11, an important event occurred that changed my previously negative attitude toward sign language. I happened to meet two deaf adults who had recently moved to the Virgin Islands to pursue their very successful careers. On meeting them, I was struck not only by their obvious competence and self-assurance, but also by their comfortable reliance on a combination of sign language, speech, and writing for effective communication. I saw immediately that these were the kind of role models I had needed to see and that I wanted Stephanie also to see. This encounter, in itself, was all that was required to convert me from an oral to a total communication philosophy.

Consequently, in 1976, when Stephanie was about 12, we moved to Washington, D.C., so she could attend Gallaudet's Model Secondary School for the Deaf (MSSD), which follows a total communication approach. Looking back, this move was probably the single most significant positive step in Stephanie's educational life.

The 5 years spent in that program—sometimes as a day student and sometimes as a residential student—brought more growth and challenge to Stephanie and the rest of our family than anything else we had experienced. We began to see the "real" Stephanie emerge from behind that beautiful, smiling, but often confused-looking face. She quickly mastered a communication system that was socially and emotionally satisfying to her. She developed friendships, both long lasting and short term. She fulfilled dreams of doing things her older sister had done that she thought she would never be able to do, such as cheerleading and acting in plays. Also, Stephanie was finally developing the self-confidence that has become so important in her pursuit of academic achievement.

About the same time Stephanie entered MSSD, Public Law 94-142 was beginning to have an impact on America's approach to the education of deaf children. By using all the professional knowledge I had gained about education, all the information I could gather about MSSD's curriculum, and everything I knew firsthand about Stephanie as her parent and former teacher, I decided to take full advantage of that law. For example, I worked long and hard with Stephanie's advisor to design her first individualized education program (IEP). With modifications here and there and constant monitoring, the plan worked out fairly well. We had designed an IEP that was extremely basic, including English, math, science, and social studies. I had insisted on adding reading, which to my surprise was not a traditional part of the curriculum. Through negotiations, we were able to get reading included.

Under these generally positive circumstances I at last began to put into perspective, and disregard, a psychological report entered into Stephanie's records several years earlier by two hearing psychologists who had come to the Virgin Islands from the "mainland" to test our deaf students. At that time, I was sure Stephanie's report would doom her forever, if anyone ever read it, because its only positive statement was that "Stephanie is a well-mannered, well-dressed, black female." I now regard that report as representing little more than the particular biases of those psychologists.

"What do you want to do in life?"

We experienced good, humdrum, and bad times—all of which served to make Stephanie a stronger person. At age 13, she was being asked questions such as, "What do you want to do in life?" or, "What are your goals?" She replied with career choices such as flight attendant and immigration officer, which were undoubtedly based on her somewhat unusual background. She had probably traveled by air and ship more than most kids her age, and she had idolized the friendly, glamorous flight attendants who had given her so much attention. Her desire to become an immigration officer was surely sparked by the frequent abrupt disappearances of babysitters, friends, and neighbors who were not allowed to renew or extend their passports. She had a strong humanitarian impulse to save people she cared about from what she considered unfair treatment.

The idea of becoming an immigration officer, in fact, seemed for some time to be foremost in her mind, and it certainly seemed to me to be an achievable goal. When Stephanie was 15, however, and we wrote to the U.S. Department of Immigration requesting information on employment opportunities, that department's response was one of the first to shatter a long-harbored dream. One requirement, the department's brochure said, was that she "must be able to hear a whisper." Although we had managed to reason out why being a flight attendant might be difficult for Stephanie, it was not easy for her to understand or accept this particular requirement for an immigration officer.

Each time we reviewed her IEP and found we had all the basics in place, we would add a few electives from various potential career areas. First, we added typing, then word processing. Stephanie did well in those areas and her teachers were encouraging, but she wanted no part of them, saying they were, "okay, but boring." She explained that—partly because she was a deaf person—she yearned most to work with people, not stare at machines. If I have ever seen my child adamant about anything, it was, and is, this strong preference for working with people.

Stephanie's Dream: A Career in Fashion Design

We decided to explore the possibility of a summer job. She was selected to work for the U.S. Department of Justice, Tax Division, as a messenger/mail clerk and was somewhat excited. It was her first job and she was successful at it. She enjoyed the money and wanted to return the next summer. She visited all the nearby museums during her lunch times and began to acquire an almost obsessive interest in Washington, D.C. More important, perhaps, she managed to establish a few rewarding friendships with hearing peers at work. I definitely saw a more independent person emerging.

A second successful summer experience at the same job encouraged us to explore a new idea at the final IEP meeting. Stephanie loved clothes and dressing well; she had taken one basic course in sewing and had enjoyed it. We selected an advanced sewing class for her and also a drafting class. She had taken a shop class and had acquired experience in using household and other tools, making a tool box, printing various items, and—most impressive to me—learning to change a tire on a car, something many females never learn to do. From her shop class experience, she had developed an interest in and had become quite skilled in drafting. So, encouraged by her female drafting teacher, she continued to the next level.

Gradually, Stephanie's successful experiences in drafting and sewing, her desire to work with people, and her love of dressing well and visiting high-fashion stores began to inspire her to pursue a career in fashion design. I had conferences with her drafting and sewing teachers and was encouraged by their comments about her skills in both areas. They never gave any false hopes about Stephanie's new dream, but they never said "she couldn't." I had these conferences in secret with her teachers because, too often, when discussing career possibilities with her vocational specialist, I found myself labeled as "over-ambitious," "a stage mother," and "unrealistic." I had gotten my fill of such put-downs! I did not need to hear anything that might make me feel pessimistic because I knew the feeling could easily transfer to Stephanie, who did not deserve or need negative influences.

Seeking an Appropriate Postsecondary Program

As Stephanie's graduation from MSSD got closer, I did not panic. She and I had gotten used to tackling obstacles as a team. We knew that, ultimately, we were the ones who had to figure out how best to manage her transition from school to work, and we felt that we were generally doing a good job, taking or leaving the good and not-so-good advice we got from others. Gallaudet College (now Gallaudet University) had recently published a listing of most postsecondary programs around the country with special programs and support services for deaf students. MSSD made this publication available to its students and parents, and Stephanie and I avidly combed through it looking for programs offering drafting, fashion design, or any facsimile thereof. We particularly noted those programs that had open enrollment, dormitory programs, and courses in apparel design (which usually meant training for factory or assembly-line garment construction).

About mid-year, Stephanie began to work with her school counselor on postsecondary plans. Although I believed this person's intentions were good, I was concerned because I had been repeatedly "warned" by a vocational specialist that Stephanie probably would not be well suited to any of her first career choices. I therefore suggested to Stephanie that she limit the amount of information to be shared with any school staff about future academic plans. We were both experiencing a "high" related to her fashion-design goal, and I suppose that, frankly, I was guarding that high from anything I feared might deflate it. I was also worried that negative feedback from others might somehow get to a postsecondary institution considering Stephanie's application for admission. Stephanie and I realized that success on the postsecondary level would, for many reasons, be an uphill battle that would require high self-esteem built of positive thoughts and evaluations.

What a pleasant surprise it was, then, when we finally met with the vocational rehabilitation and school counselors and revealed our choice of programs for Stephanie. The news—along with information about Stephanie's career aspirations—was greeted quite favorably.

We had chosen a program with open enrollment, dormitory accommodations, a major area of study close enough to what Stephanie wanted that she was willing to settle for it, and a reputation of offering good support services. I had no real concerns about the college being located entirely across the United States from Stephanie's home in Maryland. Her previous travel experiences, her cosmopolitan flair (acquired as a result of our many relocations), her curiosity about other parts of the country and world, and her love for various cultures and people assured me that she could get along anywhere.

Much of the next few months was devoted to completing applications both for admission into the college and for various types of financial assistance. Applying for admission to the college turned out to be a rewarding experience, in part because of the many positive things I then had good reason to say about Stephanie. Concerning references, I chose very carefully those teachers and others from her past who knew Stephanie, cared about her, and had seen what a hard worker she was. They understood her determination to succeed at anything she tried. As a result, extremely good references were written, and she was quickly accepted into the postsecondary program of her choice.

The Trouble with "Vocational Rehabilitation"

I had so much experience in the area of filling out applications for financial assistance that the paperwork involved was not difficult. However, I was caught quite off-guard by the strict requirements placed by vocational rehabilitation (VR) regulations on applications for financial assistance to deaf students. Stephanie seemed to be subjected to rigid dictates concerning what she could and could not do. We were told bluntly what kinds of choices VR would and would not fund. The guidelines seemed to be phrased in such a way that if she did not follow the recommendations made by VR, she simply would not receive funding. Also, it seemed that it had to be somehow predictable that she would be successful at her chosen career for life.

I began to compare Stephanie's experiences in getting financial assistance with those of my hearing daughter, Terre. Terre had decided very early in high school where she wanted to attend college and had applied for financial aid and scholarships that were granted to her without any dictation of what her major should be. No counselor had attempted to tell her what she could or could not do or tried to predict her success or failure. Everyone involved seemed to realize that she was a young adult and that it was up to her to make the most of her opportunities.

It is my impression, however, that with deaf children VR professionals seem to be in the business of predicting success or failure according to certain preestablished levels of expectation, of making pronouncements about what the student/client will *not* be able to do. Maybe they do this to ensure that their funding is not wasted in futile efforts, but my concern for Stephanie was that she be enabled to pursue her interest, even if doing so contained an element of risk. I felt that she should be given the chance to try to succeed in her chosen course of study without threats of funding cuts constantly hanging over her head.

Stephanie's financial dilemma became even clearer to me after she had been admitted into the postsecondary program and had completed what I considered to be a very successful first semester. She took a normal courseload, consisting of some prep courses and courses taken in the mainstream. As I recall, she received Cs and one D. Her cumulative grade-point-average was at a level that allowed her to remain at the school with probationary status, but without funding. To say she was caught between the proverbial rock and a hard place is to put it mildly. How can a student improve her grade point average to become eligible for refunding if she can't afford to enroll in classes?

Needless to say, these questions were posed to the VR counselor, who responded, predictably, with long pauses on the phone and, to my ear, flippant remarks such as, "These are not my rules, but state regulations." Most VR counselors can recite those words with, what seemed to me, extreme coldness. Furthermore, they are capable of asking their clients (our children) to come in by themselves and sign critically important documents, filled with regulations in fine print that would take most of us and our lawyers a few hours to make sense of. Yet, the deaf client—who may read at a fifth-grade level—is then held accountable for adhering to all of those regulations, even if he or she did *not* understand them in the first place.

I would hesitate to share such information for fear of biasing other parents if I believed I alone or only a few other parents had ever had such experiences. But as I have traveled around the country, sharing information about VR counselors with other parents of deaf children, I have discovered that we all usually end up singing the same sad song—at least those of us who have at some time or another needed or wanted the service. One parent shared with me that, because of the apathetic attitude of a VR counselor assigned to work with her daughter, she had decided to minimize her daughter's contact with the counselor. Another parent recently said, "I wouldn't let them near my child."

I should add that, in my years of working with parents and professionals, I have talked with VR counselors around the country who feel and admit that their agencies are not perfect and that they sometimes have to slightly bend state regulations to make these rules truly serve the needs of clients. It would be a blessing if more VR counselors adopted that attitude.

There are some very basic things that I, as a parent, would like to suggest to make the VR system more functional for clients.

1. More consumer input should be considered by federal and state governments when VR regulations and legislation are first being

planned. These rules should be designed so that they help, rather than hinder, clients' progress.

2. VR should evaluate or analyze failure and success rates with more subtlety, so that the exceptionally motivated client's aspirations are not cavalierly nipped in the bud.

3. VR should set realistic goals or guidelines for deaf clients that are in accord with the statistics and studies available from such locations as Gallaudet's Center for Assessment and Demographic Studies or the research department at the National Technical Institute for the Deaf. There are many studies that reveal the functional levels of the majority of deaf students at the secondary or postsecondary levels, none of which is congruent with the expectations or guidelines of most state requirements.

The Trouble with "Vocational Counseling"

For those who don't know, I should point out that VR services include more than financial assistance. Among other VR services is vocational counseling. I am sorry to say, however, that each time my daughter sought such assistance—usually on an annual basis when the VR agency sent out its notices—she would leave so depressed that we tried to be sure someone would be home to console her when she arrived.

Once, some counselors at the VR agency tried to persuade me that Stephanie was not well suited for her chosen career in fashion design. They had her tested and, when the tests did not prove their point, they requested a second set of tests. I eagerly awaited the results, since I had great respect for the noted psychologist who administered the tests. Again, his evaluation did not substantiate the counselors' opinions. Rather than admit they had been mistaken, however, they merely sent me a copy of the test results, and they did that only after I insisted on seeing them! Disgusted, I decided to boycott VR services. Although I am generally pessimistic, I do hope for a changing of the guard that will one day make VR services be what they should be: "designed for the consumers."

My decision never again to contact a VR agency was made while Stephanie and I were ahead. We had a favorable report from the psychologist giving her what we considered a "green light" on her career choice and encouraging her to continue her chosen postsecondary training. Evidently, however, the negative attitude of the VR counselors had been passed on to the academic counselor at Stephanie's school. Previously, this counselor had always worked with us in a positive way, but now she too began to look at all the negative aspects and actually seemed *disappointed* when the test results were different from what she had anticipated.

Finding a Better Program

During this entire time (thanks, largely, to unflagging family support), Stephanie was still enrolled in her classes, doing well in some classes and not so well, *grade-wise*, in others. I stress grade-wise because, for the most part, she was enjoying school and felt she was learning consistently, something that seemed to be important only to the two of us. The classes she had selected, although vocational or skill oriented, also involved academic requirements that required a high reading level. The demands on Stephanie were numerous and exhausting. She was becoming discouraged.

The rest of the family tried hard to keep her spirits up with phone calls and mail, but at the end of that semester we decided she would withdraw. The program, supposedly designed for deaf consumers, was not working. Several of Stephanie's deaf friends had exited from the program even before she did, and others left at or about the same time. Over the years, as these friends visited our home, I found that they all had had similar experiences.

Once again, Stephanie was fortunate. We had heard of a program in our local metropolitan area that offered a major in fashion design. I knew Stephanie would not want a break in her education; so I contacted the school and found that it was not too late to register for the second semester. The school's director of special services assured us that Stephanie would have interpreters for all her classes. Stephanie arrived home mid-December and by early January was enrolled at this local university. Her nonresident status made the program a bit expensive for us; so she started with only one class. A few basic courses were waived because she had taken similar classes at her previous school.

When Stephanie came home the first day, she was quite excited. She said the students were all friendly, professional, and serious about their majors. The semester went by quickly and ended with an exotic, outdoor fashion show on campus that made me feel extremely proud. It was thrilling to see the camaraderie Stephanie had developed with the other students. If they missed class or a rehearsal and were not sure where to go, they telephoned her to ask about times and locations for rehearsals. They knew that if they called Stephanie, they would get the information because she never missed a class or a rehearsal. This was serious business to her, and she was loving every minute of it.

That summer Stephanie was fortunate to get another summer job with the federal government. She saved her money to pay part of her fall semester tuition costs. She wanted to be able to take a full, 15-semester-hour load. This became very expensive because some of her classes required that she use natural fabrics such as silks, leathers, or ultra suedes that we would have to buy ourselves. As a teacher, I normally had summers off, but Stephanie and I both worked that summer to ensure that we could afford the upcoming semester.

When fall came, Stephanie eagerly registered again with a confidence founded on the preceding successful semester. This is not to say there were no problems. There were interpreter problems, for instance, but most of these were easily worked out. More important, Stephanie did not have service providers telling her, "You must take a certain number of credits," "You can't take this or that course," or, "Your grades must be this."

Stephanie stayed in the fashion design program at this university for 2 years, and her grade point average was never lower than 2.325 and was once as high as 3.00. She accomplished this while working up to 20 hours per week in the Stay-In-School Program. There was good communication with her teachers. It was refreshing to work with teachers who had positive attitudes, who would get upset if the interpreter did not show up, and who would phone us at home to work out a make-up session or ask if Stephanie's sister Terre could fill in as an interpreter for a 2-hour class or lab. The sincerity and caring added humanity to the situation—something that had been absent for such a long time.

Social Security Problems

Work and school kept Stephanie extremely busy—too busy at times. It was sometimes a little eerie to see things going so well. Then it happened. Stephanie's working and earning some of her own money did not sit well with Social Security. She was not receiving Supplemental Security Income (SSI), but Social Security Disability Insurance (SSDI), which she was eligible for because of her disability and her prior service with the federal government. She was summoned to the Social Security office and told that she would have to pay back some of the money now that she had reported she was employed part time.

I questioned why she was being penalized for her self-help efforts. Again, I got the old refrain: "It's not my rule, but the agency's regulations." After a 2-year hiatus from combat, however, I had gathered enough confidence and steam to take on the bureaucracy. I felt very strongly about all the sacrificing Stephanie and our family had endured to have her *not* develop an SSI mentality ("free money"), and I felt this was an injustice; we appealed.

Stephanie has always been well organized and efficient. She had saved every check stub from every job she had ever had. She had made photocopies of every check from Social Security and had saved copies of every piece of correspondence with that agency. The merit of our appeal was accepted, and a date for a hearing was set. The hearing was before a magistrate judge. The setting was a bit intimidating. The judge let me act as Stephanie's spokesperson, and we went through the entire stack of papers Stephanie had carefully organized in sequential order. We discussed every annual conference she had had with Social Security officers in the past, all of the documents she had previously signed, and what she had used her funds for. At the end of this long discussion, the judge thanked Stephanie for being so well organized and told her she would hear from him in about 30 days. When the news finally came, it was good. He had ruled in her favor.

Stephanie Takes Charge of Her Life

Stephanie continued to take fashion design classes in the Department of Human Ecology at the University of the District of Columbia (UDC) until I decided I needed to move away from the Washington, D.C., area. She, of course, wanted to stay near UDC, Gallaudet, and her friends. But the time was just not right for me, financially and in other ways. The years of hard work had taken a toll on my body. I was physically and mentally exhausted and didn't feel that I could take on another battle, should one come up. Stephanie knew I had made many sacrifices on her behalf; so she accepted the new situation for the time being, and left with me.

Prior to our leaving, a new idea had come up. We had discussed what the next step toward an actual career might be with a teacher who had shown particular interest in Stephanie's future. We all agreed that some sort of apprenticeship program would be good for her at this time. We had done a brief search in the Washington, D.C., area, but I did not have enough time and energy to investigate the possibility thoroughly there. The thought that VR might be able to help came to mind, but I quite honestly was not up to another confrontation with VR, nor was I prepared to risk any more damage to Stephanie's growing self-esteem.

Once we had settled in Florida and had devoted more time to considering this plan, Stephanie decided to return to the Virgin Islands where she would try to secure an apprenticeship with a silk-screen manufacturing company. She had sent inquiries to this company previously and had gotten some encouragement. When she arrived there, though, the tourist season was at its lowest; and the company she had hoped to work for was laying off workers. Upon her return to Florida, she complained that her life here was too boring and announced that she intended to return to the D.C. area as soon as possible.

Stephanie spent the next few months designing and constructing some garments that a close friend is now exhibiting in her jewelry and consignment shop. Needless to say, Stephanie is quite curious to see whether her designs will sell.

In the meantime, her excellent work record has enabled her to secure a civil service position at the U.S. Nuclear Regulatory Commission, a job that gives her some financial security and independence, even though it doesn't in itself fulfill her dream. The rest remains to be seen, but one thing is certain: Stephanie is holding onto her dream. She is intensely curious as to what will happen with her designs, and she recently informed me that she plans to take more fashion design classes at UDC. I support her completely, and I'm convinced that one day Stephanie will find her place in the world of fashion design.

If I Had It All To Do Over

I often wonder: If I had known all that I know now and had the chance to do it all over again, what would I do differently? The only thing that comes quickly to mind is that I wish I had made my transition from an oral to a total communication philosophy much sooner. All else, I think, even though it has not always been smooth or easy, has helped create the lovely young woman my daughter has become.

My own hopes for Stephanie are that she have high self-esteem, happiness, effective coping skills, stability, and success in the workplace of her choice.

Luckily, these are exactly the things she appears to be reaching for herself.

Parent and Rehabilitation Partnerships

Gloria Wright

Chapter 3 was originally conceived as a companion piece to be included with the presentations by parents of deaf students in Chapter 2. However, because the involvement of vocational rehabilitation (VR) in transition is very often such an important part of that process and because the function of the agency seems unclear in some minds, the volume authors decided that the following material should be a separate chapter. Gloria Wright, president of the American Deafness and Rehabilitation Association and a member of the Council of State Administrators of Vocational Rehabilitation, Committee on Services for Individuals with Hearing Impairments, was asked to prepare a manuscript describing the role of state rehabilitation agencies in transition, and clarifying, from the perspective of those within the profession, some of the complicated issues arising from the interaction of students, their families, and rehabilitation counselors and administrators.

THE PARENT DILEMMA

Transition from high school brings an unexpected dilemma for parents who have spent 12 years fighting for educational services and programs for their deaf child. Armed with the knowledge of legislation, regulations, and requirements for developing individualized education programs (IEPs), they quickly find themselves talking with rehabilitation counselors, evaluators, and others who use different terminology and operate under different sets of rules. For many parents, the transition from education, an "entitlement program," to rehabilitation, an "eligibility program," can be confusing as well as frustrating.

Under Public Law 94-142, the Education for All Handicapped Children Act, the deaf child is entitled to a free and appropriate public educa-

The following members of the Council of State Administrators of Vocational Rehabilitation, Committee on Services for Individuals with Hearing Impairments, also contributed to this chapter: W. Calvin Melton, Chair, Florida; Richard Hehir, New York; James Hilber, Utah; Sherry Holland, Colorado; Jack LeBlond, Connecticut; Richard Sample, Florida; Patricia Tomlinson, New Jersey.

tion, as is any other child with disabilities. Since this legislation was enacted in 1975, additional federal funds have been made available to ensure basic educational services as well as expanded services. The federal law also provides for the parents, and the child acting on his or her own behalf at age 18, to participate in the decision-making process through a mandated IEP.

LANDMARK LEGISLATION

In 1973, approximately 2 years prior to the landmark legislation in education, Congress enacted Public Law 93-112, probably the most significant piece of legislation to date for persons with disabilities seeking services from state rehabilitation agencies. The concept of the individual's (or, in appropriate cases, parents' or guardians') participation in his or her own program came about because of testimony before Congress by people with disabilities and their advocates. (The 1975 Education for All Handicapped Children Act modeled the IEP after the individualized written rehabilitation plan [IWRP] found in the Rehabilitation Act of 1973, Public Law 93-112.)

Subsequent legislation encouraged the joint development of the IEP and the IWRP, and many states have initiated closer working relationships with secondary school programs and state rehabilitation agencies to assure a smoother student transition from the educational system into the postschool rehabilitation system.

PARENT PERCEPTIONS AND REHABILITATION REGULATIONS

Because preparation for employment begins early for most individuals through incidental learning, time of referral for the deaf student is critical. If referral is postponed until the student is near graduation or has graduated, opportunities for career preparation are lessened. Collaboration between rehabilitation agencies, schools, and parents can begin as early as the 9th or 10th grade by inviting the rehabilitation counselor to participate in IEP staffings, by conducting joint training sessions, or through other activities that encourage vocational exploration and increased knowledge about the world of work and rehabilitation.

Problems arise when the state rehabilitation agency is seen only as a bill payer or is mistakenly thought of as just another college scholarship provider. Too often, these misunderstandings happen when the rehabilitation agency has not been involved at the earliest point possible. Like education, the rehabilitation program is federally funded, with additional support from state funds. However, the level of such funding is not comparable with funding provided to elementary and secondary education programs, nor does the state rehabilitation agency have access to the additional funds that school districts have through taxes on real estate. Because of these fiscal restrictions, some states must utilize an order of selection—based on severity of disability—and/or financial means criteria to ensure that as many adults with disabilities as possible receive services.

Parents accustomed to receiving many and all services indicated in the IEP are surprised to learn that, although educational services were provided at no cost, rehabilitation services may require parent or client financial contribution. Although it is understandable why some parents become disgruntled and disappointed, family or client contributions to one's rehabilitation program can foster ownership, control, and shared responsibility on the part of the consumer.

ENTITLEMENT VERSUS ELIGIBILITY

Establishing eligibility for rehabilitation services has always been an integral part of the program. When the Education for All Handicapped Children Act was authored in the mid-1970s, no one could have guessed that parents and their children with disabilities would be caught between the twin realities of entitlement and eligibility. "Deaf, therefore eligible" is an erroneous assumption of many persons when making application for rehabilitation services. (If all deaf people were eligible, vocational rehabilitation, like education, would be an entitlement, a disability-based program, based solely on medical evidence.) The burden for determining eligibility is placed on the rehabilitation counselor, who, by law, must complete a thorough diagnostic study of each client. Through this study, the counselor must document that the client meets the following criteria: that a diagnosed physical or mental disability exists, that this disability results in a vocational handicap, and that there is a reasonable expectation that vocational rehabilitation services will lead to employment.

The thorough diagnostic study requires gathering information in ten different areas: 1) personality, 2) intelligence level, 3) educational achievement, 4) work experience, 5) personal considerations, 6) vocational and social adjustment, 7) employment opportunities, 8) patterns of work behavior, 9) ability to acquire occupational skills, and 10) capacity for successful job performance. The information gained from the study is critical to the rehabilitation process; it forms the basis by which the state agency establishes eligibility or ineligibility. The study also becomes the basis for the joint development of the IWRP and the counseling relationship where the counselor and client explore vocational options, goals, and intermediate objectives to meet the final goal of employment. If the need for the study is not fully explained, the stage is set for conflict and misunderstanding.

INDIVIDUALIZED WRITTEN
REHABILITATION PLAN: MEANS TO AN END

The individualized written rehabilitation plan can have as its objective the attainment of a college degree, but the attainment of the degree is the means whereby the deaf student receives the training necessary to get a job. The important distinction then, is that the degree is not the final objective but rather is the means whereby the student/client receives the training necessary to become employed. Parents frequently focus on the attainment of the degree and the growth and development of their young adult in a college setting; the vocational rehabilitation counselor focuses on the training in the college setting that enables the student/client to obtain a job in the world of work. The rehabilitation counselor must also review the availability of job opportunities in the geographic area in which the client intends to live after school training is completed.

Although the main goal of vocational rehabilitation is successful job placement for the individual, a number of services may be necessary to achieve that goal. These services include diagnosis and evaluation, physical restoration (surgery), counseling and guidance, job training, job placement, follow-up services, and postemployment services. All these services are based on individual needs and should be mutually agreed upon by the deaf client and the rehabilitation counselor.

When a client (or parent/guardian) is not satisfied with the decisions made by the rehabilitation counselor or with services provided, there are several avenues available for appeal. These rights by law should be explained to the client at time of referral, during the development of the plan, and when his or her case is closed. Each state also has a client assistance program (CAP) that can be very helpful in assisting clients or applicants in their efforts to secure services from the state rehabilitation agency. Such assistance can include pursuing legal, administrative, or other appropriate remedies for the protection of the client's rights to services under the Rehabilitation Act of 1973.

State agencies can be improved by clients actively pursuing the appeals process if they are unhappy with the outcome of their contact with the rehabilitation agency. Sometimes calling attention to certain policies or procedures with which the client is in disagreement can either get that client a clearer explanation of why a decision was made or can cause the state agency to rethink the rationale for such decisions.

Other very important opportunities for parents to influence the system come with their willingness to serve on advisory committees or their efforts to review their state's formalized plan for rehabilitation services and to make comments about it. This parental involvement can be very constructive and informative for both the state rehabilitation agency and the parent. The more parents know and understand the rehabilitation program, the better advocates they can be for themselves and for other parents. It is unfortunate when one parent has a bad experience and generalizes that experience for all parents to the point that it negatively influences others who could potentially benefit. In addition to seeking an active dialogue with the rehabilitation agency, parents can also be helpful toward establishing productive partnerships between education and rehabilitation to the benefit of deaf youth.

The combination of increased economic independence and reduced dependence on public assistance has made vocational rehabilitation one of the most popular and cost-effective programs in this country. During 1985, 931,779 individuals with disabilities were served through state vocational rehabilitation programs. Of these, 577,200 were still being served and 354,579 were closed as of September 30, 1985. Among these the rehabilitated closures amounted to 227,652 and the nonrehabilitated to 126,927. An examination of these closure outcomes reveals that 20,151 hearing impaired (primary and secondary disability codes) persons were closed as rehabilitated; 5,506 were closed as nonrehabilitated (L. Mars, personal communication, August, 1988).

COLLABORATIVE EFFORTS

The Committee on Services for Individuals with Hearing Impairments of the Council of State Administrators of Vocational Rehabilitation (CSAVR) is constantly working with programs and organizations to improve services. In collaboration with the Arkansas Rehabilitation Research and Training Center on Deafness and Hearing Impairment, the committee's efforts to review, evaluate, and recommend guidelines for state agencies to follow has resulted in the *Model State Plan for Rehabilitation of Deaf Clients: Second revision* (Schein, 1980). The committee also has entered into cooperative agreements with Gallaudet University and the National Technical Institute for the Deaf (NTID) to help address concerns of rehabilitation counselors sponsoring students at those institutions. An outgrowth of the agreement with NTID is a training package called *Connections* (Egelston-Dodd, 1988). Developed at NTID in consultation with state rehabilitation agency staff, this package provides an orientation to rehabilitation for postsecondary institutions. The committee has also taken the lead in encouraging states to establish communication skills assessment programs and provide training based on those assessments. It has also encouraged parents to become involved with the rehabilitation agencies in their home states and to work closely with rehabilitation personnel to make programs and services more responsive and productive for people with disabilities.

REFERENCES

Egelston-Dodd, J. (1988). *Connections: Vocational rehabilitation training package*. Rochester, NY: Rochester Institute of Technology.

Schein, J.D. (Ed.). (1980). *Model state plan for rehabilitation of deaf clients: Second revision*. Silver Spring, MD: National Association of the Deaf.

Study of Deaf Students in Transition from School to Work

Method and Demographics

Having set the stage in Chapter 1 with a legislative history of transition issues in the education of deaf students, in Chapter 2 with a description by two parents of their experiences with the transition process, and in Chapter 3 with an essay by members of the Council of State Administrators of Vocational Rehabilitation on parental and vocational rehabilitation (VR) partnerships, the remaining chapters of this book will report on a national study of deaf students in transition from school to work. The purpose of this study was to provide descriptive data on current high school experiences of deaf youth in America related to transition. A review of recent transition literature leads to an inescapable conclusion: There is a lack of adequate studies of high school students with disabilities and their transition experiences. This is particularly true for deaf students. Empirical studies have either focused on mentally retarded and learning disabled students, or they have considered the combined experiences of students with many different disabilities (Bellamy, 1985; Edgar, 1985; Hasazi, 1985; McDonnell, Wilcox, & Bowles, 1986; Mithaug & Horiuchi, 1983; Wehman, Kregel, & Barcus, 1985). The study described in this chapter was designed to focus solely on the experiences of deaf students and their schools.

The present chapter describes the methodology employed by this study and presents statistics related to the demographic characteristics of the sample. As is described in the pages that follow, the student sample was drawn from a national data base containing demographic, audiological, and educational information on the majority of students in America with significant levels of hearing loss. With such a well-defined target population, it was possible to assess the representativeness of the responding sample in order to determine whether the findings can be generalized to the target population. Finally, the degree to which selected demographic variables are associated with one another in the population is described. Since these demographic variables serve as the major independent measures in subsequent chapters (with the transition variables serving as dependent measures), it is important to understand how these characteristics covary.

STUDY RATIONALE

The research described in this book focuses on elements of transition as they occur in high schools. There is universal agreement among researchers, educators, rehabilitation counselors, and policy makers that schools should form the basis for successful transitions. Yet schools are complex organizations, their relationships to the adult service network are often not well defined, and they operate with limited resources. Thus, coordination and cooperation between intraschool divisions of vocational education and special education and among schools and outside service providers such as Vocational Rehabilitation, community training agencies, and the business community have often been viewed as the ultimate, if elusive, goals of exemplary transition programs. Filling in the gaps along the continuum of services leading to employment while avoiding costly duplication through interagency cooperation has been the more specific objective (Ashby & Bensberg, 1981).

In cooperative models of transition, high schools are being viewed as responsible for establishing the foundation for successful transitions from school to work for students with disabilities. Specifically, the role of vocational education in the transition of disabled students has received increased emphasis (Corthell & Van Boskirk, 1984; Hasazi, Collins, & Cobb, 1988). As the caseloads of vocational counselors in the adult postsecondary service network grow to unprecedented and unmanageable levels, the services that disabled students receive in their schools increase in their importance. In fact, schools are assuming a predominant role in coordinating the transition programs for many disabled students.

For deaf students, as Chapter 1 has shown, the need for early and effective transition programming has clearly been established. A major emphasis of the 1988 report to the President and Congress by the Commission on Education of the Deaf (COED) was the lack of adequate vocational training for the large number of unemployed and underemployed deaf adults in the United States. The COED report recommends that Congress establish 10 regional vocational training centers for the deaf.

The services to be provided by the proposed centers include: evaluation and diagnosis, general education, counseling and guidance, vocational training, work transition, supported employment, job placement and follow-up, and community outreach (COED, 1988).

Other authors outside the field of deafness have outlined nearly identical service agendas for adoption by vocational education systems within the schools. For example, Corthell and Van Boskirk (1984) delineate service responsibilities for each of the three primary service units— education, vocational education, and vocational rehabilitation. The services they prescribe for vocational education include: identification, assessment, individualized program planning, vocational training, provision of appropriate support staff (such as tutors, interpreters, and notetakers), employment services (including on-the-job work experiences), and architectural barrier removal. The National Conference on Transition for Youth with Handicapping Conditions to Work, held in Albany in 1984 (New York State Education Department, 1984) recommended that transition services begin in elementary school with assessment services and career-awareness programming.

The difference between the COED (1988) recommendations and those of Corthell and Van Boskirk (1984) and the National Conference on Transition for Youth with Handicapping Conditions to Work (New York State Education Department, 1984) pertain only to the timing of the services. While the proposed COED regional centers would serve deaf adults, the National Conference proposals and those advanced by Corthell and Van Boskirk involve developing increased services from within currently existing high school programs. Given the recent emphasis placed on early transition planning (Will, 1985), it is clear that proposals that stress school involvement should receive a great deal of attention.

As is described in Chapter 5 in this book, a large number of deaf youth remain in secondary programs beyond the time of normal graduation. This fact underscores the heightened transition responsibilities that schools have in serving older students. Particularly among special educational facilities designed to serve deaf students—which serve a proportionally larger number of the students in the 18 to 22 age range—the distinctions between secondary and postsecondary services become blurred. Clearly, vocational education is important for the school-to-work transitions of students enrolled in these programs.

The current study was designed to describe the vocational education experienced by deaf students in high schools throughout the United States. In this design, the broad definition of vocational education given by Corthell and Van Boskirk (1984) formed the basis for formulating research questions and developing research tools. In this definition, vocational education involves a large number of activities, ranging from vocational training and assessment to work experience. In this context, the following research objectives were defined:

1. To characterize the vocational coursework and training received by deaf students in schools throughout the United States
2. To describe the involvement of VR and other outside agencies in the vocational education of deaf students while in school
3. To describe the work experiences that deaf students obtain while they are still high school students
4. To describe the role of assessment in the making of placement decisions for deaf students and to provide a compendium of the most commonly used assessment tools
5. To study the degree to which formal interagency agreements exist between schools and VR
6. To present data related to dropping out and the graduation status of deaf students

These research objectives are not exhaustive; many other aspects of vocational education (e.g., career education) need to be explored. However, the questions posed here provide a starting point that will lead, eventually, to a better understanding of the appropriate roles that schools play in fostering successful school-to-work transitions of deaf students.

STUDY METHODOLOGY

The Annual Survey of Hearing Impaired Children and Youth

For the past 20 years, the hearing impaired school-age population in the United States has been monitored through the Annual Survey of Hearing Impaired Children and Youth, conducted by the Center for Assessment and Demographic Studies, one of several research units of the Gallaudet University's Research Institute. Since the current transition study was designed as a series of supplemental surveys to the Annual Survey, a brief description of this larger effort is provided.

In 1964, the National Institute of Neurological Diseases and Blindness convened a group of experts at a "Conference on the Collection of Statistics of Severe Hearing Impairments and Deafness in the United States." Those attending expressed a need for accurate data for planning educational, medical, and social services for this population. The proceedings of this conference recommended the establishment of a program for collecting information on the number and characteristics of hearing impaired persons in the United States (Public Health Service, 1964). Two projects resulted from this conference. One was the National Census of the Deaf Population conducted in 1971 with grant funds provided by the Rehabilitation Services Administration (Schein & Delk, 1974); this study described the demographics of the adult deaf population, with an emphasis on those who had lost their hearing prior to 19 years of age.

The other project focused on the school-age population. In 1965, the Office of Education, Bureau of Education for the Handicapped (BEH), awarded Gallaudet College (now Gallaudet University) a 2-year grant to determine the feasibility of establishing a national data base on hearing impaired children. With the success of this pilot study, limited to data collection in the District of Columbia and 4 states, BEH provided additional funding for the expansion of data collection activities to all 50 states. Support for the project was later provided by the National Institute of Education; survey activities are now funded by Gallaudet University.

To conduct the Annual Survey, the Center for Assessment and Demographic Studies (CADS) was established at Gallaudet. The mission of CADS remains consistent with the original goals of the Annual Survey— that is, to determine the size of the school-age hearing impaired population of the United States and to describe its characteristics in ways that are useful to educators, program planners, legislators, and other re searchers. The center has, in addition to maintaining its Annual Survey activities, conducted numerous supplemental studies on topics ranging from academic achievement to communication methods, to the current study of school-to-work transition. Choice of topics for in-depth supplemental studies has always been made through consultation with people who represent the major consumers of the information. An examination of the first 15 years of data collection has been published in a book entitled *Deaf Children in America* (Schildroth & Karchmer, 1986).

Currently, the Annual Survey data base contains individual data records for nearly 50,000 hearing impaired students from all 50 states, the District of Columbia, Puerto Rico, Guam, and the Virgin Islands. Although it is not possible to know how representative the programs on the Annual Survey list are in relation to the total number of programs educating deaf students across the nation, some indication of this relationship may be had by comparing the numbers of handicapped children reported to the federal government by the states each year with the numbers reported to the Annual Survey. If the special education "child count" figures for hearing impairment are accepted as accurate, then recent Annual Surveys have collected information on approximately 65% to 70% of the hearing impaired children receiving special education services in the United States. The 1986–1987 Annual Survey, the school year discussed in this chapter, gathered information on 47,162 deaf and hard of hearing students. As a comparison, 66,761 deaf and hard of hearing students were reported to the federal government by the states during that year (Office of Special Education and Rehabilitative Services, 1988). It appears, therefore, that although there is not a complete overlap of the Annual Survey and the "child count" numbers due to slight differences in age and program inclusions, the Annual Survey data file represents a sizable majority of the hearing impaired students receiving special education services in the United States.

Methodology

The Annual Survey identifies its target population as all hearing impaired children who are receiving some special services in a preschool through secondary level education program in the United States. To reach this population, CADS attempts to identify as many special education programs serving hearing impaired students as possible. All state departments of special education are routinely requested to report the programs in their states that serve hearing impaired students; directories of public and private education programs are reviewed and potential programs contacted to verify that they serve hearing impaired students. The CADS list of special education programs serving hearing impaired children in 1986–1987 contains over 1,400 agencies and school districts providing services to hearing impaired students enrolled in over 8,000 school facilities.

Each year CADS contacts these programs and invites their participation in the Annual Survey. If the program agrees, school personnel complete a questionnaire on each hearing impaired child receiving services. For programs that participated in the survey during the previous school year, the school updates information on children already in the data base and completes forms for newly enrolled children. When the questionnaires are returned to CADS, they are edited, verified, and optically scanned to create a computerized data base. Using this data base, CADS then prepares a variety of reports for the participating programs, summarizing information at the local, state, regional, and national levels.

Target Population and
Sampling Strategy for Transition Study

To establish a data base of deaf high schoolers, the center used the 1985–1986 Annual Survey of Hearing Impaired Children and Youth. All students who met the following criteria were defined as the target population for the current study:

- Age 16 through 22 as of December 1, 1985
- Unaided average hearing threshold of 71 dB or greater in the better ear across the three frequencies of 500, 1,000, and 2,000 Hz (i.e., severe to profound hearing loss)

This selection process resulted in a list of 8,285 youth enrolled at 645 education programs in the United States. Due to uncertainty as to how many of the students selected would have graduated or left between the sampling year and the survey year and also uncertainty as to the projected response rates, all 8,285 students were selected for the study.

One of the survey instruments was designed to gather individual student information from the student's career or guidance counselor. Because of concern that individual counselors in the larger programs would be asked to fill out survey forms for large numbers of students, a special sampling procedure was used to reduce the survey burden for these individuals. In this procedure a random sample of 40 students was selected from any program containing more than 40 students who fit the target criteria, and counselor surveys were sent only for these sampled students. In the data files created by this procedure, counselor data were weighted by the ratio of the total students in the program to 40. This weighting assured adequate representation in the data base for the larger programs.

Instrumentation

Information for this transition study was collected using the following four separate survey tools. These are reproduced in Appendix A at the end of this book and described extensively in subsequent chapters.

Program Survey: Career Training of Deaf Youth Program administrators in each of the programs supplying data to the Annual Survey were asked to provide information regarding the program and its relationship to the office of vocational rehabilitation in the state where the program was located.

Annual Survey of Hearing Impaired Children and Youth The Annual Survey form for the 1985–1986 school year provided demographic data on students. In addition to age, sex, and ethnic information, detailed information on the individual's hearing loss was obtained, which included degree of loss and cause of loss. Information on educationally significant additional handicapping conditions and descriptions of the type of special education program were also reported to the survey office.

Student Questionnaire: Survey of Job Training for Hearing Impaired Youth The questions on this form related to employment either after school or during the previous summer, the type of job, hours worked, and wages earned. Students were asked to indicate if they had a vocational rehabilitation counselor and, if so, the types of services requested and received. Information was also sought on other income or benefits received from federal or state agencies.

Counselor Questionnaire: Survey of Career Training for Hearing Impaired Youth The content of this questionnaire focused on the career training opportunities utilized by the students. Information was also requested on the educational placement of the students and on factors associated with their career planning.

Survey Procedures

In January, 1987, the center mailed the Program Survey to administrators of programs on the Annual Survey mailing list. Questionnaires returned to the center were entered into a computerized data base.

As indicated earlier, the demographic information for the study was obtained from the 1985–1986 Annual Survey, since this was the data base from which the original student population was selected; for many students, it was the most current demographic information available at the time of the study.

Copies of the Student Questionnaire and Counselor Questionnaire were mailed to education programs in March, 1987. The program administrators received a letter describing the project and soliciting the assistance of their staff. They were asked to distribute the Student Questionnaires, to assist students in completing the information if necessary, and to collect the questionnaires for return to the center. The administrators were asked to forward the Counselor Questionnaires to the students' career or guidance counselors for completion.

CHARACTERISTICS OF STUDY SAMPLE

Table 4.1 presents response rate information for the three transition surveys. There were 8,285 deaf youth, ages 16 through 22, receiving special

Table 4.1. Program, student, and counselor response rates: Transition study, 1987

Questionnaire	Target population[a]	Respondents	
	N	N	%
Program Survey			
Students	NA	NA	NA
Programs	1,452	881	61%
Student Questionnaire			
Students	8,285	6,196	75%
Programs	645	489	75%
Counselor Questionnaire			
Students	5,895	4,513	77%
Programs	645	489	76%

NA indicates "not applicable," as Program Survey was not sent to students.

[a]The target population of programs was all programs on the 1986–1987 mailing list of the Annual Survey of Hearing Impaired Children and Youth. The target population of students included all students in the 1985–1986 Annual Survey data base between the ages of 16 and 22 with severe to profound hearing loss.

education services at 645 programs reporting information to the 1985–1986 Annual Survey. (This is the "target population" in Table 4.1.) Each of these students received a Student Questionnaire to complete; 6,196 (75%) questionnaires were returned to the center. These responding students were enrolled at 485 (75%) of the 645 education programs contacted.

As previously mentioned, the Counselor Questionnaire was mailed to a sample of the counselors of 5,895 students at the 645 education programs. A slightly higher response rate (77%) was achieved from the counselors, some of whom completed multiple forms; the center received 4,513 completed Counselor Questionnaires from 489 (76%) of the programs. When the weighting factor was applied to the data records for those sampled from the large programs, the resulting weighted N for the counselor data was 6,659.

The information in Table 4.2 provides an overview of the characteristics of the target population and each of the two analysis samples defined by the student and counselor survey respondents. Percentage distributions are shown for selected characteristics. Because of the sampling procedures, the distribution of the responses for the Counselor Questionnaire are based on the weighted records in the file.

Age

Almost half (48%) of the target population was born in 1968 or 1969. At the time of the survey—Spring, 1987—these students were 17 and 18 years old. The age distribution of the responses to the student and counselor questionnaires mirrored the total Annual Survey population very closely; 46% of the students responding were 17 and 18 years old.

Sex

The sex distribution for all three groups was identical: 55% of the youth were males and 45% were females.

Ethnic Background

Of the 8,285 students in the target population, 64% were white, 21% were black, and 11% were Hispanic (4% had "other" ethnic backgrounds). The distribution of responses for the two questionnaires represented a similar distribution of ethnic backgrounds: 65% of both the student and counselor questionnaires contained information from white, non-Hispanic students.

Degree of Hearing Loss

The study was limited to youth with severe (32%) and profound (68%) hearing losses. Thirty percent of both the student and counselor question-

Table 4.2. Percentage comparison of student characteristics: Transition study, 1987

Characteristics	Target population (N = 8,285)	Student Questionnaire (N = 6,196)	Counselor Questionnaire (N = 6,659)
		Respondents	
Birth year			
1963	*	*	*
1964	7%	7%	7%
1965	10%	11%	11%
1966	13%	14%	13%
1967	21%	22%	22%
1968	24%	23%	24%
1969	24%	23%	22%
Sex			
Male	55%	55%	55%
Female	45%	45%	45%
Ethnic background			
White, non-Hispanic	64%	65%	65%
Black, non-Hispanic	21%	21%	21%
Hispanic	11%	10%	11%
Other	4%		
Degree of hearing loss			
Severe	32%	30%	30%
Profound	68%	70%	70%
Selected etiologies of loss			
Maternal rubella	24%	24%	24%
Heredity	11%	11%	12%
Meningitis	8%	8%	8%
Additional handicap status			
No additional handicap	67%	67%	68%
One additional handicap	21%	22%	21%
Two or more additional handicaps	12%	11%	11%
Selected types of additional handicaps			
Mental retardation	11%	11%	10%
Legal blindness/visual problem	9%	9%	8%
Learning disability	8%	8%	7%
Emotional/behavioral Problem	7%	8%	7%
Cerebral palsy	4%	4%	4%
Region of country			
Northeast	21%	19%	20%
Midwest	21%	21%	20%

(continued)

Table 4.2. (continued)

| | Respondents | | |
| | Target population (N = 8,285) | Student Questionnaire (N = 6,196) | Counselor Questionnaire (N = 6,659) |
Characteristics			
South	39%	43%	42%
West	20%	18%	18%
School setting			
Special facility, not integrated	47%	58%	53%
Special facility, integrated	10%	4%	10%
Regular/local facility, not integrated	7%	7%	6%
Regular/local facility, integrated	35%	32%	30%

* = less than 1%.

naires returned were for youth with severe losses. Thus, both the student and counselor data are slightly biased in favor of students with profound hearing loss.

Etiology of Hearing Loss

Among the target population, maternal rubella was the leading cause of hearing loss, reported for almost one fourth (24%) of the students, followed by hereditary factors (11%), and meningitis (8%). Virtually identical response distributions were found for the respondents to both the student and counselor questionnaires.

Additional Handicapping Conditions

One third (33%) of the target population had one or more educationally significant handicapping conditions in addition to hearing impairment. Among the students responding to the Student Questionnaire and the students for whom counselors responded on the Counselor Questionnaire, the percentages of students with additional handicapping conditions was virtually identical. For all three groups, mental retardation was the most frequently reported additional handicap. Legal blindness/visual problems, learning disabilities, emotional/behavioral problems, and cerebral palsy were the other handicaps most frequently reported for the total population and for the two samples.

In the analyses presented in the remaining chapters of this book, the importance of this variable to various transition variables is made evident. Multihandicapped deaf students are a distinct subgroup of the deaf population, and their needs are different. In the analyses described in

Chapters 5 through 8 in this book, an attempt is made to approximate the level of additional handicaps through categorizing the sample into three subgroups: those with no reported handicaps in addition to hearing impairment, those with one reported handicap in addition to hearing impairment, and those with two or more reported additional handicaps.

The presence and number of additional handicaps are obviously significant factors in the education of a deaf student. However, equally important is the kind of additional handicap. Table 4.3 shows the percentages of students with no, one, and two or more additional handicaps reported as having each of the individual handicaps listed on the Annual Survey form. As can be seen from these figures, students with two or more handicaps differ significantly from those with only one additional handicap. A large majority of the students in the "two or more" category (60%) were classified as mentally retarded, and over one third had emotional/behavioral problems. Almost one half were blind or had severe visual problems in addition to their hearing impairment. These facts should be kept in mind when interpreting the results of the study.

Regional Distribution

As Table 4.2 shows, the largest percentage of students in the target population was from the South (39%); the other three regions were equally represented with 21% from the Northeast, 21% from the Midwest, and 20% from the West. The largest percentage of survey responses was also from the South: 43% of the Student Questionnaires and 42% of the Counselor Questionnaires. This higher representation of targeted hearing im-

Table 4.3. Percentage of students reported to have specific additional handicaps: Transition study, 1987[a]

Type of handicap	One additional handicap ($N = 1,760$)	Two or more additional handicaps ($N = 987$)
Legal blindness	3%	23%
Visual problems	11%	24%
Brain damage	2%	17%
Epilepsy	2%	9%
Orthopedic problems	3%	15%
Cerebral palsy	8%	19%
Heart disorder	2%	13%
Other physical handicap	7%	11%
Mental retardation	19%	60%
Emotional/behavioral problem	13%	34%
Learning disability	23%	24%
Other cognitive/social handicap	6%	5%

[a]No additional handicaps were reported for 5,468 students.

paired students in the South and the corresponding higher response rates for the two surveys are partially attributable to the extensive Annual Survey coverage in the state of Texas. For over 10 years, the Texas Education Agency (TEA) has contracted with the center to maintain a data-based management system on the hearing impaired school-age population in the state; this has resulted in close cooperation between the center and the education programs in Texas and in the high rates of response to survey projects.

School Setting

Students were categorized by the type of educational facility they attended (special facility designed to serve only deaf students versus regular/local facility designed primarily for hearing students) and by their receiving academic instruction with hearing students in an integrated classroom. While 82% of the target population were either nonintegrated students attending special facilities (47%) or integrated students attending regular/local facilities (35%), it is important to take note of the students in the other categories. Ten percent of the target population were students attending special facilities who received some integration with hearing students for instruction. This is an emerging group within the population of hearing impaired students. The remaining 7% of the students were those in self-contained special education classrooms in the regular/local schools.

In comparison to these figures, the student and counselor data bases are somewhat biased in favor of students attending special facilities. While 57% of the target population attended special facilities (combining the nonintegrated and integrated groups), 62% of the Student Questionnaires and 63% of the Counselor Questionnaires were returned for students attending special facilities.

Summary Comments
Related to Sample Representativeness

The most important fact to keep in mind when considering the representativeness of the sample of the current study is the definition of the target population, which has two basic criteria: All students were between the ages of 17 and 23 in the *survey year*, and all students had severe to profound hearing losses. By naming this study "Deaf Students in Transition from School to Work," it was intended to limit the sample to those students with substantial hearing losses (i.e., deaf students). Students with lesser degrees of impairment are not included.

Regarding the degree to which the samples for the student and counselor questionnaires represent the target population, the results of this analysis are extremely encouraging. Response rates for both surveys were 75% or greater, and, as noted in Table 4.2, the sample demographic characteristics are nearly identical to the target population characteristics. The two caveats to this conclusion pertain to facility type in a geographic region: Students attending regular/local facilities were slightly underrepresented in the survey samples and those from the South were overrepresented.

ASSOCIATION OF DEMOGRAPHIC CHARACTERISTICS

In the analyses in the following chapters in this book, the general strategy is to present breakdowns of important transition variables by relevant demographic characteristics. While this approach reveals important individual bivariate relationships between the demographic variables and the transition variables, it does not clarify the higher order relationships that exist among the variables.

For example, it may be shown in many instances that the age of the student is related to a given transitional outcome variable. However, if age itself were considered the dependent measure, it would be noted that the younger and older students in the data set differ as to demographic characteristics. Thus, the original relationships that were noted between age and the transitional outcome variable may be due to the effects of the other characteristics for which the age groups differ.

While statistical techniques would have permitted the isolation of independent effects and assessment of the higher order interrelationships of the variables, it was decided that such techniques would have made the individual chapters long and overly technical. Additionally, from a policy point of view, the higher order effects may be less relevant than would at first appear. For example, if older and younger students differ on the number of contacts with state vocational rehabilitation counselors, it is sufficient to note that the data suggest that more contacts with younger students may have a positive impact on their transition experiences.

Tables 4.4 and 4.5 are presented to show the degree of bivariate covariation among the main independent variables used in subsequent chapters. In these tables, each of the characteristics considered has been dichotomized as follows: age (17- and 18-year-olds versus students who were 19 or older during the survey year); sex (males versus females); ethnic background (white, non-Hispanic versus minority); additional handicap status (those with no additional handicaps versus those with one or more reported additional handicaps); and school setting (those attending special facilities designed solely for hearing impaired students versus those attending regular/local schools designed for hearing students).

Most important, the data in Tables 4.4 and 4.5 show the high levels of association between additional handicap status and each of the demo-

Table 4.4.   Association of student characteristics: Transition study, 1987

Category	Total N	Age: % 19 or older	Sex: % male	Ethnic background: % minority	% with additional handicaps	% in special facility
Target Population	8,285	52%	55%	36%	33%	58%
Age						
17–18 years		—	54%	33%	27%	55%
19 and older		—	56%	38%	40%	61%
Sex						
Male		53%	—	35%	36%	60%
Female		50%	—	37%	31%	55%
Ethnic background						
White, non-Hispanic		50%	56%	—	31%	58%
Minority		55%	54%	—	37%	59%
Additional handicap status						
No additional handicap		47%	47%	34%	—	58%
With additional handicaps		62%	59%	40%	—	57%
School setting						
Special facility		54%	57%	36%	33%	—
Regular/local facility		48%	52%	36%	34%	—

Note: These percentages were derived from the total target population as it was drawn from the data of the Annual Survey of Hearing Impaired Children and Youth.

Table 4.5. Summary of the association of student characteristics: Transition study, 1987

Considering age:

Compared to 17- and 18-year-olds,
students age 19 and older were:

MORE likely to be males	by 2% points
MORE likely to be minorities	by 5% points
MORE likely to have additional handicaps	by 13% points
MORE likely to attend special facilities	by 6% points

Considering sex:

Compared to females, males were:

MORE likely to be 19 or older	by 3% points
LESS likely to be minorities	by 2% points
MORE likely to have additional handicaps	by 5% points
MORE likely to attend special facilities	by 5% points

Considering ethnic background:

Compared to white, non-Hispanic students,
minority students were:

MORE likely to be 19 or older	by 5% points
LESS likely to be male	by 2% points
MORE likely to have additional handicaps	by 6% points
EQUALLY likely to attend special facilities	(% difference <2% points)

Considering additional handicap status:

Compared to those with *no* additional
handicaps, those students *with* additional
handicaps were:

MORE likely to be 19 or older	by 15% points
MORE likely to be male	by 12% points
MORE likely to be minorities	by 6% points
EQUALLY likely to attend special facilities	(% difference <2% points)

Considering the school setting:

Compared to those students attending
regular/local facilities, students attending
special facilities were:

MORE likely to be 19 or older	by 6% points
MORE likely to be male	by 5% points
EQUALLY likely to be minorities	(% difference <2% points)
EQUALLY likely to have additional handicaps	(% difference <2% points)

graphic characteristics age, sex, and ethnic background. Older students, male students, and minority students are all more likely than their respective counterparts to have additional handicapping conditions. These correlations should be kept in mind as the relationships of each of these characteristics with important transition variables are explored in future chapters in this book.

REFERENCES

Ashby, S., & Bensberg, G.J. (Eds.). (1981). *Cooperative occupational preparation of the handicapped: Exemplary models.* Lubbock: Texas Technical University.

Bellamy, G.T. (1985). Transition progress: Comments on Hasazi, Gordon & Roe. *Exceptional Children, 51*(6), 474–478.

Commission on Education of the Deaf. (1988). *Toward equality: Education of the deaf.* Washington, DC: U.S. Government Printing Office.

Corthell, D., & Van Boskirk, C. (1984). *Continuum of services: School to work.* Menomonie, WI: Stout Vocational Rehabilitation Institute.

Edgar, E. (1985). How do special education students fare after they leave school? A response to Hasazi, Gordon, and Roe. *Exceptional Children, 51*(6), 470–473.

Hasazi, S.B. (1985). School-to-work transition: Policies and practices. *American Rehabilitation, 11*(3), 9–11.

Hasazi, S.B., Collins, M., & Cobb, R.B. (1988). Implementing transition programs for productive employment: New directions. In B.L. Ludlow, A.P. Turnbull, & R. Luckasson (Eds.), *Transitions to adult life for people with mental retardation: Principles and practices* (pp. 177–195). Baltimore: Paul H. Brookes Publishing Co.

McDonnell, J., Wilcox, B., & Bowles, S. (1986). Do we know enough to plan for transition? A national survey of state agencies responsible for services to persons with severe handicaps. *Journal of The Association for Persons with Severe Handicaps, 11,* 53–60.

Mithaug, D., & Horiuchi, C. (1983). *Colorado statewide follow-up survey of special education students.* Colorado Springs: State Department of Education.

New York State Education Department. (1984). *A report on the National Conference on Transition for Youth with Handicapping Conditions to Work, Coordination of State Policies and Practices.* Albany, NY: Author.

Office of Special Education and Rehabilitative Services. (1988). To assure the free appropriate public education of all handicapped children. In *Tenth annual report to Congress on the implementation of the Education of the Handicapped Act* (p. B–3). Washington, DC: U.S. Department of Education.

Public Health Service. (1964). *Proceedings of the conference on the collection of statistics of severe hearing impairments and deafness in the United States, 1964* (PHS Publication No. 1227). Washington, DC: U.S. Government Printing Office.

Schein, J., & Delk, M. (1974). *The deaf population of the United States.* Silver Spring, MD: National Association of the Deaf.

Schildroth, A.N., & Karchmer, M.A. (Eds.). (1986). *Deaf children in America.* San Diego: College-Hill Press.

Wehman, P., Kregel, J., & Barcus, J.M. (1985). From school to work: A vocational transition model for handicapped students. *Exceptional Children, 52*(1), 25–37.

Will, M. (1985). OSERS programming for the transition of youth with disabilities: Bridges from school to working life. *Rehabilitation/WORLD, 9*(1), 4–7, 42–43.

Staying, Leaving, and Graduating

Enrollment and Exiting Patterns among Deaf High Schoolers

Failure to obtain a high school diploma may impede the successful school-to-work transitions for a large number of deaf students. However, little research has been reported that studies the high school exiting patterns of this group. This chapter presents the results of a study of the various high school outcomes for deaf students and assesses the degree to which members of selected demographic subgroups differ with respect to the various means for exiting high school. Methodologically, the analysis presented takes advantage of the fact that the sample for the Center for Assessment and Demographic Studies' (CADS) transition study was drawn 1 year prior to the actual survey; many students were reported to the survey as having left without graduating between the 2 years. Since demographic information was available for the school leavers from the previous year's Annual Survey of Hearing Impaired Children and Youth (see Chapter 4), an extensive study of the demographic correlates of the various reported means for exiting school is possible. While the subsequent chapters of this book focus on the school and employment experiences of the deaf students in the sample who were still enrolled during the survey year, the current chapter focuses on describing the characteristics of those who had left school. Comparisons with those who were still enrolled are also made.

BACKGROUND

There can be little doubt that, in general, dropping out of school adversely affects a person's chances for success in later life. While statistics have not specifically been reported for deaf youth, United States government statistics for the general population, reported by Rumberger (1987), show higher rates of unemployment for high school dropouts than for graduates. In an analysis of students attending school during the 1981–1982 school year, dropouts showed an unemployment rate of 42% in the fall of 1982, compared to a rate of 23% for those who had graduated the previous spring. Furthermore, those dropouts able to obtain full-time employment earned 12%–18% less than those who graduated.

Other studies have shown correlations between dropping out and various adverse individual and societal affects. Alexander, Natriello, and Pallas (1985) reported lower levels of academic skill among dropouts than among graduates. This is cause for particular alarm if other predictions about the nature of jobs in the future come true. These predictions suggest that dropouts in the future will be at even greater disadvantages due to the increasing technical nature of available jobs requiring higher levels of educational skill (National Academy of Sciences, 1984; Rumberger, 1987). Danek and McCrone, in the first chapter of this volume, note the potential impact of this trend on deaf students.

In terms of the effects on society of dropping out, Levin (1972) noted that high school dropouts are more likely to require a wide range of social and rehabilitative services. This finding has particular relevance for deaf students who may require extensive support services in order to be able to compete in the marketplace. The potential increase in the need for social and rehabilitative services, combined with the decreased earning power of dropouts, suggests that a high incidence of deaf high school students who leave school without graduating is very costly to society.

In addition to the potential costs of dropping out to individuals and society, various trends in the general population and in the population of deaf students make the study of dropouts and graduates particularly crucial now. The first is the changing demographics of the student population of the United States. Students from minority groups, who traditionally have higher drop-out rates (U.S. Bureau of the Census, 1986), are constituting larger proportions of the population (Rumberger, 1987). Demographic studies of the deaf student population (Schildroth, 1988) reveal a similar trend. If deaf students, in general, are more likely to drop out than hearing students, it is important to ascertain the degree to which deafness and minority status affect a student's chances for remaining in school and in succeeding in later life.

A second trend that underscores the importance of studying dropouts among deaf students is the tendency among states for adopting more stringent academic requirements for high school graduation (Levin, 1986; McDill, Natriello, & Pallas, 1985; Rumberger, 1987). Bloomquist (1986) presents a discussion of minimum competency testing and its potential impact on hearing impaired students. She reports that, as of 1985, 40 states employed some form of minimum competency testing, 19 of the 40 required some form of minimum competency test for graduation, and 14 of the 19 imposed the same requirements for hearing impaired students as they did for hearing students in regular education. Yet, studies of the academic achievement levels of deaf students reveal that these students lag behind their hearing counterparts in academic achievement (Allen, 1986; Trybus & Karchmer, 1977; Wolk & Allen, 1984). Thus, if the trend toward "excellence" in education yields greater academic pressure with more stringent requirements, the number of hearing impaired students likely to drop out or leave school without a diploma will increase.

Previous estimates of the incidence of dropping out have varied widely, due largely to differences in definitions and in the different methods used to assess graduation or drop-out status (Rumberger, 1987). The most widely quoted statistics on dropping out come from the U.S. Bureau of the Census, which publishes school enrollment figures annually. The census bureau defines a "dropout" as someone in a given age cohort who has not completed school and who is no longer enrolled. To derive estimates of the overall rates of dropouts, age cohorts are combined. The most recent data available from census studies show an overall drop-out rate of 15% for individuals age 18 and 19 years (reported in Rumberger, 1987). Other studies have reported slightly different rates. For example, a 4-year longitudinal study of high school sophomores from 1980 showed a drop-out rate of 18.6% for nonhandicapped students (Harnisch, Lichtenstein, & Langford, 1986).

Drop-out rates for students in special education have rarely been reported. Harnisch et al. (1986) performed secondary analyses of a large longitudinal data base from the National Center for Educational Statistics survey called, "High School and Beyond" (HSB). Using data from the HSB, Harnisch et al. (1986) reported the drop-out rate for handicapped students as being 21.7%. For the hearing impaired subgroup, the rate was 28.3%, a higher rate than for any other handicapped subgroup except students with learning disabilities.

Caution should be used in interpreting these HSB figures, however, due to the nature of the HSB special education sample. First, the sample was small. Graduation and drop-out status data were available for only 371 hearing impaired students in the HSB file. Second, the sample did not include students attending special facilities, such as residential schools for the deaf. According to recent demographic reports, 30%–50% of the deaf students in the United States receiving special education services attend such schools (Center for Assessment and Demographic Studies [CADS], 1988); as was reported in Chapter 4, a higher percentage of older hearing impaired students attend special facilities. The HSB sample was limited to those who were enrolled in diploma tracks in regular education programs. Thus, the hearing impaired students in the sample were more typical of mainstreamed hearing impaired students, who have very different demographic characteristics from those in special programs (Allen & Karchmer, in press; Schildroth, 1987; Wolk, Karchmer, & Schildroth, 1982). They are characterized by less severe audiological impairment and better speech intelligibility. Finally, caution needs to be exerted when interpreting the HSB rates due to the means by which students were classified as handicapped (i.e., through self-reporting on a questionnaire). Requesting high school respondents to identify themselves as handicapped may not lead to an entirely reliable sample.

Given that the HSB hearing impaired sample comprises students likely to be more academically qualified than more typical students in special education programs, the high drop-out rate reported by Harnisch et al. (1986) is especially alarming. Given the association of dropping out with poor academic performance, one might expect the rate for the population of hearing impaired students nationwide to be even higher. However, it might be true that, in spite of having lower achieving students, special facilities may have greater success in seeing students through to graduation. This possibility needs to be thoroughly explored, particularly in light of recent criticism of mainstreaming practices for hearing impaired students in the United States (Commission on Education of the Deaf, 1988).

Although hearing students enrolled in regular education most often drop out or graduate with a diploma, additional categories are needed to adequately describe the experiences of deaf students. First, many deaf students remain in school beyond the age of 18. Since these students remain in their high school programs up to 3 or 4 years longer than their hearing cohorts, their vocational experiences during the extended time in school warrant separate study. Second, many deaf students graduate with "certificates" rather than with diplomas. In studying deaf dropouts, it is necessary to determine whether these students are more similar to the diploma recipients or to the dropouts in terms of their future job successes and failures. Although the certificate recipients are not thought of as "dropouts," they nonetheless fit the Census Bureau criterion: They leave school without a high school diploma. It is particularly important to assess the value of completing a program with a certificate versus completing one with a diploma.

One recent statistical report considered certificates as an outcome. In this report (Office of Special Education and Rehabilitative Services, 1988) the following categories and rates of exiting for hearing impaired students were reported: graduated with diploma (56%); graduated with certificate (19%); reached maximum age (2%); dropped out (13%); and left for other reasons (10%). Combining all categories not leading to diplomas or certificates yields a rate of 25%—similar to the HSB figure for dropping out. Also, a significant number, nearly one in five, received certificates rather than diplomas.

These data, reported by the Office of Special Education and Rehabilitative Services (OSERS, 1988), have limitations. First, they rely on aggregated "child-count" figures supplied by school districts to state education agencies and, in turn, to OSERS. There is no mechanism for assessing the reliability of the figures. Second, the deaf and hard of hearing students have been combined into one category, and the multiply handicapped deaf students have been excluded. There is no basis for generalizing the expected rates to a population comprising deaf students, which includes multiply handicapped students. Finally, as aggregated data, there is no way to explore subgroups of the population through cross-tabulation of characteristics. Thus, conclusions or policies based on these figures cannot be targeted to specific demographic subgroups of the population.

The current study presented in this book overcomes some of the limitations of the U.S. child-count data. The target population has been specifically defined as including deaf students only, and the merging of demographic and exiting information for individual students permits a more detailed exploration of exiting patterns among deaf high schoolers.

Three research questions are addressed by the analysis presented in this chapter: 1) What is the prevalence of dropping out, graduating with diploma, and graduating with certificate among deaf high school students? 2) What demographic characteristics are associated with different school-leaving patterns? and 3) What characteristics are associated with staying in school beyond the age of 18?

METHOD

As described in Chapter 4, all students from the 1985–1986 Annual Survey who were between the ages of 16 and 22 on December 31, 1985, and who were reported to the survey as having a severe or profound hearing loss were included in the CADS' transition study. Surveys were distributed to each of these students in the spring of 1987 through their school counselors. Simultaneously, surveys were sent to the counselors of roughly 70% of these students for additional information about vocational and career training. In programs containing more than 40 students in the target group, a random sample of 40 students was selected in order to reduce the amount of survey work for individual counselors. In the final data file, the counselor forms for students from these larger programs where sampling had been carried out were weighted appropriately, as described in Chapter 4.

The Counselor Questionnaires asked if individual students, whose names were preprinted on labels affixed to each form, were still enrolled in the spring of 1987. For those students reported as no longer enrolled, counselors were asked to categorize the leavers into one of the following categories:

Graduated with diploma
Graduated with certificate
Dropped out
Transferred to another program
Left, whereabouts unknown

The weighted distribution of counselor responses to these questions appears in Table 5.1. In order to estimate the overall drop-out rates for deaf students from these figures, two assumptions were made; one pertains to the treatment of missing data, the other to the validity of longitudinal conclusions based on cross-sectional data.

Statistical Assumptions

Treatment of Missing Data

As noted in Table 5.1, a large number of students (1,295, or 20%) were reported by counselors as having left, with their whereabouts unknown. For this analysis, it was assumed that the counselors knew precisely which students were still enrolled and which students had graduated with diplomas and certificates. Thus, to compute rates of different exiting categories, the students in the "Left, whereabouts unknown" category were redistributed only among the "Dropped out" and "Transferred" categories. Furthermore, the method by which these students were redistributed was determined by the proportion of dropouts and transfers in each of those two categories.

Table 5.2 shows the results of this redistribution. In contrast to Table

Table 5.1. Enrollment and graduation status of students in survey year, 1 year after sampling

Category	N	%
Still enrolled	3,220	48%
Graduated, diploma	1,332	20%
Graduated, certificate	493	7%
Dropped out	145	2%
Transferred	174	3%
Left, whereabouts unknown	1,295	20%

Table 5.2. Estimates of drop-out and graduation rates for deaf sample based on redistributions of students whose whereabouts were unknown, Spring, 1987[a]

Category	Original N	N adjusted for unknowns	Adjusted %	Estimated % for leavers only
Still enrolled	3,220	3,220	48%	—
Graduated, diploma	1,332	1,332	20%	52%
Graduated, certificate	493	493	7%	19%
Dropped out	145	734	11%	29%
Transferred	174	880	13%	—
Left, whereabouts unknown	1,295	—	—	—

[a]See text for further explanation.

5.1, which revealed only 145 (2%) known dropouts, Table 5.2 estimates that the total number of dropouts in the sample was 734 (11%).

Longitudinal Assumption

Although drawing longitudinal conclusions about cross-sectional data is often not warranted due to the presence of factors that differentially affect specific age cohorts, the current analysis proceeds somewhat hesitantly with such a presentation. Adequate longitudinal studies of deaf students leaving school are nonexistent. Therefore, the cross-sectional estimates of drop-out rates are presented in hopes that they will be replicated and validated in the future by better studies.

It is assumed in this analysis that the deaf students who leave programs between the ages of 16 and 22 represent a large majority of the deaf students who leave school for any reason. Few deaf students leave school prior to the age of 16, and very few remain in programs beyond the age of 22. Thus, if one sums across the age cohorts of students between the ages of 16 and 22, one is likely to be able to describe most of the means by which deaf students leave school.

The final column of Table 5.2 presents the percentages of students in each of the three school-leaving categories after eliminating those who were still enrolled from the denominators of the percent fraction. In these computations, transfers were assumed to be still enrolled. As noted in Table 5.2, estimates for the percentages of deaf students in each of the three leaving categories are: 52% graduated with diploma; 19% graduated with certificate; and 29% dropped out. These rates are very close to those reported by OSERS (1988) when the categories "dropped out," "reached maximum age," and "left for other reasons" are combined. The current study does not differentiate among these three categories.

RESULTS

School-Leaving Patterns
by Demographic Characteristics

Table 5.3 presents the percentages of students in the three school-leaver categories for various subgroups of the population. To derive these percentages, the two statistical assumptions described above were applied to each subgroup being analyzed. For each subgroup, students in the "Left, whereabouts unknown" category were redistributed to the "Dropped out" and "Transferred" categories, and the age cohorts were aggregated. Breakdowns of Annual Survey data collected on the following characteristics have been presented: sex, ethnic background, handicaps in addition to hearing impairment, and school setting. (The Annual Survey form is presented in Appendix A at the end of this book.) Additionally, students were categorized as to whether they resided in states that required minimum competency tests for deaf students.

Table 5.3 presents summary data for the subgroups of the population defined by these variables. The subgroups defined by the sex, ethnic status, and minimum competency test variables are self-explanatory. For additional handicap status, three subgroups have been defined: 1) students with no additional handicapping conditions, 2) students with one reported additional handicapping condition, and 3) students with two or more reported additional handicapping conditions. A fuller description of these subgroups is presented in Chapter 4. For facility and integration status, students were categorized as to the type of educational facility (special or regular/local) they attended and whether they were integrated with hearing students for any or all of their academic instruction. Special facilities included residential or day school facilities that served only deaf students. Regular/local facilities included public or private schools designed for hearing students enrolled in regular education. Since many residential school students are now being reported as integrated for at least part of their academic instruction through cooperative programs with regular/local schools, and, conversely, many of the deaf students attending regular/local schools receive only minimal or no academic integration with hearing students, a school setting status variable was defined to account for both the type of facility and whether the student received any academic integration. The following paragraphs summarize the percentages reported in Table 5.3.

A higher percentage of females than males dropped out. Higher percentages of males graduated with both certificates and diplomas. A higher percentage of whites graduated with diplomas, compared to blacks and Hispanics. However, blacks and whites did not differ substantially in percentages of dropouts. Black students were much more likely

Table 5.3. Estimated graduation and drop-out rates for population subgroups

Category	N	Total	Graduated, diploma	Graduated, certificate	Dropped Out
Sex					
Male	1,359	100%	54%	21%	25%
Female	1,188	100%	49%	18%	33%
Ethnic background					
White, non-Hispanic	1,624	100%	59%	12%	29%
Black, non-Hispanic	554	100%	38%	36%	26%
Hispanic	323	100%	36%	28%	36%
Additional handicap status					
No additional handicap	1,710	100%	59%	17%	24%
One additional handicap	464	100%	51%	27%	22%
Two or more additional handicaps	331	100%	19%	24%	57%
School setting					
Special facility, not integrated	1,400	100%	52%	25%	23%
Special facility, integrated	99	100%	58%	25%	17%
Regular/local facility, not integrated	182	100%	36%	9%	54%
Regular/local facility, integrated	781	100%	55%	8%	37%
Minimum competency test (MCT)					
MCT required by state for diploma	732	100%	39%	34%	27%
MCT *not* required by state	1,812	100%	57%	14%	29%

to receive certificates than white students or Hispanics. Hispanics had a noticeably higher drop-out percentage than the other groups.

The presence of two or more handicapping conditions substantially increased the likelihood of dropping out. In general, students with two or more reported additional handicaps included a larger number of students categorized as mentally retarded, as described in Chapter 4. Only 19% of the students with two or more additional handicapping conditions graduated with diplomas. The majority of these students dropped out of school without receiving diplomas or certificates. Students with only one additional handicapping condition received diplomas at a lower rate than did students with no additional handicapping conditions; similarly, they received certificates at a higher rate.

Those deaf students in regular/local programs who received no academic integration with hearing students were less likely to receive diplomas than students in the other situations. This finding covaries with the above finding revealing that receipt of diplomas was related to additional handicapping status, since students with additional handicaps are less likely to be integrated during academic instruction. (See Schildroth [1988] for a discussion of the relationship between integration and additional handicaps in the regular/local schools.) This finding is significant, given the relatively high rate of diploma graduation for nonintegrated students attending special facilities. Interestingly, the diploma rates for the two groups from special facilities and from integrated regular/local education programs did not differ markedly. The group most likely to graduate with diplomas comprised students attending special schools who were also integrated for part of their instruction with hearing students in neighboring regular/local programs. Evidently, special facility programs select their highest achieving students for interprogram integration at the regular/local school. These are the students most likely to receive diplomas.

Granting certificates is a practice employed mostly by special facilities. Only a few students (less than 9%) were reported as having been granted certificates from regular/local facilities, whereas one quarter of the students from special facilities received such documents.

Deaf students attending regular/local facilities were more likely to drop out than were deaf students from special facilities. This fact is related to the finding described above pertaining to the granting of certificates. Since regular/local schools are not likely to grant certificates, the students who fail to complete graduation requirements are more likely to drop out.

These results pose additional questions worth considering: If special schools are likely to grant certificates to their students who fail to meet graduation requirements, and regular/local schools are likely to allow these students to drop out, then how do these students differ demographically, and might there be an advantage to one type of program over another? Table 5.4 presents a demographic profile comparison of school leavers (age 18 or older during the sampling year) who received certifi-

Table 5.4. Demographic comparison between special school certificate recipients and regular/local school dropouts

Category	Special school certificate recipients	Regular/local school dropouts
Age: Percent 20 or older	59%	75%
Sex: Percent female	42%	43%
Ethnic background: Percent minority	59%	35%
Additional handicaps: Percent yes	43%	84%
Integrated with hearing students: Percent yes	6%	23%

cates from special facilities versus those from regular/local schools who were reported as dropouts.

The percentages reported in Table 5.4 reveal interesting differences between these two groups of students. The regular/local school dropouts were older than the special school certificate recipients, they were less likely to be minority students, a higher percentage of the regular/local school dropouts were reported with additional handicaps, and more of the regular/local school dropouts had experienced some degree of academic integration during the year before they dropped out. These percentages reveal that special school certificate recipients and regular/local school dropouts are very different demographically. Facility type is not the only characteristic on which they differ. Special facilities are not simply granting certificates to those who would otherwise drop out of regular/local education programs.

The final comparison made in this part of the analysis is between those deaf students who resided in the 14 states reported by Bloomquist(1986) requiring their students to pass minimum competency tests (MCTs) prior to graduation and those students who resided in states not requiring such a test. Clearly, the granting of diplomas was less prevalent in states where minimum competency tests were required for the receipt of high school diplomas. As noted in Table 5.3, only 39% of the deaf students exiting programs from the MCT states graduated with diplomas, compared to 57% from states not requiring the tests. Although the dropout rates were similar for these two groups, a large difference existed in the percentage of students receiving certificates from the two different sets of states. When the receipt of a diploma was dependent upon the passing of a state-mandated test, the diploma rate went down and the certificate rate rose commensurately.

One possible explanation for these results is that the demographic characteristics of students from MCT states differ from those of students in the non-MCT states. Given the finding above that black students are more likely to receive certificates than white students, an obvious question asks whether the ethnic distributions differ for the MCT and the non-MCT states. Table 5.5 presents a breakdown of the ethnic distributions for the two state subgroups. The percentages show that a much higher proportion of the black students in the sample reside in states that require MCT tests. Thus, the negative impact of these tests on drop-out status may be proportionally higher on black students nationwide.

Characteristics of Younger and Older Students Still Enrolled in Programs in Survey Year

For this part of the analysis, the focus is on comparing enrolled students age 17 or 18 during the survey year with those who were 19 and older. The purpose of this analysis is to describe characteristics of students who remain in their programs after the age of 18.

The results of this analysis appear in Table 5.6. A higher percentage of the older students were male, a larger percentage of the older students were minorities, and older students were more likely to have additional handicaps. Finally, older students were more likely than the 17- and 18-year-olds to be enrolled in special facilities serving hearing impaired students only. Seventy-two percent of the enrolled students who were 19 or older at the time of the survey were enrolled in special facilities. This compares to 63% of the enrolled 17- and 18-year-olds in the data base.

SUMMARY AND DISCUSSION

The purpose of this chapter was to estimate the drop-out rate of deaf high school students and to determine the demographic correlates of various high school exiting patterns. By the use of statistical assumptions pertaining to the treatment of missing data and to the longitudinal interpretability of cross-sectional data, the drop-out rate was estimated at 29%, a rate that is virtually identical to the rate reported by Harnisch et al. (1986). Unlike the Harnisch study, however, the current analysis considered a

Table 5.5. Relationship between ethnic status and residence in states requiring minimum competency test (MCT) for high school diploma

Ethnic status	Residing in MCT states		Residing in non-MCT states	
	N	%	N	%
White, non-Hispanic	587	27%	1,623	73%
Black, non-Hispanic	343	42%	481	58%
Hispanic	78	18%	350	82%

Table 5.6. Demographic characteristics: Two age categories

| | Still enrolled | | | |
| | 17–18 years | | 19 or older | |
Category	N	%	N	%
Sex				
Male	1,276	54%	604	59%
Female	1,089	46%	416	41%
Ethnic background				
White, non-Hispanic	1,602	68%	621	61%
Black, non-Hispanic	455	19%	224	22%
Hispanic	210	9%	117	12%
Other	87	4%	52	5%
Additional handicap status				
No additional handicap	1,696	72%	568	56%
One additional handicap	489	21%	266	26%
Two or more additional handicaps	170	7%	183	18%
School setting				
Special facility, not integrated	1,400	59%	694	69%
Special facility, integrated	94	4%	34	3%
Regular/local facility, not integrated	124	5%	75	7%
Regular/local facility, integrated	741	32%	212	21%

high school outcome other than dropping out and graduating with diploma —that is, receiving a certificate. A substantial number of deaf students (19%) exited high schools with such a document, leaving an alarmingly low 52% earning a high school diploma. The figures reported in the current analyses are similar to those reported by the Office of Special Education and Rehabilitative Services (1988) on the federal child-count data.

Demographically, the receipt of a diploma is strongly correlated to three factors studied here: ethnic background, additional handicap status, and residence in a state requiring deaf students to pass minimum competency tests in order to qualify for a diploma. Regarding ethnic status, diploma rates for blacks and Hispanics in the current data set were only 38% and 36% respectively. As alternatives, blacks tended to receive certificates and Hispanics tended to drop out. The drop-out rates for whites and blacks did not differ substantially.

The presence of two or more additional handicaps had the greatest effect on receiving a diploma: Only 19% of the students with two or more additional handicaps were estimated as having received a high school diploma. The majority of students with two or more additional handicapping conditions were estimated as having dropped out without receiving either diploma or certificate. As described in Chapter 4, the group of students reported with two or more additional handicaps were highly likely to be classified as being mentally retarded. Students with only one reported additional handicap received diplomas at a rate of 51%, which was only slightly less than the 59% reported for students with no additional handicaps.

Finally, residence in a state requiring a minimum competency test as a prerequisite for a high school diploma had a detrimental effect on the likelihood of obtaining a diploma. However, students residing in states requiring minimum competency tests did not have a higher likelihood of dropping out; rather, they were more likely to receive certificates.

As noted in the introduction to this chapter, many deaf students, unlike their hearing peers, remain in school beyond the age of 18. A set of analyses of this group of students, compared to those younger students who were still enrolled, revealed that staying in school beyond the age of 18 was related to sex (a higher percentage of older students were male), ethnic background (a higher percentage of older students were from minority ethnic groups), additional handicap status (a higher percentage of older students were reported with additional handicaps), and type of educational facility (a higher percentage of older students attended special facilities designed exclusively for deaf students).

Although some statistical assumptions were made at the outset of the analysis, it is clear that a large number of deaf students remain in programs beyond the age of 18 and eventually leave without a high school diploma. This fact underscores the need for early and comprehensive transition services at the secondary school level, especially for those deaf students less likely to obtain diplomas (i.e., those with additional handicaps, those from minority ethnic groups, and those residing in states where testing requirements preclude the likelihood of graduation). Furthermore, community-based and vocational rehabilitation services must pay particular attention to the needs of a large number of deaf students entering the work force without a high school diploma. Services designed for multiply handicapped deaf youth exiting school are clearly needed. For those leaving school prior to the age of 18, concern must be raised over the fact that they are entering the work force without the benefit of full transition programming that they would have received had they stayed in school.

Since a large number of deaf students are granted certificates in lieu of diplomas upon completion of high school programs, it is important that future research be directed at determining the value, in terms of future job success, of obtaining certificates versus that of obtaining diplomas. In the current data set, the receipt of certificates was more prevalent in states that impose minimum competency tests as prerequisites for diplomas for all students, including deaf students. The validity and appropriateness of this testing with hearing impaired students needs to be considered carefully. (The issue of testing and its role in the tracking and class placements of deaf students is discussed in Chapter 8 in this book.)

Given the large number of deaf students who remain in their high school programs beyond the age of 18, especially those with additional handicaps attending special facilities for deaf students, it is important to evaluate the extent and nature of the vocational training that these older students are receiving. It is clear from the data presented here—72% of the deaf students older than 18 in the data base attended special facilities—that the residential and day schools for the deaf are viewed as playing an important role in the vocational training of older deaf students. In the chapters to follow, the nature of this training and the employment opportunities offered to students as a part of their secondary school experience is explored.

REFERENCES

Alexander, K.L., Natriello, G., & Pallas, A.M. (1985). For whom the school bell tolls: The impact of dropping out on cognitive performance. *American Sociological Review, 50,* 409–420.

Allen, T. (1986). Patterns of academic achievement among hearing impaired students: 1974 and 1983. In A.N. Schildroth & M.A. Karchmer (Eds.), *Deaf children in America* (pp. 161–206). San Diego: College-Hill Press.

Allen, T., & Karchmer, M. (in press). Communication in classrooms for hearing impaired students: Student, teacher, and program characteristics. In H. Bornstein (Ed.), *Manual communication in American education.* Washington, DC: Gallaudet University Press.

Bloomquist, C.A. (1986). Minimum competency testing programs and hearing impaired students. In A.N. Schildroth & M.A. Karchmer (Eds.), *Deaf children in America* (pp. 207–229). San Diego: College-Hill Press.

Center for Assessment and Demographic Studies. (1988). *Annual Survey of Hearing Impaired Children and Youth, 1986–87 School Year.* Washington, DC: Gallaudet University.

Commission on Education of the Deaf. (1988). *Toward equality: Education of the deaf.* Washington, DC: U.S. Government Printing Office.

Harnisch, D.J., Lichtenstein, S.J., & Langford, J.B. (1986). *Digest on youth in transition.* Champaign: Transition Institute at Illinois.

Levin, H.M. (1972). *The costs to the nation of inadequate education* (Study prepared for the Select Committee on Equal Educational Opportunity, U.S. Senate). Washington, DC: U.S. Government Printing Office.

Levin, H.M. (1986). *Education reform for disadvantaged students: An emerging crisis.* West Haven, CT: National Education Association.

McDill, E.L., Natriello, G., & Pallas, A.M. (1985). Raising standards and retaining students: The impact of the reform recommendations on potential dropouts. *Review of Educational Research, 55*(4), 415–433.

National Academy of Sciences. (1984). *High schools and the changing workplace: The employers' view* (Report of the Panel on Secondary School Education for the Changing Workplace). Washington, DC: National Academy Press.

Office of Special Education and Rehabilitative Services. (1988). *Tenth annual report to Congress on the implementation of Public Law 94-142: The Education for All Handicapped Children Act.* Washington, DC: U.S. Department of Education.

Rumberger, R.W. (1987). High school dropouts: A review of issues and evidence. *Review of Educational Research, 57*(2), 101–121.

Schildroth, A.N. (1987). Two profiles of deaf adolescents: Special schools and the mainstream. In G.B. Anderson & D. Watson (Eds.), *Innovations in the habilitation and rehabilitation of deaf adolescents* (pp. 31–38). Little Rock, AR: National Deaf Adolescent Conference.

Schildroth, A.N. (1988). Recent changes in the educational placement of deaf students. *American Annals of the Deaf, 133,* 61–67.

Trybus, R., & Karchmer, M. (1977). School achievement scores of hearing impaired children: National data on achievement status and growth patterns. *American Annals of the Deaf, 122,* 62–69.

U.S. Bureau of the Census. (1986). *Statistical abstract of the United States, 1986.* Washington, DC: U.S. Government Printing Office.

Wolk, S., & Allen, T. (1984). A 5-year follow-up of reading comprehension achievement of hearing-impaired students in special education programs. *Journal of Special Education, 18,* 161–176.

Wolk, S., Karchmer, M., & Schildroth, A. (1982). *Patterns of academic and nonacademic integration among hearing impaired students in special education* (Series R, No. 9). Washington, DC: Gallaudet College, Center for Assessment and Demographic Studies.

Vocational Training and Coursework of Deaf Students in School

6

While contemporary views of the role of high schools in the vocational preparation of students encompass a wide range of activities ranging from career awareness to assessment, the provision of curricula designed to train students with specific job skills has, historically, been the centerpiece of vocational education programs. This emphasis has not been without criticism. Researchers have failed to demonstrate a clear link between skills learned in high school vocational education programs and eventual career choices. Furthermore, given the rapid technological changes associated with particular careers, it is unrealistic to assume that high schools can keep pace and retool their vocational training shops in a timely fashion. Nonetheless, considerable time is spent in school programs developing and implementing vocational curricula in specific skill areas. The appropriateness of these training programs can legitimately be questioned.

For deaf students, the question of whether high schools should be providing skill training is extremely important. For hearing students, the potential for acquiring skills after graduation through postsecondary education and through on-the-job training is far greater than for deaf students. This is true for two basic reasons. First, deaf youth need considerable support such as sign language or oral interpreting in order to take advantage of postsecondary training opportunities. These may not be available, or employers may be unwilling to hire untrained youth who need this kind of support during the time in which they are mastering appropriate job skills. Second, many deaf youth who have left high school either as diploma or certificate recipients or as dropouts have limited proficiency in the English language. Thus, a common employer attitude that, in effect, says, "Give me a graduate with a solid general education in the three Rs and I will teach the appropriate skills," will frustrate a large number of deaf high school graduates who can demonstrate a reading level of no higher than the third grade.

The issue regarding the role of vocational training for deaf students in high schools is therefore a very complicated one. From one perspective, the difficulty of obtaining postsecondary training suggests that schools, which already employ interpreters and special educators with expertise in deafness, should play a major role; from another perspective one could argue that if basic English literacy were the most important ingredient to future job success, then schools should devote more energy to the development of reading and writing skills and less to the development of technical job skills. It might also be argued that large deficits in English language abilities exhibited by deaf 15- and 16-year-olds are extremely difficult to remediate, and therefore vocational training should predominate in the curricular offerings for these students. From yet a different viewpoint, the mandate for schools to serve older students in the 18 to 22 age range, and the increasing number of deaf students in this age range attending special schools for the deaf, is tantamount to a mandate for vocational instruction. (Chapter 9 in this book notes the historical role of vocational training in these special facilities.)

Whatever philosophical point of view is taken regarding the appropriate role of vocational skills training in high school for deaf students, it is apparent that considerable educational resources are devoted to this type of activity. The purpose of the analysis presented in the current chapter is to describe the extent and nature of this activity as it currently exists in programs serving deaf students throughout the United States. The questions addressed include: 1) What are the overall levels of vocational training in the schools educating deaf students and to what degree is training being provided by agencies outside the schools? 2) What specific vocational course areas are most often selected by deaf students, and are these consistent with current labor market needs? 3) What is the relative mix of academic and vocational coursework in the schools, and to what degree are deaf students tracked into vocational and academic coursework? and 4) What percentage of deaf students have individualized written rehabilitation plans (IWRPs) developed through cooperative arrangements between the schools and rehabilitation agencies?

RESULTS

Vocational Training

The extent of vocational training among deaf high school students and the degree to which the training is provided by schools and outside agencies is described in this section. Also presented are data describing the degree to which members of specific subgroups are receiving vocational training in the schools.

Table 6.1 and Figure 6.1 indicate that 21% of the students did not receive vocational training. Of the 79% of the students receiving some training, most received training only as part of their school curricula and not through agencies outside the school. One-half of the students receiving training outside the schools were receiving it directly through state rehabilitation agencies. Eleven percent of the students in the sample were engaged in employment activities that the counselors classified as "on-the-job vocational training." Relatively low percentages of students received training through other programs such as the Job Training Partnership Act (JTPA), through private training agencies, or at rehabilitation centers or other educational agencies outside the schools.

Since rehabilitation agencies often refer clients to other groups outside the school, the column categories on the right side of Table 6.1 are not exclusive. Students receiving rehabilitation services are likely to be receiving services through one of the other types of agencies listed. Table 6.2 shows the relationships of JTPA, private agencies, on-the-job training, and rehabilitation centers to state rehabilitaion offices. That is, the percentages in Table 6.2 show the degree to which students receiving help from state agencies were also receiving training through these other agencies. A fairly high percentage of the students reported by their counselors to be receiving direct training through state rehabilitation were reported to be receiving training through no other outside agency. Of those who had been referred to other agencies, most were receiving some form of on-the-job training, some arranged through the Job Training Partnership Act. About one fifth of the state rehabilitation referrals were to rehabilitation centers.

Breakdowns by Subgroups

Age In Table 6.1 and in the subsequent tables presented in this chapter, students have been divided into two age groups: those who were 17 or 18 years old during the survey year and those who were 19 or older in the survey year. This division was made in order to study differences in vocational training experiences between those students who would normally be expected to still be in school (i.e., those 18 years of age and younger) and those who would normally be expected to have graduated (i.e., those who were 19 years of age or older). Chapter 5 in this book presents a demographic comparison of these two groups in a discussion of high school enrollment and exiting patterns. In this chapter, the concern is to study the differences in vocational training experiences among students of different ages.

Table 6.1 reveals that a higher percentage of older students were receiving vocational training. A study of where these students were receiving their training shows that affiliations with outside agencies account for

Table 6.1. Frequency of participation in vocational training and enumeration of which agencies most frequently provide training: Transition study, 1987

Category	Total N[a]	No training	Training by school only	Some training by outside agency	Outside agency providing training[b]				
					VR	JTPA	Private agency	On-the-job	Rehab ctr/other school
Full sample									
Number	3,188	658	1,709	821	409	151	63	351	179
Percent		21%	53%	26%	13%	5%	2%	11%	6%
Age									
17–18 years	2,213	24%	55%	21%	11%	5%	1%	8%	4%
19 and older	975	14%	50%	36%	17%	5%	3%	17%	9%
Sex									
Male	1,758	19%	54%	27%	14%	5%	2%	11%	6%
Female	1,412	22%	53%	25%	11%	5%	2%	11%	5%
Ethnic background									
White, non-Hispanic	2,073	23%	53%	24%	12%	4%	2%	9%	5%
Black, non-Hispanic	651	15%	60%	25%	14%	5%	2%	9%	6%
Hispanic	309	18%	47%	35%	16%	6%	4%	18%	7%
Additional handicap status									
No additional handicap	2,122	23%	54%	23%	13%	4%	1%	10%	4%
One additional handicap	708	14%	53%	33%	12%	7%	4%	13%	9%
Two or more additional handicaps	336	22%	52%	26%	8%	3%	1%	10%	11%
School setting									
Special facility, not integrated	1,825	13%	63%	24%	11%	3%	2%	10%	5%
Special facility, integrated	315	25%	32%	43%	23%	14%	3%	15%	14%
Regular/local facility, not integrated	174	22%	56%	22%	10%	7%	2%	11%	5%
Regular/local facility, integrated	859	35%	41%	24%	12%	5%	1%	11%	3%

VR = Vocational rehabilitation.

JTPA = Job Training Partnership Act.

[a]Ns do not always sum to 3,188 due to missing information on the demographic variables.

[b]Outside agency categories are not mutually exclusive (e.g., VR often contracts with outside agency to provide training for VR clients). The sum of the percentages in these columns, therefore, will be greater than the percentage of students receiving at least some training from outside agencies.

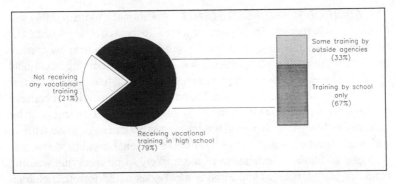

Figure 6.1. Vocational training of deaf students in schools and prevalence of training by outside agencies.

most of the differences between the two age groups. Higher percentages of older students were receiving training through VR, through on-the-job training, and through rehabilitation centers or other educational agencies.

Sex Males and females did not differ appreciably in the degree to which they were receiving vocational training, although a slightly higher percentage of males were reported to be receiving vocational training. Also, the distributions of agencies providing training to males and females were nearly identical.

Ethnic Background Minorities received vocational training more often than did white students. Only 15% of the black students in the sample, for example, were reported as receiving no vocational training. Furthermore, ethnic differences existed in the agencies reported as having provided the training. Blacks were more likely to receive all their training through the schools. Hispanics, however, were more likely than whites and blacks to receive training from outside agencies. On-the-job training accounted for most of this difference. Hispanics were twice as likely to be receiving some form of on-the-job training than whites and blacks.

Table 6.2. Percentage of students receiving direct training support from vocational rehabilitation (VR) also receiving other sources of outside agency training: Transition study, 1987

Agency providing training	%
VR students not served by other agencies	42%
VR plus:	
Job Training Partnership Act	17%
Private training agencies	8%
On-the-job training	31%
Rehabilitation centers	20%
Other agency	4%

Additional Handicap Status Additional handicap status was related to whether students were reported to be receiving vocational training in the schools; students with one additional handicap were more likely than those with no additional handicap to be receiving vocational training. However, those with two or more additional handicaps were *less* likely than those with no additional handicaps to be receiving vocational training. The provision of training by outside agencies accounted for most of the differences between the training experiences of those with no additional handicaps and those with one additional handicap; students with one additional handicap were more likely to be receiving training from outside agencies. Unlike the comparisons noted for other characteristics, however, the additionally handicapped students who received more training from outside agencies were *not* more likely to receive training through VR offices. Rather, they were more likely to receive training through all other sources listed (i.e., JTPA, private agencies, on-the-job training, rehabilitation centers, or other schools). Use of rehabilitation centers was directly related to the degree of handicap: The percentages of students with no additional handicap, one additional handicap, and two or more additional handicaps who received training through rehabilitation centers was 4%, 9%, and 11%, respectively.

School Setting Of the deaf students attending special facilities who were not integrated with hearing students in regular/local education, 87% received some vocational training. Of the integrated students attending regular/local facilities, 65% received vocational training. Thus, while vocational education is widespread in both types of facilities, it is even more prevalent among those students attending special schools. The differences could be accounted for by the differences in the percentage of students receiving training in the schools only. A much higher percentage of students at special facilities received training only as part of their curricula.

Students who attended special facilities and who had some integration with hearing students were more likely to receive no vocational training and more likely to receive training in outside agencies than their non-integrated peers. In all likelihood, some of the special school students are selected for integration into vocational courses at the local school and some for integration into academic courses in the regular/local education program.

Topic Areas of Vocational Study

The numbers and percentages of students reported to be receiving vocational training in selected topic areas are presented in Table 6.3. The percentages are based only on the subgroup of students who were reported to be receiving some vocational training overall. Thus, the 21% noted in

Table 6.3.   Number and percentage of students receiving training in different vocational topic areas: Transition study, 1987

Vocational topic area	All Students Receiving Training	
	N	%
Office work	491	20%
Computer related	487	20%
Home economics	379	16%
Food occupations	340	14%
Construction trades	320	13%
Commercial arts	302	12%
Automative trades	237	10%
Drafting	180	7%
Agriculture	112	5%
Custodial service	99	4%
Photography	95	4%
Machine shop	91	4%
Welding	83	3%
Clothing industry	67	3%
Printing	63	3%
Sheltered workshop	59	2%
Sales	48	2%
Upholstery	41	2%
Electronics	40	2%
Factory work	30	1%
Health related	21	1%
Cosmetology	16	1%
Total number of responses	3,601	[a]
Total N	2,426	

[a]The percentages add up to more than 100 since students may receive vocational training in more than one area.

Table 6.1 as receiving no vocational training have been excluded from the computations presented in this section of the analysis. The two most often cited vocational course areas were office work (reported for 20% of the vocational students) and computer-related topics (also reported for 20% of the students). Other areas reported for at least 10% of the students included home economics (16%), food occupations (14%), construction trades (13%), commercial arts (12%), and automotive trades (10%).

Breakdowns By Subgroups

Table 6.4 lists the five most often reported vocational training areas for each of the demographic subgroups analyzed in this chapter.

Age   Younger students were likely to be receiving training in computer-related topics and in office-work topics. In contrast, the modal

Table 6.4.   Top five vocational training areas reported by different demographic subgroups of the deaf high school population: Transition study, 1987

Category and training area	%[a]
Full sample	
1. Office work	20%
2. Computer related	20%
3. Home economics	16%
4. Food occupations	14%
5. Construction trades	13%
By age	
18 and under	
1. Computer related	24%
2. Office work	22%
3. Home economics	18%
4. Commercial arts	15%
5. Construction trades	12%
19 and over	
1. Food occupations	19%
2. Office work	17%
3. Construction trades	15%
4. Computer related	13%
5. Home economics	11%
By sex	
Male	
1. Construction trades	22%
2. Computer related	18%
3. Automotive trades	17%
4. Food occupations	13%
5. Drafting	11%
Female	
1. Office work	34%
2. Home economics	25%
3. Computer related	23%
4. Commercial arts	15%
5. Food occupations	15%
By ethnic background	
White, non-Hispanic	
1. Computer related	25%
2. Office work	21%
3. Home economics	16%
4. Commercial arts	14%
5. Construction trades	12%
Black, non-Hispanic	
1. Food occupations	21%
2. Office work	17%
3. Home economics	15%
4. Construction trades	13%
5. Automotive trades	11%
Hispanic	
1. Food occupations	20%
2. Office work	17%

(continued)

Table 6.4. *(continued)*

Category and training area	%[a]
3. Construction trades	15%
4. Home economics	12%
5. Commercial arts	10%
By additional handicap status	
No additional handicap	
1. Computer related	24%
2. Office work	23%
3. Home economics	16%
4. Commercial arts	14%
5. Construction trades	14%
One additional handicap	
1. Food occupations	19%
2. Home economics	16%
3. Construction trades	16%
4. Office work	15%
5. Computer related	12%
Two or more additional handicaps	
1. Food occupations	23%
2. Office work	15%
3. Home economics	13%
4. Sheltered workshop	13%
5. Agriculture	12%
By school setting	
Special facility, not integrated	
1. Computer related	20%
2. Office work	19%
3. Commercial arts	15%
4. Home economics	14%
5. Construction trades	14%
Special facility, integrated	
1. Office work	25%
2. Food occupations	21%
3. Computer related	20%
4. Home economics	14%
5. Construction trades	11%
Regular/local facility, not integrated	
1. Food occupations	22%
2. Office work	21%
3. Home economics	15%
4. Construction trades	11%
5. Automobile trades	9%
Regular/local facility, integrated	
1. Computer related	23%
2. Office work	22%
3. Home economics	21%
4. Food occupations	16%
5. Construction trades	13%

[a]The base for these percentages includes those students who are reported as receiving some vocational training.

topic area for older students was food occupations, a topic that does not appear in the top-five list for the younger students. Commercial arts, reported as a top-five topic area for the younger students, does not appear on the list for older students.

One important feature for these age data is the percentages that appear for each of the top five areas. For the younger students, the percentages for the five most prevalent areas are higher than for the top five areas listed for the older students. This indicates that, overall, the training received by the younger students is more homogeneous (i.e., more of the students are clustered in computer and office work courses). Older students are more scattered throughout the list of topic areas, resulting in fewer students reported for each area.

One conclusion that can be drawn from these results is that the successful younger students who will graduate are more likely to be enrolled in vocational courses such as computer operations or word processing, as opposed to less technical areas such as food occupations. It should be kept in mind that the older students in the data base represent those students who do not graduate by age 18. This may explain the difference in course areas taken by younger and older students. It appears that vocational course placement is not independent of demonstrated academic ability. Computer course placement may be dependent on demonstrated competence in mathematics, and office work training may require a minimum level of literacy. Training in areas related to computers or in the operation of office equipment will likely lead to higher paying jobs than some of the other areas. The data suggest that underlying fundamental academic skills are important for successful transitions.

Sex Comparisons of the top five reported areas of vocational training for males and females reveal overlap in only two areas: computer-related courses and food occupations. As for the remaining three, males were more likely to be enrolled in construction trades, automotive trades, and drafting; females were more likely to be enrolled in office work, home economics, and commercial arts. The percentages of females enrolled in the top five course areas are higher than are reported in the top five areas for males, revealing more homogeneity among the vocational training for females: over one third of the females receiving vocational training were enrolled in office work courses, and one quarter of the female students were enrolled in home economics. The data suggest that deaf students, like their hearing counterparts, are concentrated in training areas that will lead to gender-specific occupations, reflecting the influence of gender socialization on vocational course placement.

Ethnic Background In spite of the fact that computer-related courses represent the modal vocational training area for the full sample, especially for students under the age of 19, this training area is not among the top five listed areas for blacks or for Hispanics. Furthermore, food occupations is the modal training area for both minority groups. Additionally, commercial arts appears as a top-five area for whites and Hispanics, but not for blacks. In its place, automotive trades appears as a top-five choice for blacks.

As noted for the different gender subgroups, the vocational placements for the different ethnic subgroups reflect societal stereotypes. Probably, they also reflect a different level of academic preparation as prerequisites for entry into different fields. Previous research has shown that white deaf students outperform black and Hispanic deaf students on academic achievement tests (e.g., Allen, 1986). Thus, to the extent that entry into computer courses is limited to the higher achieving students, it would be expected that minority deaf students would be excluded from these courses in greater numbers.

Additional Handicap Status Consistent with the notion that vocational course assignment correlates with levels of academic preparation, the vocational course areas reported for deaf students with different levels of additional handicapping conditions follows an expected pattern: Those with no additional handicapping conditions were more likely to be enrolled in computer-related courses. Also, food occupations appears as the modal choice for multihandicapped deaf students. Thirteen percent of the vocational students reported to have two or more additional handicaps were being trained in sheltered workshop activities.

School Setting The top-five lists for the two largest subgroups defined by this variable (i.e., the nonintegrated students attending special schools and the integrated students attending regular/local schools) are strikingly similar. Four of the five topic areas are the same, and they appear in the same order.

The percentages reported for students in regular/local facilities are slightly higher than those reported for students attending special facilities, indicating a greater concentration of students in the top-five reported areas. This may indicate that special school students are more diverse in their training experiences.

The vocationally trained students from special facilities who were selected for integration with regular/local programs have a similar list to their nonintegrated peers; however, they were more likely to be enrolled in food preparation courses. Food preparation appears as a top-five area in all three of the four groups involving regular/local schools, but not for the nonintegrated special school students. There is some indication, therefore, that food preparation courses are more emphasized in the regular/local schools.

The nonintegrated regular/local school students, a group largely comprising students with additional handicaps, show a pattern of training seen before to be typical of students with additional handicaps: Training in food occupations was the most common course area, and computer training was not listed among the top five.

Mix of Academic and Vocational Training

For each student in the study, counselors were asked about the relative mix of academic and vocational coursework. On the basis of responses to this question, students were placed into one of three categories: those whose coursework included *all or almost all vocational courses*, those whose coursework was composed *equally* of academic and vocational coursework, and those whose coursework included *all or almost all academic courses*. The resulting distributions for the full sample and for the demographic subgroups are presented in Table 6.5.

Nineteen percent of the students were reported as having all or most of their training in vocational areas, 25% were reported as having an equal mix of academic and vocational training, and 57% were reported as having all or most of their training in academic courses. Since, as noted in Table 6.1, 21% were reported as receiving no vocational training, it can be concluded that 36% of the sample were enrolled primarily in academic courses, but were receiving some vocational training as well.

Breakdowns by Subgroups

Age The relative mix of academic and vocational training differed substantially for younger and older students. Younger students were much more likely to be reported as receiving all or most of their training in academic courses; older students were more likely to be reported as receiving all or most of their training in vocational areas. This finding is consistent with what has been seen earlier: The younger group comprises the academically oriented students likely to graduate (and therefore not represented in the cohort of older students studied). Those who do not graduate and who remain in schools beyond the age of 18 were more likely to pursue vocational training in the schools.

Sex Females were more likely than males to be receiving all or most of their training in academic areas. Males were not likely to be receiving mostly vocational courses or an equal mix of academic and vocational coursework.

Ethnic Background Blacks and Hispanics were much more likely than whites to be receiving all or most of their training in vocational areas. The difference between white students and the other ethnic groups in reported prevalence of receiving all or most of school training in academic areas was overwhelming: 62% of the whites in the sample were reported in predominantly academic course areas; only 44% and 42% of blacks and Hispanics were reported in this category. These find-

Table 6.5.   Relative mix of academic/vocational training for deaf students: Transition study, 1987

Category	N	All or most vocational training	Equal mix academic and vocational	All or most academic training
Full sample	3,164	588 19%	788 25%	1,788 57%
Age				
17–18 years	2,200	14%	23%	63%
19 or older	964	30%	29%	41%
Sex				
Male	1,749	20%	26%	54%
Female	1,407	17%	23%	60%
Ethnic background				
White, non-Hispanic	2,064	13%	24%	62%
Black, non-Hispanic	639	30%	26%	44%
Hispanic	308	28%	29%	42%
Additional handicap status				
No additional handicap	2,108	12%	23%	65%
One additional handicap	700	26%	33%	41%
Two or more additional handicaps	334	45%	23%	31%
School setting				
Special facility, not integrated	1,808	21%	25%	54%
Special facility, integrated	306	21%	36%	43%
Regular/local facility, not integrated	174	30%	32%	37%
Regular/local facility, integrated	861	10%	20%	69%

ings add to what has been observed before related to the vocational topic areas studied by whites and by minority students. Minority deaf students were not only less likely to be enrolled in predominantly academic courses, but the specific vocational areas of their training required lower levels of academic skill. The impact of these school training differences on later job success implies a bleaker success picture for minority students than for white students.

Additional Handicap Status As noted in Figure 6.2, 65% of the students with no additional handicaps were reported to be receiving all or almost all academic training. This percentage decreased as the number of reported additional handicaps increased. The percentage of students with one additional handicap receiving all or almost all academic training was 41%; the percentage for those with two or more additional handicaps 31%. Forty-five percent of the students with two or more additional handicaps were reported as receiving all or almost all vocational training. It is clear from these figures that the importance of vocational training to the educational experiences of deaf youth increases to the degree that they have other educationally relevant handicaps.

School Setting Deaf students integrated in regular/local schools were more likely than nonintegrated deaf students in special facilities to be reported as receiving all or almost all academic training. A

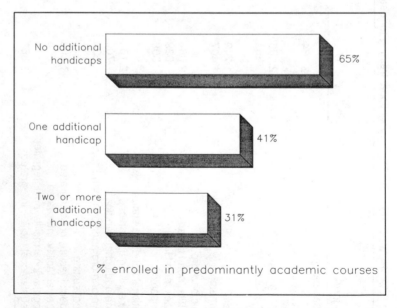

Figure 6.2. Influence of additional handicaps on likelihood deaf students will be enrolled in predominantly academic courses.

more interesting comparison is between the integrated and nonintegrated students in the regular/local schools. While, of the four groups reported, the integrated regular/local school students were the most academically oriented, the nonintegrated students in the regular/local schools were the least. As noted before, deaf students in this latter group were likely to have additional handicaps.

Academic and Vocational Tracking

As can be seen from Table 6.6, many deaf students from the sample attended schools where separate vocational and academic tracks formed a basis for placements in different school curricula. Seventy percent of the students from the current study were attending schools with such tracking policies. One quarter of the tracked students were in vocational tracks, 29% were in academic tracks, 38% were in combined academic and vocational tracks, and 7% were in some "other" defined curricular track. The breakdowns of tracking categories by demographic categories are presented in Table 6.6.

Individualized Written Rehabilitation Plans

In the survey, counselors were asked if students had IWRPs. As noted in Table 6.7, 25% of the students in the entire data base were reported to have such a plan. Students in various demographic subgroups differed in the likelihood of having such a plan.

Older students were more likely than younger students to have IWRPs. Males were a little more likely than females to have IWRPs. Whites and blacks were more likely than Hispanics to have IWRPs. Students with no additional handicaps and those with one additional handicap differed little with respect to the degree to which they had IWRPs. However, only 17% of the students with two or more additional handicaps had IWRPs, indicating that this group had fewer contacts with VR agencies.

Students attending special schools who had been selected for integration into a regular/local school program were much more likely to have an IWRP than students in other groups. This finding suggests that, for these few students, VR may be serving the role of facilitating the relationship between the special facility and the regular/local program. The group least likely to have IWRPs was the nonintegrated students in the regular/local schools. As discussed earlier, this group was composed largely of students with additional handicaps. The two largest groups in the population (i.e., the nonintegrated students from the special facilities and the integrated students from the regular/local programs) differed very little as to the percentage of students reported to have IWRPs.

Table 6.8 and Figure 6.3 present a comparison of the group of stu-

Table 6.6. Percentage of deaf students in educational or vocational tracks: Transition study, 1987

Category	N	Schools with separate vocational/ academic tracks	Tracks for those enrolled in tracking schools			
			Vocational[a]	Academic[a]	Combined[a]	Other[a]
Full sample	3,157	2,208 70%	556 25%	640 29%	837 38%	156 7%
Age						
17–18 years	2,194	70%	22%	34%	38%	6%
19 or older	963	70%	33%	19%	38%	9%
Sex						
Male	1,749	69%	29%	28%	37%	6%
Female	1,399	70%	21%	31%	40%	8%
Ethnic background						
White, non-Hispanic	2,060	69%	20%	35%	38%	7%
Black, non-Hispanic	652	75%	37%	15%	42%	6%
Hispanic	300	69%	32%	24%	35%	8%
Additional handicap status						
No additional handicap	2,112	70%	21%	36%	41%	2%
One additional handicap	700	71%	37%	18%	35%	11%
Two or more additional handicaps	325	68%	30%	8%	29%	33%
School setting						
Special facility, not integrated	1,806	70%	27%	24%	43%	5%
Special facility, integrated	315	82%	33%	26%	30%	10%
Regular/local facility, not integrated	168	82%	39%	19%	31%	10%
Regular/local facility, integrated	852	62%	15%	45%	33%	6%

[a]The percentages in the four columns on the right side of this table are based on the number of students counted as being tracked, not on the total sample N.

Table 6.7. Percentage of deaf students with individualized written rehabilitation plans (IWRPs): Transition study, 1987

Category	Total N	Students with IWRPs
Full sample	2,926	726
		25%
Age		
17–18 years	2,028	21%
19 or older	898	33%
Sex		
Male	1,616	26%
Female	1,310	23%
Ethnic background		
White, non-Hispanic	1,938	26%
Black, non-Hispanic	584	26%
Hispanic	267	21%
Additional handicap status		
No additional handicap	1,960	26%
One additional handicap	660	25%
Two or more additional handicaps	293	17%
School setting		
Special facility, not integrated	1,668	24%
Special facility, integrated	303	34%
Regular/local facility, not integrated	151	19%
Regular/local facility integrated	798	23%

Table 6.8. Vocational and work characteristics of deaf students with and
without individualized written rehabilitation plans (IWRPs)

Characteristic	Students with IWRPs	Students without IWRPs
Currently working for pay	35%	30%
Currently have an assigned state VR counselor	94%	57%
Have met with a VR counselor dur-ing the last 12 months	89%	40%
Of those receiving some vocational training, those receiving training through outside agencies	55%	24%
Of those in tracked curricula, those in vocational *or* combined voca-tional and academic tracks	68%	62%

VR = vocational rehabilitation.

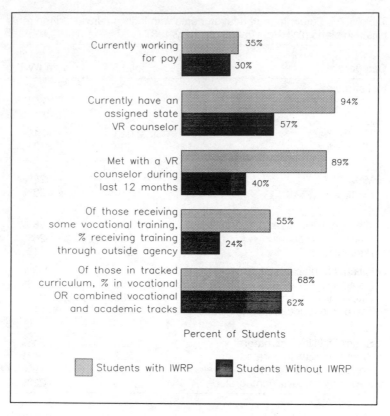

Figure 6.3. Vocational and work characteristics of students with and without an individualized written rehabilitation plan.

dents with IWRPs and those without. Some of the comparison variables come from the student employment questionnaire and receive a more extensive analysis in the next chapter. Here, their relationship to students having (or not having) IWRPs is considered.

As evident in Table 6.8, the employment and vocational experiences of students with IWRPs differ markedly from those without IWRPs. In considering these findings, however, it should be noted that having an IWRP is highly associated with being a member of a particular demographic group, as discussed above and shown in Table 6.7. Thus, differences in vocational and work experiences for students with and without IWRPs may be due to underlying demographic factors, and causal relationships cannot be assumed.

A greater number of students with IWRPs were working for pay than were students with no IWRPs. IWRP students were more likely to have an assigned state VR counselor. As indicated in Table 6.8, 94% of the students reported with IWRPs reported that they had a VR counselor. Since having an IWRP implies that a plan has been worked out involving VR, the schools, the parents, and the student (See Chapter 1), the 6% of the students reported by their counselors as having IWRPs who reported not having a VR counselor are somewhat of a mystery. It is possible that some of the students responding to the survey were uncertain as to whether they, in fact, had a VR counselor. It is also possible that some school counselors developed plans on their own for their students that they are calling IWRPs. Nonetheless, the data confirm the fact that having a state VR counselor assigned to a student is crucial for the development of an IWRP. More important, 57% of the students with no IWRPs indicated on the student survey that they did not have a VR counselor. Having a state VR counselor and having an IWRP are highly associated.

Students were asked if they had met with a state VR counselor within the last 12 months. Of those with an IWRP, 89% reported that they had met with a counselor. Of those with no IWRP, only 40% reported that they had met with a counselor.

The likelihood of receiving at least some vocational training through agencies outside the school was also correlated with whether students had IWRPs. Limiting this analysis to those students who received some vocational training as part of their education programs, it was found that 55% of the vocational students with IWRPs were receiving training at agencies outside the school, and only 24% of the students with no IWRPs were receiving training at agencies outside the schools. Thus, having an IWRP was a factor in facilitating arrangements between students and training agents outside the school.

Finally, tracked students who had IWRPs were more likely to be enrolled in vocational tracks than were those tracked students without IWRPs. However, 29% of the tracked students with IWRPs were actually reported as being in academic tracks. Having an IWRP does not necessarily imply enrollment in a vocational track.

SUMMARY AND DISCUSSION

The purpose of the analyses presented in this chapter was to study patterns of vocational training in schools serving deaf students. Throughout the analyses, the strategy was, first, to provide data relative to the group of deaf students as a whole, and, second, to study differences in the patterns of training for selected demographic subgroups of the deaf high school–age population. Four topic areas guided the structure of the analyses: 1) the overall levels of vocational training and the determination of which agencies were providing this training; 2) the specific content of vocational courses and training areas; 3) the relative mix of academic and

vocational coursework and the extent of vocational and academic tracking in the schools; and 4) the existence and function of the IWRP as an
educational and vocational planning tool. These topic areas are discussed
separately.

Overall Levels of Vocational Training

A large majority of deaf students were receiving some degree of vocational training as part of their schooling; typically this meant that they
were taking vocational courses as part of their curricula. Only about one
quarter of the students were reported to be receiving training through
agencies outside the school. Among these students who were receiving
training outside the school, they most often acquired training either
through VR services directly or through on-the-job training.

Older and younger students did not differ in the degree to which they
took vocational courses as part of their school coursework; however,
older students were much more likely to receive training through outside
agencies. The previous chapter compared the characteristics of older and
younger students in an attempt to describe the demographic correlates of
graduating and staying in school beyond the normal graduation age. The
current chapter has demonstrated that older students remain in schools to
obtain additional vocational training. It is significant that the provision of
training by outside agencies accounts for the differences between these
two groups. This fact underscores the importance of interagency participation by schools and other training sources for older deaf students in
these transition years. PL 94-142 mandates that local education agencies
provide appropriate educational services to students up to the age of 22.
The data indicate that these extra years of schooling often involve agencies other than the schools.

Minorities were more likely than whites to be receiving vocational
training. However, the pattern of school versus outside agency training
for Hispanics and blacks differed markedly. The vocational training received by blacks was more often limited to school coursework, while a
higher proportion of Hispanics were receiving training through outside
agencies. To the extent that these outside experiences are viewed as contributing positively to a student's transition, these findings are disturbing.
The data suggest that more extramural opportunities need to be found for
black deaf students. Chapter 7 considers more specifically the employment of black deaf students while in school.

The vocational training experiences for students with additional
handicapping conditions reveal that those students who were reported
with one additional handicapping condition were more likely to be receiving vocational training than those with no additional handicapping conditions. Unfortunately, those with two or more additional handicapping

conditions were *less* likely than others to be receiving vocational training. These findings are worrisome, especially in light of the findings of the previous chapter indicating that those students with two or more additional handicaps were more likely than other students to drop out of school with neither diploma nor certificate. The diminished likelihood that multiply handicapped students were enrolled in vocational training experiences may help explain the higher drop-out rates (i.e., insufficient educational programming is provided for students with considerable educational needs). Attention in the future needs to be directed toward providing appropriate vocational instruction and transition services to students with compounding handicapping conditions.

In terms of facility and integration status, vocational training was almost universal for those students at special facilities who were not integrated. This finding is correlated to the one noted above that older students were more likely than younger students to be receiving vocational training, since, as noted in Chapter 4, special facilities had higher proportions of older students. Much has been written about the enrollment patterns at special schools for deaf students. The number of students attending these facilities has decreased dramatically in recent years due to three factors: 1) the departure from the secondary school system of the so-called "rubella bulge" (i.e., the large number of children born in 1963 and 1964 with deafness caused by maternal rubella) (Brown & Karchmer, 1987); 2) the implementation of PL 94-142, which has resulted in an increase in placing deaf students in integrated classroom settings (Allen & Karchmer, 1987); and 3) the overall decline in the birth rate in the United States resulting in the decline in the number of children born with deafness due to congenital factors.

The greater prevalence of older students attending special facilities and the overwhelming proportion of students attending special facilities and receiving some vocational training suggests a future important role that these institutions may serve in the area of transition and vocational training and preparation. The recent Federal Commission on Education of the Deaf (1988) took particular note of the lack of vocational training centers for young deaf adults. At the same time, legislation through the last decade has continued to expand the age range of students to be served through the special education network. The logical culmination of these trends is to envision the special schools evolving into resource centers and focal points for transition and vocational training.

Developing such a plan for the special facilities need not undermine the mandate of PL 94-142 and the principles of "least restrictive environment." In fact, the subgroup of the current data set with the most interesting pattern of vocational training was the group of students from the special facilities who received some degree of integration with hearing students. These students were the most likely to receive training through outside agencies, and they were the group most likely to have IWRPs. (These two facts are obviously not independent; training through outside agencies is often arranged by virtue of the IWRP.) Students in these mixed programs that include the involvement of VR, academic integration, and training through a variety of outside agencies should be monitored carefully over the next decade in order to judge the efficacy of such multiagency programming arrangements.

Specific Content Areas

The findings of this study as they pertain to the specific training areas prevalent in the vocational programs in schools serving deaf students suggest that these programs are keeping pace with the job market, at least in terms of the subject areas offered. Traditional—and somewhat stereotyped—fields for deaf workers (e.g., printing and cosmetology) were being studied by only a few of the respondents in the sample selected for the current inquiry. The modal subject areas, computer-related topics and office work, are consistent with the prevailing labor conditions.

However, these findings should lead only to a cautious optimism. That many students were studying computer-related topics in their vocational programs is no guarantee that they will find employment in that field. Clearly, longitudinal research is needed to determine the degree to which the study of a particular vocational area in high school leads to employment in that field.

In terms of the specific course offerings, special schools and regular/local programs serving deaf students were remarkably similar: Four of the five most prevalent course areas for the nonintegrated special school students and the integrated regular/local school students were the same and appeared on the lists in the same prevalence order. While the current findings do not assess the quality of the training in different settings, it is clear that the relative emphasis in vocational areas is similar across settings.

The different demographic subgroups studied differed dramatically in regard to the prevalent vocational subject areas studied; the differences followed predictable ethnic and gender stereotypes. The lists of the five most prevalent vocational areas studied by males and females overlapped only for the topics of computer-related courses and food occupations. Otherwise, the top five choices for males included construction trades, automotive trades, and drafting; the female list included office work, home economics, and commercial arts.

Regarding ethnic comparisons, the most prevalent area for blacks and Hispanics was food occupations, which failed to appear on the top five list for whites. At the same time, the most prevalent choice for whites was computer-related topics; this area failed to appear on the top-five lists for blacks or Hispanics.

Clearly, paths toward stereotyped occupations for subgroups of deaf high school students have already begun in high school. This finding has obvious implications related to students' eventual abilities to obtain high-paying jobs after they leave high school.

Another implication of the current findings is that there is an "academic factor" to the selection of vocational courses. For example, while computer-related topics were not, in the current analysis, specifically demonstrated to be associated with academic achievement, it was clearly associated with demographic variables known to be highly correlated with academic performance, particularly ethnic background and additional handicap status. This leads to a suspicion that the selection by students of—or, perhaps, the placement of students into—vocational courses does not proceed independently from consideration of a student's academic competence.

Tracking and the Mix of Academic and Vocational Courses

It is clear from the data presented in this chapter that the importance of vocational training to the educational experiences of deaf youth increases with the student's age and with the likelihood that the student has additional handicapping conditions. The relative proportion of time spent by students in vocational coursework increased with age and with handicapping conditions. Younger students and students with no handicapping conditions other than deafness were more academically oriented.

Blacks were more often found in programs with tracking than were whites and Hispanics. Chapter 5 noted that blacks more often resided in states that imposed minimum competency requirements for the receipt of a high school diploma, and, as a possible consequence, were more often awarded certificates rather than diplomas. The finding that blacks were more often in vocational tracks is consistent with this. Tracking as school policy is associated with mandated diploma requirements. Much further research is needed to determine whether such practices facilitate quality vocational training and transition planning or whether they are more detrimental by limiting the opportunities available to individuals after they leave high school.

Students attending special facilities who had been selected for integration with hearing students for instruction were more likely to come from programs where tracking occurred. This suggests that official mechanisms, such as tracking, for customizing education plans are associated with innovative (or, at least, atypical) education programming (e.g., integrating special school students at regular/local schools).

Individualized Written Rehabilitation Plans

Only one quarter of the deaf students reported to the current study had official IWRPs as part of their education programs. Two groups—older students and students attending special facilities who had been selected for integration—were more likely than other groups to have prepared IWRPs. Older students were more likely than younger students to be receiving vocational training through outside agencies. Furthermore, by definition, selecting students from special facilities for integration involves an interagency agreement between two school programs. Thus, the data suggest that IWRPs are serving their intended function of facilitating interagency participation in the planning for individual students. Unfortunately, the prevalence of this activity remains low.

IWRPs for students with two or more additional handicapping conditions were especially rare. This is unfortunate since these students have the greatest need for special planning. It was noted above that students with multiple handicapping conditions were: 1) more likely to drop out, and 2) less likely to be receiving vocational training. Combined with their lowered likelihood of having an IWRP, the data strongly suggest that attention should be given to this group of students.

CONCLUSION

In keeping with the theme of this book, the data presented in this chapter substantiate the conclusion that there are reasons to be both optimistic and pessimistic about the future with respect to the role of vocational training in the transition of deaf students from school to work. On the optimistic side, this chapter has documented the substantial involvement of vocational rehabilitation in the development of specific training programs for individual students, and, for students with IWRPs, enhancements to training programs such as on-the-job training, integration with hearing students, and involvement with outside training agencies have occurred. Furthermore, the specific training areas offered as courses appear to be keeping pace with the needs of society.

On a more pessimistic note, although participation in vocational curricula is high, the actual existence of IWRPs remains at approximately 25%. For many, the direct involvement of personnel from the adult service network, namely VR counselors, in the designing of specific transition plans is not occurring.

Also, the examination of vocational education variables for different subgroups of the population reveals wide disparities that foretell different futures for students with different characteristics. Of particular concern are minority deaf students and deaf students with compounding additional handicaps. Black students had lesser involvement with agencies outside the schools; Hispanics had fewer IWRPs; students with two or more additional handicaps had fewer relationships with VR. Furthermore, minority students and students with additional handicaps were enrolled in vocational subject areas requiring less academic skill. As noted in Chapter 1, the barriers to advancement imposed by limited levels of English language literacy are perhaps the most difficult to overcome. This is particularly true for these specific subgroups of the population.

REFERENCES

Allen, T. (1986). Patterns of academic achievement among hearing impaired students: 1974 and 1983. In A.N. Schildroth & M.A. Karchmer (Eds.), *Deaf children in America* (pp. 161–206). San Diego: College-Hill Press.

Allen, T.E., & Karchmer, M.A. (1987). *Changing patterns of educational placement for hearing impaired students under the influence of P.L. 94-142* (Paper prepared as testimony for the deliberations for the Commission on Education of the Deaf). Washington, DC: Gallaudet University.

Brown, S.C., & Karchmer, M.A. (1987). Who will be served? Charting the trends. *Gallaudet Today, 18*(1), 4–7.

Federal Commission on Education of the Deaf. (1988). *Toward equality: Education of the deaf; a report to the President and the Congress of the United States.* Washington, DC: Government Printing Office.

Establishing an Employment History

$\boxed{7}$

Deaf Students and Their Jobs While in School

Recognizing the role employment experience plays in training youth for future careers, the "Study of Deaf Students in Transition from School to Work," conducted by the Center for Assessment and Demographic Studies (CADS), sought information from deaf students regarding their employment during the 1986–1987 school year. For those not working, the study attempted to identify reasons that prevented these youth from holding afterschool or weekend jobs. This information provides a picture of the actual work experiences of deaf high school students.

This chapter examines these data and attempts to answer the following questions: When do deaf students get jobs? What percentage of deaf high school students hold jobs during the school year? How does this employment rate compare to that of their hearing peers? How many hours a week do deaf youth work? What types of jobs are deaf students getting? Who gets summer jobs? What are the hourly salaries of deaf youth? Who helped students obtain jobs? Why do deaf students quit or get fired from jobs? Why do deaf students not look for work? and Are there certain demographic characteristics of deaf youth that make them more or less likely to be employed?

THE ROLE OF WORK EXPERIENCE IN THE TRANSITION PROCESS

After-school, weekend, and summer jobs expose students to the world of work. Some education programs provide work-study options, permitting students to work while attending school. These employment experiences introduce students to the skills, responsibilities, and roles they will need

119

when they enter the job market in search of full-time employment. Madeleine Will (1985) speaks of the goal of the transition process as paid employment that ". . . offers opportunities to expand social contacts, contribute to society, demonstrate creativity, and establish an adult identity" (p. 5). Employment experience while students pursue their secondary education can also offer these same opportunities and aid in the transition process.

The recognition of the importance of employment experience for disabled individuals is not a recent phenomenon and is noted by many as an important component of successful transition models. In the 1960s the Rehabilitation Services Administration urged education and vocational rehabilitation agencies to develop cooperative work-study programs (Szymanski & Danek, 1985).

Rusch, Mithaug, and Flexer (1986) discuss the "special education work experience model" that links the services of special education agencies with those of vocational rehabilitation. They attribute the development of this model to the positive relationship observed between work experience during school and employment after completion of school for disabled students. The work-experience opportunities that are part of their model include: 1) classroom simulation, 2) work experience at a job within the school, 3) part-day off-campus work experience, and 4) full-day off-campus jobs.

The advantages provided by special education work-experience programs are numerous (Rusch et al., 1986). The obvious primary advantage is introduction to actual work settings. Since some disabled students encounter difficulties and failures with academic coursework, the work experience can provide an opportunity to demonstrate achievement in a school-related activity. Students become more motivated by the change in the traditional class schedule and the introduction of new activities.

A study supported by the National Institute of Handicapped Research (1985) examined exemplary special education and vocational rehabilitation programs. A common element in these programs was the incorporation of work-experience opportunities. Among the benefits offered by the work experience was the opportunity for students to demonstrate success in a school-related program.

Bellamy, Rose, Wilson, and Clarke (1982) report that the work-experience or work-study programs were most successful with students whose handicaps were less than severe. The actual skills gained by the students, the interaction of students with nonhandicapped individuals in the workplace, and the contacts with potential future employers are among the benefits they cite.

Rudrud, Ziarnak, Bernstein, and Ferrara (1984) also discuss the importance of handicapped students obtaining actual work experience.

They attribute some of the postschool employment failures of disabled youth to the lack of previous opportunities to interact in real-life situations. In the model of vocational transition described by Wehman, Kregel, and Barcus (1985), one key component is the utilization of "community based instruction." The students learn skills in the curriculum-based classroom instruction but have an opportunity to practice and improve these skills on job sites within the community.

A study of factors associated with post–high school employment of disabled youth reported a positive correlation between students' employment during school and their employment status after school (Hasazi, Gordon, & Roe, 1985; Hasazi, Gordon, Roe, Hull, Finck, & Salembier, 1985). This study distinguished between work experience gained in "real jobs" versus participation in "work-experience programs." Students with real jobs for which they earned money were more likely to be employed after leaving school. Students who held part-time jobs during high school also were more likely than those students who did not hold such jobs to obtain higher wages in their jobs after high school. The authors attributed the lack of correlation between participation in work-experience programs and future employment to the fact that the programs in which the students participated were for short periods of time, and often volunteer in nature rather than salaried.

Work-experience opportunities offered to high school students either as part of their vocational training program or gained by the student's own resourcefulness have the potential for playing an important role in the transition process. The extent to which deaf students obtain employment experience while in high school is addressed in the following sections.

STUDENT QUESTIONNAIRE: SURVEY OF JOB TRAINING FOR HEARING IMPAIRED YOUTH

As part of the CADS transition study, 6,196 severely and profoundly deaf youth 17 through 23 years of age returned a questionnaire that sought information related to their work experience. A copy of the Student Questionnaire mailed to students in March, 1987 appears in Appendix A at the end of this book. Chapter 4 provides detailed information on the study methodology and the demographic characteristics of the respondents; Chapter 5 discusses those youth who had graduated, dropped out, or transferred to other programs.

Of the 6,196 returned questionnaires, 3,312 youth were no longer enrolled in Spring, 1987 at the education program contacted. The analyses presented in this chapter are based on the 2,884 students enrolled in special education programs in the spring of 1987 who completed a Student Questionnaire. On all demographic characteristics, except age, the distribution of responding students was nearly identical to those of the target population (i.e., the group of students originally selected for the study). Many of the older students had left the educational setting and did not return to school in the fall of 1986; while 48% of the target population of the study were 17 or 18 years of age, 71% of those still enrolled in the spring of 1987 and who returned questionnaires were in this age group. Thus, the results that follow can be assumed to represent the work experiences of deaf high school students nationally.

When Do Deaf Students Get Jobs?

One goal of this study was to establish a picture of employment experiences of deaf youth. Students reported employment experience during the summer of 1986 and jobs held during the spring of 1987. Work experience included competitive employment within the community, subsidized employment, and sheltered workshop settings.

More than one half (59%) of the hearing impaired youth had obtained some kind of work experience during either the summer or spring (Figure 7.1). Twenty percent held paid jobs both during the summer and while they attended school. Twenty-eight percent worked in the summer of 1986 only, and another 11% worked only during the spring of 1987.

Summer vacations appear to be the preferred time to schedule work;

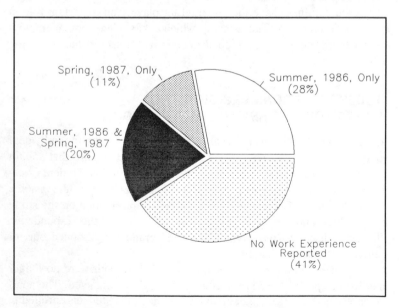

Figure 7.1. Employment history of deaf youth, 1986–1987.

48% of the youth held jobs during the summer. This compares with 31% of the students who held jobs in the spring of 1987. These figures are conservative indications of overall work experience, however, as some students may have had jobs at times other than the summer of 1986 or the spring of 1987; for the purposes of this study, those students would be counted among those with no work experience.

What Percentage of Deaf High School Students Hold Jobs During the School Year?

Three out of every 10 deaf youth in the study held jobs during the spring of 1987. Certain demographic characteristics of the youth were associated with their employment status, as can be seen Table 7.1. The following statements summarize these results:

- Older students (38%) were more likely to be working than younger students (27%).
- A larger percentage of males (32%) than females (27%) held jobs.

Table 7.1.   Employment status of deaf youth: Transition study, 1987

Category	N	Employed	Not employed
Full sample	2,884	869 30%	2,015 70%
Age			
17–18 years	2,044	27%	73%
19 or older	840	38%	62%
Sex			
Male	1,590	32%	68%
Female	1,288	27%	72%
Ethnic background			
White, non-Hispanic	1,849	31%	69%
Black, non-Hispanic	591	29%	71%
Hispanic	295	24%	76%
Additional handicap status			
No additional handicap	1,933	30%	70%
One additional handicap	625	33%	67%
Two or more additional handicaps	305	25%	75%
School setting			
Special facility, not integrated	1,718	29%	71%
Special facility, integrated	115	29%	71%
Regular/local facility, not integrated	188	26%	75%
Regular/local facility, integrated	843	34%	66%

- Ethnic background also was associated with employment status. Whites (31%) were slightly more likely to be employed than blacks (29%). Hispanic youth (24%) were least likely to hold jobs while attending school.
- Deaf students with no additional handicaps (30%) or only one additional handicap (33%) were more likely to work for pay than those with two or more additional handicaps (25%).
- The type of school setting in which the student was enrolled was also related to employment status. A higher percentage of deaf youth attending regular/local programs and integrated in classrooms with hearing students (34%) held jobs than those students in other educational settings.

What Types of Jobs Are Deaf Students Getting?

Students working in the spring of 1987 provided information to two questions regarding their jobs. The initial question asked, "What kind of job do you have?" The follow-up question was "What do you do in this job?" The responses to both of these items were used to classify the occupation into categories used by the U.S. Bureau of the Census. Nearly all (97%) of those working provided information allowing classification of their job title.

Figure 7.2 presents a summary of the major occupational categories in which students were employed for pay. Of those employed, the largest percentage (44%) held jobs in service-related occupations. Technical, sales, and administrative support jobs accounted for another quarter (24%) of the occupations in which deaf students found employment.

Students indicated over 100 different job titles. Forty-two percent of the students were employed in one of four occupations. The most frequently reported job titles were "kitchen worker, food preparation" (16%), "janitor and cleaner" (13%), "stock handler and bagger" (8%), and "file clerk" (5%) (Table 7.2). When demographic variables were considered for the various subgroups, these same four occupations were the most frequently reported, with minor exceptions. For males, the job title of "groundskeeper" was among the top four jobs reported; for females, "teacher's aide" was among the top four job titles. In considering ethnic background, "child-care aide" was listed by Hispanic youth as the fourth most frequent job title. For students with one additional handicap, "assembler" was a frequently held job; for students with two or more additional handicaps, "production helper" ranked among the leading jobs. When school setting was considered, those at special facilities and integrated with hearing students reported "freight, stock and material handler" as the fourth most frequent job title; youth in regular/local programs

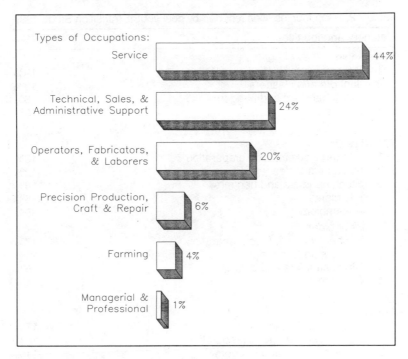

Figure 7.2. Types of occupations held by deaf youth, Spring, 1987.

and not integrated with hearing students included jobs as "short-order cook" among the most frequent occupations.

How Many Hours a Week Do Deaf Youth Work?

The number of hours a student works per week provides an added dimension to the work-experience picture and an indication of the amount of experience being obtained (Table 7.3). The reported number of hours worked per week ranged from 1 hour to 50 hours. One third of the youth reported working less than 10 hours a week, another third worked 10–19 hours, and another third worked 20 hours or more a week. Seven percent worked 40 or more hours.

Some of the students' demographic factors were associated with the number of hours worked each week. The following statements illustrate these data:

- Males were more likely to work longer hours each week. Forty percent of the males worked 20 hours a week or more, as compared to 24% of the females.

Table 7.2.   Top four job titles reported by deaf youth: Transition Study, 1987

Category and job title	%
Full sample	
1. Kitchen workers, food preparation	16%
2. Janitors and cleaners	13%
3. Stock handlers and baggers	8%
4. File clerks	5%
Age	
17–18 years	
1. Kitchen workers, food preparation	16%
2. Janitors and cleaners	12%
3. Stock handlers and baggers	10%
4. File clerks	5%
5. Assemblers	5%
19 years or older	
1. Kitchen workers, food preparation	17%
2. Janitors and cleaners	15%
3. Stock handlers and baggers	5%
4. File clerks	4%
Sex	
Males	
1. Janitors and cleaners	17%
2. Kitchen workers, food preparation	16%
3. Stock handlers and baggers	11%
4. Groundskeepers	3%
Females	
1. Kitchen workers, food preparation	17%
2. File clerks	8%
3. Janitors and cleaners	7%
4. Teacher's aides	7%
Ethnic background	
White, non-Hispanic	
1. Kitchen workers, food preparation	16%
2. Janitors and cleaners	11%
3. Stock handlers and baggers	9%
4. File clerks	4%
Black, non-Hispanic	
1. Janitors and cleaners	21%
2. Kitchen workers, food preparation	15%
3. Stock handlers and baggers	7%
4. File clerks	6%
Hispanic	
1. Kitchen workers, food preparation	19%
2. Janitors and cleaners	10%
3. Stock handlers and baggers	9%
4. File clerks	7%
5. Child-care aides	7%

(continued)

Table 7. 2.   (*continued*)

Category and job title	%
Additional handicap status	
No additional handicap	
1. Kitchen workers, food preparation	16%
2. Janitors and cleaners	10%
3. Stock handlers and baggers	8%
4. File clerks	5%
One additional handicap	
1. Kitchen workers, food preparation	18%
2. Janitors and cleaners	17%
3. Stock handlers and baggers	9%
4. File clerks	5%
5. Assemblers	5%
Two or more additional handicaps	
1. Janitors and cleaners	26%
2. Kitchen workers, food preparation	15%
3. Stock handlers and baggers	10%
4. Production helpers	8%
School setting	
Special facility, not integrated	
1. Janitors and cleaners	15%
2. Kitchen workers, food preparation	15%
3. File clerks	6%
4. Stock handlers and baggers	5%
Special facility, integrated	
1. Stock handlers and baggers	28%
2. Kitchen workers, food preparation	22%
3. Janitors and cleaners	6%
4. Freight, stock, and material handlers	6%
Regular/local facility, not integrated	
1. Janitors and cleaners	20%
2. Kitchen workers, food preparation	13%
3. Short-order cooks	11%
4. Stock handlers and baggers	9%
Regular/local facility, integrated	
1. Kitchen workers, food preparation	20%
2. Stock handlers and baggers	12%
3. Janitors and cleaners	9%
4. File clerks	4%

- Minority students tended to work more hours than white youth. Blacks and Hispanics worked 20 hours a week or more at rates of 36% and 39%, respectively; 33% of whites worked 20 hours a week or more.
- Students with no or only one additional handicap were more likely to work longer hours compared to students with two or more additional

Table 7.3. Hours per week worked by deaf youth: Transition study, 1987

Category	N	Less than 10 hrs.	10–14 hrs.	15–19 hrs.	20–24 hrs.	25–39 hrs.	40 hrs. or more
Full sample	820	281 34%	151 18%	115 14%	139 17%	80 10%	54 7%
Age							
17–18 years	510	35%	19%	13%	17%	10%	5%
19 or older	310	33%	18%	15%	16%	10%	9%
Sex							
Male	487	33%	16%	11%	19%	13%	8%
Female	329	35%	23%	18%	14%	5%	5%
Ethnic background							
White, non-Hispanic	545	34%	18%	15%	15%	11%	7%
Black, non-Hispanic	161	35%	17%	12%	22%	8%	6%
Hispanic	68	28%	22%	10%	22%	10%	7%
Additional handicap status							
No additional handicap	545	33%	17%	15%	17%	11%	7%
One additional handicap	196	33%	21%	13%	17%	9%	8%
Two or more additional handicaps	72	49%	19%	11%	13%	6%	3%
School setting							
Special facility, not integrated	471	42%	17%	12%	13%	7%	9%
Special facility, integrated	30	33%	13%	10%	27%	7%	10%
Regular/local facility, not integrated	45	18%	27%	30%	4%	18%	4%
Regular/local facility, integrated	270	23%	21%	16%	24%	14%	2%

handicaps. Nearly one half (49%) of those with two or more additional handicaps worked less than 10 hours per week, while only 33% of those with no or only one additional handicap worked less than 10 hours per week.

- The student's educational placement was also related to the number of hours worked each week. Students in integrated settings were more likely to work longer hours than those in nonintegrated settings. Forty-four percent of those from special facilities who were integrated with hearing students at local schools and 40% of those youth in integrated regular/local programs worked 20 or more hours per week. Only 29% of those nonintegrated students from special schools and 26% of those in regular/local programs in self-contained classes worked 20 or more hours.

What Are the Hourly Salaries of Deaf Youth?

The median hourly salary of the students employed during the school year was at the minimum wage of $3.35 an hour; 28% received salaries below $3.35, and 21% received $3.35 an hour; 51% received more than $3.35 an hour.

Table 7.4 shows demographic factors related to the salaries received. Highlights of these data include the following:

- There was a negative association between age and salary. Fifty-five percent of the 17- and 18-year-olds earned wages above the minimum wage; only 42% of those over 19 earned salaries above the minimum wage.
- Males reported higher hourly wages than did females. Fifty-three percent of the males earned salaries above the minimum wage, compared to only 48% of the females.
- Over one half of the white (54%) and Hispanic (51%) students received salaries of more than $3.35 an hour; 37% of the black students earned similar wages.
- Deaf youth with no additional handicaps were more likely to earn above the minimum wage than those students with one or more additional handicaps; over half (54%) of those with no additional handicaps earned more than $3.35 an hour, compared to 48% of youth with one additional handicap and one fourth (24%) of those with two or more additional handicaps.
- Youth integrated with hearing students earned higher hourly salaries than nonintegrated students—73% of those from special facilities selected for integration and 63% of those integrated at regular/local programs earned wages above $3.35 an hour. Only 43% of the nonintegrated students attending special facilities and 42% of the nonin-

Table 7.4. Hourly salaries of deaf youth: Transition study, 1987

Category	N	Less than $3.35 per hr.	$3.35 per hr.	$3.36–$3.99 per hr.	$4.00–$4.99 per hr.	$5.00 or more per hr.
Full sample	778	219 28%	165 21%	181 23%	129 17%	84 11%
Age						
17–18 years	501	25%	21%	26%	18%	11%
19 or older	277	34%	22%	18%	14%	10%
Sex						
Male	461	24%	24%	22%	18%	13%
Female	313	35%	18%	25%	15%	8%
Ethnic background						
White, non-Hispanic	515	27%	18%	23%	19%	12%
Black, non-Hispanic	154	38%	26%	17%	12%	8%
Hispanic	65	18%	31%	37%	6%	8%
Additional handicap status						
No additional handicap	531	24%	21%	24%	18%	12%
One additional handicap	179	30%	22%	23%	16%	9%
Two or more additional handicaps	62	53%	23%	16%	5%	3%
School setting						
Special facility, not integrated	450	38%	20%	19%	13%	11%
Special facility, integrated	26	8%	19%	19%	50%	4%
Regular/local facility, not integrated	37	32%	24%	32%	5%	5%
Regular/local facility, integrated	261	14%	24%	30%	21%	12%

tegrated students attending regular/local programs earned wages in this range.

Who Helped Students Obtain Jobs?

Students use many different individuals to help them in obtaining jobs. High school counselors or teachers assisted over one half of the students in locating jobs. Almost one third of the students reported finding jobs by themselves. Family members aided 22% of the students in locating employment, and vocational rehabilitation (VR) counselors helped 11% of the students. Friends (10%) and job placement agencies (4%) also assisted some youth in locating their most recent job.

As stated, high school counselors and teachers were the most frequently reported source of assistance for all demographic subgroups (Table 7.5). There were, however, interesting differences in the response patterns:

- Seventy-one percent of older students used high school counselors or teachers, compared to only 45% of those under 19. These younger students reported a higher usage of family and friends than did the older students, 37% and 21%, respectively. Thirty-eight percent of the younger students found jobs on their own, compared with only 21% of those age 19 or over.
- Female students (59%) used high school counselors or teachers in their job search slightly more than did male students (52%).
- Differences in the methods used to obtain jobs were observed among the various ethnic groups in the study. Minority students were more likely to use high school counselors or teachers in obtaining jobs than were white students. Less than one half (48%) of the white students reported that a high school counselor or teacher helped them locate their current job, compared with 70% of the black students and 69% of the Hispanic students.
- Multiply handicapped deaf youth were more likely to use the services of a high school counselor or teacher than deaf youth with no additional handicaps (72% of those with one additional handicap and 78% of those with two or more additional handicaps received this assistance).
- Nonintegrated youth reported significantly more frequent use of high school counselors and teachers and VR assistance than did those students integrated with hearing students.

Who Gets Summer Jobs?

Summer vacations provided an opportunity for many students to obtain employment experience; 48% of the youth held jobs during the summer of 1986. Some youth, however, were more likely than others to have summer jobs (Table 7.6):

Table 7.5. Five most frequently reported methods[a] used to obtain jobs by deaf youth: Transition study, 1987

Category	N	High school counselor or teacher	Self	Family	Vocational rehabilitation counselor	Friend
Full sample	841	458 54%	267 32%	182 22%	93 11%	82 10%
Age						
17–18 years	530	45%	38%	25%	8%	12%
19 or older	311	71%	21%	15%	17%	6%
Sex						
Male	500	52%	33%	25%	12%	11%
Female	337	59%	29%	17%	10%	9%
Ethnic background						
White, non-Hispanic	554	48%	37%	26%	9%	11%
Black, non-Hispanic	169	70%	21%	12%	14%	8%
Hispanic	71	69%	21%	10%	16%	9%
Additional handicap status						
No additional handicap	560	45%	39%	26%	10%	12%
One additional handicap	200	72%	19%	13%	14%	7%
Two or more additional handicaps	74	78%	8%	8%	14%	3%
School setting						
Special facility, not integrated	481	69%	25%	16%	15%	7%
Special facility, integrated	33	39%	33%	39%	9%	18%
Regular/local facility not integrated	47	64%	17%	21%	13%	6%
Regular/local facility, integrated	275	30%	46%	28%	5%	13%

[a]Students could report more than one method.

- Fifty percent of the 17- and 18-year-olds held summer jobs, compared to only 41% of those 19 and over.
- Fifty-five percent of the males worked in the summer, while only 39% of the females held summer jobs.
- White students (52%) were more likely to have summer jobs than Hispanic youth (43%) or black youth (38%).
- Fifty-four percent of deaf students with no additional handicaps worked in the summer, compared to 41% of those with one additional handicap and only 22% of those with two or more additional handicaps.
- Those students in integrated classes (54% at special facilities and 53% at regular/local facilities) were more likely to have summer jobs than those in nonintegrated educational settings (46% at special facilities and 53% at regular/local facilities).

Why Do Deaf Students Not Look for Work?

Seven of every 10 deaf students were not working in the spring of 1987. Nearly all of these (97%) youth who were not working indicated

Table 7.6. Summer employment status of deaf youth: Transition study, 1987

Category	N	Summer job	No summer job
Full sample	2,706	1,293 48%	1,413 52%
Age			
17–18 years	1,927	50%	50%
19 or older	779	41%	59%
Sex			
Male	1,484	55%	45%
Female	1,217	39%	61%
Ethnic background			
White, non-Hispanic	1,750	52%	48%
Black, non-Hispanic	539	38%	62%
Hispanic	277	43%	57%
Additional handicap status			
No additional handicap	1,833	54%	46%
One additional handicap	579	41%	59%
Two or more additional handicaps	273	22%	78%
School setting			
Special facility, not integrated	1,608	46%	54%
Special facility, integrated	112	54%	46%
Regular/local facility, not integrated	173	35%	65%
Regular/local facility, integrated	794	53%	47%

that school responsibilities deterred them from seeking employment (Figure 7.3).

Lack of job opportunities was given as a reason by 8% of the students, and 7% reported transportation difficulties contributed to their not working. Fear of reduction of Supplemental Security Income (SSI) was a reason cited by 6% of the nonemployed deaf youth, and 5% reported they did not work because there was no one to help them obtain a job.

Why Do Deaf Students Quit or Get Fired from Jobs?

Thirty percent of the youth indicated that at some time in the past they had held a job but had quit or been fired from the position. The most frequently reported reason for termination of employment (29%) was job dissatisfaction (Table 7.7). One quarter of those who had quit indicated it was because of school-related activities. Students may have been forced to terminate summer jobs in order to return to school in the fall or to give up after-school or weekend activities during the year because of school responsibilities. Twenty-three percent of the youth indicated they had left jobs because the job was only temporary and/or the work had been completed. Difficulties with supervisors were reported by 21% of the youth who had quit or been fired from a job. Seven percent cited transportation problems as a reason for quitting or being fired. Additional demographic-related factors are noted in the following statements:

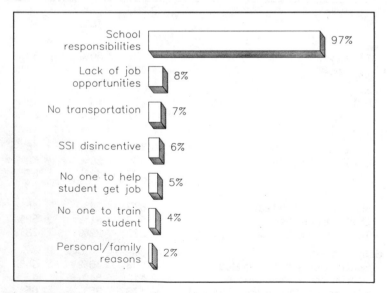

Figure 7.3. Reasons reported by deaf youth for not seeking employment while in school, Spring, 1987.

Table 7.7. Most frequently reported reasons of deaf youth for quitting or being fired from jobs: Transition study, 1987

Category	N	Disliked job	School-related activity	Job ended	Problems with supervisor	Transportation
Full sample	604	178	149	140	124	44
		29%	25%	23%	21%	7%
Age						
17–18 years	419	32%	25%	25%	21%	8%
19 or older	185	25%	24%	20%	19%	6%
Sex						
Male	374	31%	26%	22%	21%	6%
Female	229	27%	23%	25%	20%	10%
Ethnic background						
White, non-Hispanic	437	32%	24%	25%	21%	7%
Black, non-Hispanic	82	22%	29%	17%	16%	7%
Hispanic	56	21%	20%	21%	27%	7%
Additional handicap status						
No additional handicap	464	29%	28%	23%	19%	7%
One additional handicap	109	28%	14%	25%	25%	5%
Two or more additional handicaps	26	35%	8%	19%	35%	19%
School setting						
Special facility, not integrated	294	26%	32%	18%	19%	5%
Special facility, integrated	18	11%	6%	33%	33%	11%
Regular/local facility, not integrated	41	29%	22%	22%	24%	7%
Regular/local facility, integrated	249	35%	18%	29%	21%	10%

- Younger students (32%) were more likely to report job dissatisfaction as a reason for leaving a job than older students (25%). Males (31%) reported this reason slightly more frequently than females (27%).
- Differences in reasons given for quitting jobs were most noticeable when the students' responses were reviewed according to ethnic background. While nearly one third of the white youth reported job dissatisfaction as the reason for quitting a job, only 22% of the black youth and 21% of Hispanic youth indicated job dissatisfaction. Problems with supervisors was the most frequently reported reason for quitting or being fired from a job for Hispanic youth (27%). For black youth, the most frequently reported reason given was the need to return to school-related activities (29%).
- Over one third of the youth with two or more additional handicaps gave job dissatisfaction and problems with supervisors as reasons for terminating employment. Transportation problems (19%) were also a frequent problem for these multiply handicapped students.
- For those at special facilities, school-related activities were the most frequent (32%) reason reported for nonintegrated students and for integrated students, 33% reported the job ended and problems with supervisors. For students at regular/local facilities, 29% of the nonintegrated and 35% of the integrated persons reported job dissatisfaction as the most frequent reason for leaving jobs.

DISCUSSION

Work experience is only one component of the transition process, and the work history a student begins establishing while in school can affect future outcomes. The literature supports the importance of job experience for handicapped and nonhandicapped youth. In Chapter 2, the parents of two deaf youth discuss the contribution employment played in their children's transition from high school to the world of work. They indicate their children learned the rewards of earning a salary and the need to budget the use of these dollars. They also indicate the importance of learning new skills and having the chance to explore various career opportunities. From the parents' perspectives, these jobs during high school helped in the socialization of their children, allowing them to experience independence and the accompanying responsibilities. The data from the student survey provide a "snapshot" of the work experience of deaf youth, the types of jobs they obtain, their levels of compensation, and the amounts of time they spend on the job. From this picture, however, it becomes clear that not all deaf youth have equal access to work-experience opportunities.

Extent of Work Experience

Although a majority (59%) of high school–age deaf students obtained some work experience during either the summer of 1986 or the spring of 1987, the rate of employment was much lower than that reported for their hearing peers. A study conducted by the National Center for Education Statistics (Grant & Snyder, 1986) found that 95% of high school seniors reported work experience as an extracurricular activity. Among the various subgroups of deaf students studied, males and whites were more likely to be working during the school year. Also, students attending regular/local programs and integrated with hearing students were more likely to work during the school year than those in other educational placements.

The lower employment rates for students in special facilities may be attributable to the fact that many of these students reside at school and therefore may have fewer opportunities to locate after-school or weekend jobs in their home communities. The single most important reason deaf students reported for not holding a job during the school year was school responsibilities or schedules. Special education programs need to make sure they are providing sufficient opportunities and encouragement for their students to look for jobs. Work experience, both for those in academic and in vocational tracks, can provide the potential benefits of developing self-esteem, providing a positive educational experience, and introducing youth to the adult work world.

Kinds of Jobs Students Obtain

While over 100 different categories of jobs were reported by deaf youth, the majority were working in service-related activities. Many of the jobs held by deaf youth were "dead-end" jobs and entry level positions, probably very similar to those obtained by their hearing peers. Although providing an introduction into the labor force, these positions should not be viewed as definite future careers. These initial job experiences offer students the chance to explore various career options. Students not only obtain a taste of what is involved in specific jobs but they also get a first-hand view of certain industries. They can begin to frame questions and get answers as to what they would like to do and the type of organization in which they would like to work. Do they enjoy working in large hotels or do they find it more rewarding working in a neighborhood restaurant? Is office work in an insurance firm more to their liking, or do they prefer working in the office of a small construction company?

Reasons for Changing Jobs

Since jobs for teenagers are often part time, short term, or "dead end" in terms of career ladders, these youth may have frequent job changes.

When students indicate reasons why they quit or are fired from jobs, job dissatisfaction is the most frequent response. This dissatisfaction should not necessarily be viewed negatively. If career exploration is an objective of the transition process, job changes can be helpful. When job dissatisfaction occurs, it is important for the family and counselors to aid the student in identifying what specifics about the job were objectionable and to help delineate alternative and realistic job options, given the student's abilities and training.

Job dissatisfaction was not the most important reason for quitting or being fired for Hispanic students, and students with two or more additional handicaps. For these students, problems with their supervisors was the leading cause of terminating employment. Some Hispanic deaf students may bring additional English language deficits to the job, especially if English is not spoken in their homes. The multiply handicapped group might identify problems with their supervisors as reasons for leaving their job if they have been placed in jobs for which they are not physically or mentally suited. Whatever the cause, the importance of identifying worker/supervisor problems as a frequent reason for quitting or dismissal for all deaf students, but more specifically for Hispanic and multiply handicapped students, needs to be a focus of career-training programs.

Wages

It was encouraging to find that the median hourly salaries for deaf high school students was at the minimum wage; only 28% were working for wages below $3.35 an hour. As with other measures of employment, demographic factors were associated with level of compensation. A larger proportion of males, whites, and those with no additional handicaps were more likely to earn higher salaries. This discrepancy in salaries undoubtedly reflects national economic trends, which traditionally show females and minorities holding lower paying jobs. Salary differentials also reflect varying levels of job skills; multiply handicapped youth may be placed in positions requiring minimal skills. Being aware of these different rates of compensation, students, counselors, and employers should assure themselves that certain youth are not being discriminated against but are receiving equal pay for equal work.

Assistance in Obtaining Jobs

Workers entering the job market use a variety of methods to obtain employment, including the "help-wanted section" of newspapers, employment agencies, and the assistance of family or friends. Deaf high school students in this survey most frequently used high school counselors and teachers in their job search. The data indicate that minorities, multiply handicapped youth, and students who did not attend classes on an integrated basis with hearing students were more likely to use the professional resources of high school counselors and teachers and VR counselors to obtain jobs.

Some of these youth may have more difficulties locating jobs and therefore have a greater need for professional assistance in their job search. Also, the students enrolled in full-time special education settings may have greater access to the services of professionals in vocational rehabilitation and counseling than those students who are integrated in classrooms with hearing peers. (This topic of access to VR is discussed further in Chapter 9.)

CONCLUSION

The research findings on deaf students' work experience are encouraging from several viewpoints. First, students' work experience, vocational education, and national employment trends appear to be compatible. Four out of 10 employed deaf students were working in service-related occupations. As mentioned in Chapter 6, service-related occupations were also the ones in which deaf students were more likely to be receiving vocational training. Data from the Bureau of Labor Statistics (Kutscher, 1987) project that 21 million new jobs will be created between 1986 and 2000, and nearly all of this growth will be in service-producing industries.

Second, the data suggest that students needing more assistance in obtaining jobs are utilizing the professionals at the schools in order to locate employment opportunities. It is also important to note that one third of the students report they found their jobs on their own. The students also utilized the informal employment network of families and friends in their job searches. Danek and McCrone in Chapter 1, Mendelsohn and Brown in Chapter 2, and Wright in Chapter 3 emphasize the important role parents must assume in the transition process. The data indicate that families do assist in helping students acquire work experience. This continued role for families is one to be encouraged.

All of the data, however, are not optimistic. Deaf students are not getting work experience to the same degree as their hearing peers. There is a definite need for more deaf youth to get on-the-job training and to begin establishing employment histories while in secondary school when they have access to vocational training, VR counselors, and other professionals to assist them. Similar to the findings on vocational training reported in Chapter 6, various subgroups of the population studied do show different work experiences. Minority students and those with two or more additional handicaps were the least likely to hold jobs, to earn higher wages, and to work longer hours. These students are perhaps in most need of transition services from all segments of special education and vocational education programs, and vocational rehabilitation agencies.

REFERENCES

Bellamy, G., Rose, H., Wilson, D., & Clarke, J. (1982). Strategies for vocational preparation. In B. Wilcox & G.T. Bellamy (Eds.), *Design of high school programs for severely handicapped students* (pp. 139–152). Baltimore: Paul H. Brookes Publishing Co.

Grant, W.V., & Snyder, T. (1986). *Digest of education statistics: 1985–86.* Washington, DC: U.S. Department of Education, Center for Statistics.

Hasazi, S., Gordon, L., & Roe, C. (1985). Factors associated with the employment status of handicapped youth exiting high school from 1979 to 1983. *Exceptional Children, 51,* 455–469.

Hasazi, S., Gordon, L., Roe, C., Hull, M., Finck, K., & Salembier, G. (1985). A statewide follow-up on post high school employment and residential status of students labeled "mentally retarded." *Education and Training of the Mentally Retarded, 20,* 222–234.

Kutscher, R. (1987, September). Overview and implications of the projections to 2000. *Monthly Labor Review,* pp. 3–9.

National Institute of Handicapped Research. (1985). *Cooperative programs for transition from school to work* (Contract No. 300-83-0158). Washington, DC: U.S. Department of Education.

Rudrud, E., Ziarnak, J., Bernstein, G., & Ferrara, J. (1984). *Proactive vocational habilitation.* Baltimore: Paul H. Brookes Publishing Co.

Rusch, F., Mithaug, D., & Flexer, R. (1986). Obstacles to competitive employment and traditional program options for overcoming them. In W.E. Kiernan & J.A. Stark (Eds.), *Pathways to employment for adults with developmental disabilities* (pp. 7–21). Baltimore: Paul H. Brookes Publishing Co.

Szymanski, E., & Danek, M. (1985). School-to-work transition for students with disabilities: Historical, current, and conceptual issues. *Rehabilitation Counseling Bulletin, 29,* 81–89.

Wehman, P., Kregel, J., & Barcus, J. (1985). From school to work: A vocational transition model for handicapped students. *Exceptional Children, 52,* 25–37.

Will, M. (1985). Bridges from school to working life. *Rehabilitation/WORLD, 9*(1), 4-7, 42–43.

The Role of Assessment in Placing Deaf Students in Academic and Vocational Courses

8

Carol Bloomquist Traxler

Assessment plays an increasingly important role in decisions that profoundly affect many aspects of the lives of American students. The proliferation of tests for a variety of purposes is readily evidenced by the number of new entries in successive editions of Buros' *Mental Measurements Yearbook* (1953, 1959, 1965, 1972, 1978; Mitchell, 1985). It is particularly relevant to the topic of this book that vocational tests have, after psychological tests, shown the greatest number of new or revised tests in the most recent Buros edition (Mitchell, 1985, p. xv). For students who are deaf, assessment issues are particularly important since tests often require reading levels beyond those evidenced by typical deaf high school–age youth. For tests that require individual administration, the communication skills of the student and the test administrator are of paramount importance if test validity is to be assumed (e.g., see Allen, White, & Karchmer, 1983; Anastasi, 1982; Bloomquist & Allen, 1987, 1988; Cobb & Larkin, 1985; Holm, 1987; Levine, 1974; Sherman & Robinson, 1982; Sue, 1978).

This chapter focuses on one important educational decision: the role of assessment in placing deaf students in academic and vocational courses. This chapter examines current assessment practices in high school programs dealing with the transition of deaf students from school to work or to postsecondary education, and notes how assessment is used in the various types of education programs that serve deaf students. It also describes the major features of assessment instruments in current use and illuminates areas where current assessment practice does not meet the needs of transitional services and appropriate placement.

SURVEY OF SCHOOL COUNSELORS

As described in Chapter 4, a survey of career training for hearing impaired youth (Counselor Questionnaire) was mailed in March, 1987, to the counselors of a national sample of 5,895 deaf students. The Counselor Questionnaire (see Appendix A at the end of this book) contained several questions related to assessment practice. All of the questions referred to an individual student named on the questionnaire. The counselor was asked to indicate whether the student's school offered separate academic and vocational tracks and, if so, to indicate in which track the student was enrolled and the grade in which the tracking decision was made. For the analysis in this chapter, the weighted counselor data—described in Chapter 4—were used. The Ns reported are based on the weighted counselor data files.

Considering academic achievement tests, vocational assessment tests, and social-emotional assessment separately, the counselor was asked to indicate whether tests contributed to the tracking or course placement decision made for the student. For each of the three types of test given a "yes" response, the counselor listed the tests used and indicated if the tests were self-made. Space was available for listing tests in each of the three categories. Assessment information was gathered via the Counselor Questionnaire only on the 3,157 students enrolled in school at the time of the survey in the spring of 1987.

Seventy percent of the students still enrolled attended institutions offering separate academic and vocational tracks. Of these students, 25% were in vocational tracks, 29% were in academic tracks, and 38% were in a combination of vocational and academic tracks. Most tracking decisions had been made while the students were in the 9th (47%) or 10th (27%) grade; only 8% were made in or before the 7th grade, and 17% in 11th or 12th grade. Once tracking decisions were made, they usually did not change; for the few students (13%) who did change tracks, nearly all of the changes were made in seventh or ninth grade.

EXTENT OF TESTING IN DIFFERENT CATEGORIES

Tests were widely used in making tracking and course placement decisions for deaf students in the sample. Shown in Table 8.1 are the percentages of students for whom academic achievement, vocational, and social-emotional assessment instruments were used. Tests of academic achievement were used with 88% of the students to make tracking or course placement decisions, vocational assessments with 68%, and social-emotional assessments with 40%. These percentages do not represent the total number of students administered tests in these categories;

Table 8.1. Use of academic achievement, vocational, and social-emotional tests with deaf students for tracking and course placement, Transition study, 1987

Category	Academic achievement		Vocational		Social-emotional	
	%	N	%	N	%	N
Total	88%	2460	68%	1541	40%	745
Tracking						
Separate tracks	89%	1755	74%	1226	44%	544
No tracking	86%	702	57%	414	32%	202
Age						
17–18 years	88%	1731	65%	1019	39%	500
19 or older	88%	729	76%	522	42%	245
Sex						
Male	89%	1380	69%	876	41%	426
Female	87%	1073	67%	659	38%	316
Ethnic background						
White, non-Hispanic	88%	1609	65%	968	36%	430
Black, non-Hispanic	89%	507	77%	374	43%	181
Hispanic	84%	224	69%	137	55%	97
Additional handicap status						
No additional handicap	89%	1721	65%	990	36%	457
One additional handicap	89%	530	75%	391	47%	198
Two or more additional handicaps	80%	194	70%	156	48%	89
School setting						
Special facility, not integrated	96%	1540	75%	1001	36%	365
Special facility, integrated	85%	257	69%	150	68%	159
Regular/local facility, not integrated	82%	111	72%	89	47%	45
Regular/local facility, integrated	75%	545	51%	296	33%	171

Note: Values are the percentage and number of students for whom tests contribute to the tracking or course placement decision, as reported by the counselors who responded to Item C5 on the Counselor Questionnaire (see Appendix A).

they represent only those for whom tests were specifically used to help make tracking or course placement decisions.

Although achievement tests were widely and consistently used for tracked and nontracked students, vocational and social-emotional tests were used more widely for students who were placed in tracks. Similarly, vocational and social-emotional tests were used more often with older students than with students age 17 and 18. This is not surprising since, as noted in Chapter 6, older students were more likely to be receiving vocational instruction.

Although achievement testing rates were fairly comparable for the three ethnic groups examined, social-emotional tests were given relatively more often to minority students, particularly to Hispanic students (55%). Vocational tests had the highest rate of use with black students (77%). This finding underlines the importance of test validity for these students, especially when the lower levels of reading ability often found with black and Hispanic students are considered. Are these tests actually measuring what they purport to measure? Given the high verbal load of many tests and the reading ability of deaf students, these high testing rates raise an important question: Are these tests providing valid measurements of the abilities and attitudes of deaf students?

Another student characteristic related to differential rates of test usage is that of additional handicap status. Multihandicapped deaf students were tested more often with vocational and social-emotional instruments, and those with two or more additional handicaps were given academic tests for the purpose of determining course placement less frequently than were deaf students without additional handicaps. Perhaps vocational and social-emotional assessment results are considered especially informative in weighing decision options available for students with multiple handicaps. If this is so, then the validity of assessment instruments for multihandicapped students increases in importance. Multihandicapped students are commonly tested using special test formats and procedures, often with the result that available test norms cannot be applied to help in interpreting these students' scores. Consequently, the following questions arise: Are multihandicapped students being tested validly? Are their test scores being interpreted appropriately?

Regarding facility type and integration, different patterns of testing can be noted for all three categories of tests. While nearly all—96%—of the nonintegrated students in special facilities were administered achievement tests to inform course placement decisions, only 75% of the integrated students from regular/local schools were administered tests of achievement for tracking or course placement decisions. These students were the least tested with vocational (51%) and social-emotional (33%) instruments as well. It is particularly noteworthy that 68% of the students attending special facilities who were selected for integration were administered social-emotional tests. This suggests the importance of social-emotional factors in integration decisions involving students at special facilities. In contrast, only 33% of integrated students at regular/local schools were tested with social-emotional instruments; this lower testing rate may reflect lower levels of support or resources for social-emotional testing in regular/local facilities as compared to special schools.

EXTENT OF MULTIPLE TEST USE

Counselor Questionnaires containing valid responses to questions regarding the use of all three categories of tests were available for 1,797 students. These data were used to examine the extent of multiple test use, and the information is summarized in Table 8.2.

The most recurrent patterns of test use were for all three categories of tests (32%), for academic and vocational tests used together (24%), and for academic tests used alone (22%). Social-emotional tests were rarely used apart from academic and vocational tests. Only 12% of the students were given no tests at all.

When tracking is taken into consideration, the usage pattern varies. In schools that had tracking, students were more likely to get both academic and vocational tests or all three categories of tests; in schools without tracking, there was a greater tendency to use academic tests alone.

There were no sex differences in the multiple test use pattern, but when ethnic background is considered, differences were noted. White students (26%) were more likely to have been given academic tests alone than were black (13%) or Hispanic (17%) students. Black students were more likely to have been given both academic and vocational tests (34%) or all three categories of tests (33%), while Hispanic students were most often tested with all three categories of tests (44%). Black and Hispanic students who were tested were given more kinds of tests than were white students. This finding underlines the earlier-mentioned importance of determining test validity for these students.

Older students were more often tested with multiple categories of tests than were those age 17 or 18. Younger students were almost twice as likely to be given academic tests only (26%) than students age 19 or older (14%).

The consideration of additional handicap status reveals differences in multiple test use patterns. Students with two or more additional handicaps were most likely to have been tested either with all three categories of tests (42%) or with no tests at all (21%).

When type of educational facility is considered, it is striking to note that 31% of the deaf students integrated in regular/local schools were

Table 8.2. Extent of multiple test use for tracking and course placement, by student and school variables, Transition Study, 1987

Instrument	Total	Tracking		Age		Ethnic background			Sex		Additional handicap status			School setting[a]			
		Yes	No	17–18	19+	White	Black	Hispanic	Male	Female	0	1	2+	1	2	3	4
N =	1,797	1,195	599	1,241	556	1,142	407	169	1,002	792	1,212	401	178	1,008	196	94	488
Academic only	22%	18%	31%	26%	14%	26%	13%	17%	23%	22%	26%	14%	13%	24%	20%	9%	23%
Vocational only	4%	4%	4%	4%	5%	4%	4%	4%	4%	4%	4%	5%	5%	2%	9%	5%	5%
Social-emotional only	*	*	*	*	*	*	1%	0%	*	*	*	*	1%	*	0%	0%	1%
Academic and vocational only	24%	27%	20%	21%	31%	23%	34%	10%	25%	23%	24%	28%	15%	34%	3%	21%	13%
Academic and social-emotional only	4%	3%	5%	4%	3%	3%	5%	3%	4%	3%	3%	6%	3%	2%	8%	10%	3%
Vocational and social-emotional only	1%	2%	1%	1%	1%	1%	2%	6%	2%	1%	1%	1%	1%	*	10%	0%	1%
Academic and vocational and social-emotional	32%	36%	25%	31%	35%	30%	33%	44%	32%	32%	30%	36%	42%	34%	44%	36%	23%
No tests used for tracking or course placement	12%	11%	15%	13%	10%	13%	8%	16%	10%	14%	11%	10%	21%	3%	6%	20%	31%

Note: Percentages are rounded and are based on the deaf students for whom responses were given for all three test categories and for whom information on the other variables was reported. An asterisk denotes a value of less than .5%.

[a]School setting: 1 = special facility, not integrated; 2 = special facility, integrated; 3 = regular/local facility, not integrated; and 4 = regular/local facility, integrated.

given no tests at all in conjunction with the tracking or course placement decision. Students in other educational settings were more likely to be tested.

SPECIFIC INSTRUMENTS USED

A relatively small number of tests were frequently used with deaf students. Several of the tests most frequently used are included in the test reviews in the appendix that concludes this chapter. The reviews contain descriptions of the instruments and information pertinent to their use with deaf students.

Rates of usage for individual assessment instruments are shown in Table 8.3. It should be noted that these are conservative estimates. On the Counselor Questionnaires, counselors entered the names of tests used in each of the three test categories: academic achievement, vocational, and social-emotional. At most, two tests for each category were coded and entered into the data base for use in the analysis, although a small percentage of the respondents listed more than two tests for a category. Therefore, the rates calculated are based on slightly smaller frequencies of test use than were actually reported.

It should also be noted that there was lack of consensus regarding in which category several of the tests belonged. For example, the Brigance Diagnostic Inventory of Essential Skills was listed by some respondents as an academic achievement test and by others as a vocational test. The Street Survival Skills Questionnaire was listed both as a vocational and as a social-emotional instrument. For the analysis summarized in Table 8.3, each listing of a particular test was counted, even if the test was listed by respondents in several categories on the questionnaire. Tests presented in the academic achievement category primarily measure academic skills. Those in the vocational category measure vocational aptitudes and behaviors, career interests, and survival skills. Tests listed in the social-emotional category tend to assess social-emotional competencies, visual perception, and personality.

The most striking finding of the analysis of use rates for individual tests is that a very large number of different tests were used and that many tests were used with a small number of students. Figure 8.1 illustrates this finding graphically. In all three test categories—academic achievement, vocational, and social-emotional—there were many tests taken by only a few of the students tested. There were 34 different academic achievement tests, each given to less than 10% of the students tested with academic tests, and 55 different vocational tests, each given to less than 10% of the students given vocational tests. Self-made achievement tests were used in testing only 4% of the students given such tests, and self-

Table 8.3. Commercially available tests used with deaf students for tracking and course placement: Competencies assessed and percentage of students tested, Transition study, 1987

Test review number[a]	Test	Competencies assessed	% students tested
Academic achievement (N = 2,199)			
9	Stanford Achievement Test	Academic	91%
2	Brigance Diagnostic Inventory of Essential Skills	Academic, adaptive behavior, daily living, survival	5%
3	Gates-MacGinitie Reading Test	Academic, Language	5%
13	Wide Range Achievement Test–Revised (WRAT-R)	Academic	5%
Vocational assessment (N = 1,010)			
11	VALPAR Component Work Sample Series	Vocational	30%
14	Wide Range Interest-Opinion Test (WRIOT)	Career interest/attitudes	28%
10	Street Survival Skills Questionnaire (SSSQ)	Survival skills	14%
5	General Aptitude Test Battery (GATB)	Motor, general ability/intelligence	11%
4	Geist Picture Interest Inventory	Career interest	8%
7	Jewish Employment Vocational Service Work Sample System (JEVS)	Vocational service work sample evaluation of performance, interest, work behavior	7%
Social-emotional assessment (N = 360)			
8	Meadow-Kendall Social-Emotional Assessment Inventory for Deaf and Hearing Impaired Students	Social-emotional	20%
1	Bender-Gestalt Test	Visual-motor ability, personality (projective technique)	18%
12	Vineland Adaptive Behavior Scales	Social-emotional	14%
6	H-T-P: House-Tree-Person Projective Technique	Personality (projective technique)	11%

Note: Percentages are based on the number of students in each test category for whom tests were used.
[a]Numbers refer to appendix at end of this chapter.

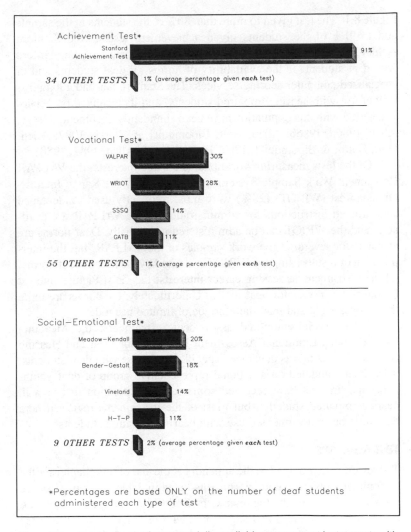

Figure 8.1. Extent of use of commercially available assessment instruments with deaf students for tracking and course placement decisions, Transition study, 1987.

made vocational instruments to 11% of the students given vocational assessments. In contrast, self-made social-emotional instruments were very widely used: 34% of the students given social-emotional tests were assessed with self-made instruments. The validity of the self-made test results and the availability of normative information to aid in interpretation of scores from self-made tests may be assumed to have sketchy documentation at best.

Of the tests measuring academic achievement, one test stands out in

Figure 8.1. The test given to more than 80% of the students in the sample and to 91% of the students given achievement tests is the Stanford Achievement Test. One probable reason for the wide use of the Stanford with deaf students is the availability of norms for deaf students and of specialized computer-scoring services. The Stanford has had a long history of use with hearing impaired students, and its technical properties when used with this population have been abundantly documented (e.g., Allen, 1986a, 1986b; Allen, Holt, Bloomquist, & Starke, 1987; Allen, Holt, Hotto, & Bloomquist, 1987; Bloomquist & Allen, 1987, 1988).

Of the tests measuring vocational skills and interests, the VALPAR Component Work Sample System (30%) and the Wide Range Interest-Opinion Test (WRIOT) (28%) were most frequently used. Videotaped standardized instructions for administration of the VALPAR are available, and the WRIOT can be administered nonverbally. Deaf norms are available for several of the work samples of the VALPAR, but the interpretation of results using the WRIOT is limited by the lack of deaf norms. Of the instruments assessing career interests, the Geist Picture Interest Inventory has norms for deaf males. Unfortunately, the norms are more than 20 years old and may therefore be of limited use today.

Of the social-emotional assessment instruments, the Meadow-Kendall Social-Emotional Assessment Inventory for Deaf and Hearing Impaired Students was developed specifically for use with deaf students; it has been validated on a national representative group of deaf youth. Other instruments have received some research attention in use with hearing impaired students, but most of the instruments reviewed here have little or no documented use with hearing impaired students.

Test Reviews

Test reviews are provided in the appendix at the end of this chapter for the 14 commercially available instruments listed in Table 8.3. For 11 of the assessment instruments, the reviews by DeStefano, Linn, and Markward (1987) were reproduced and augmented with information specific to the use of the tests with hearing impaired students. Test reviews for the remaining three instruments were modeled after those by DeStefano et al. Other sources consulted in creating and augmenting the test reviews are Botterbusch (1976); Bull, Bullis, and Sendelbaugh (no date); Buros (1965, 1972, 1978); Chun, Cobb, and French, (1975); Mitchell (1985); Reiman and Bullis (no date); Spragins, Blennerhassett, and Mullen (1987); Sweetland and Keyser (1986); Vernon and Brown (1964); Watson (1979); and Zieziula (1982).

The test reviews are organized according to the following features: name of instrument, publisher's name and address, cost, date of publication, competencies assessed, population characteristics, recommended

uses, test content and format, administration time, skill/materials required, derived scores/information, norming/standardization practices,
reliability, validity, comments, and references. Some of these features
merit comment. Under population characteristics, special attention was
given to information indicating previous use with hearing impaired students. The recommended uses are those given by the test publisher. For
the norming, reliability, and validity entries, information relevant to use
of the instrument with hearing impaired students was provided when
available in the publisher's materials or in the other sources reviewed.
The comments section includes brief summary and evaluative remarks
regarding the instrument's potential use with hearing impaired students,
especially in the context of transition. The reference section includes references judged to be especially pertinent to the use of the test with hearing impaired students and in transition settings.

SUMMARY

Academic achievement, vocational, and social-emotional tests were
widely used with deaf students, and there was heavy reliance on vocational and social-emotional tests for tracking and integration decisions.
Furthermore, large numbers of different tests were used with deaf students and in very many instances, a test was given to only a few deaf
students. Many of the vocational and social-emotional assessment instruments used were self-made tests. These findings of widespread use of
tests and many instances of an individual test being used with very few
deaf students prompt one to raise several issues concerning the assessment of deaf students.

Test Validity

How do the reading problems of deaf students affect the assessment of
their abilities and attitudes? Considering the high verbal load of many
tests and the low reading ability of many deaf students, the high testing
rates shown previously in this chapter underscore the importance of test
validity for deaf students. The English language deficits of deaf students
may pose problems in the administration of even "nonverbal" tests. The
impact of low reading ability on test validity for deaf students needs to
receive formal research attention. For example, it is necessary to be able
to say that a score indicates a level of proficiency in the content pur-
portedly measured by a test, a level that is unaffected by language deficits
in the student. When language and content knowledge are confounded in
a single test score, the test score lacks validity.

High rates of multiple test use for deaf students with additional
handicaps raise questions of test validity when special test formats and

procedures are employed. How differences in time limits and in modes of communication affect students' test scores needs to be investigated. It is not sufficient to assume test validity for tests administered under conditions different in any way from those in effect during any given validity study. The impact of changes in test administration, in test format, in time limits, or in mode of communication requires formal examination in the context of validity studies.

It is important to note that test validity does not exist in a vacuum. Validity implies validity for a particular purpose. This chapter has focused on test use for tracking and course placement decisions. Validity studies in those contexts are needed. Does test use contribute to more efficient or appropriate tracking or course placement decisions? Do students perform better or with greater enthusiasm when placement has benefited from the use of test scores?

A further research question concerns differential validity for groups of students. Do tests contribute to the decision to track white students into computer-related vocational training (see Chapter 6, especially Table 6.4), and black and Hispanic students into training for food occupations? If tests contribute to such placement decisions, are those tests equally valid for students of various ethnic backgrounds?

Test Score Interpretation

Who is interpreting the test scores? That test scores should be interpreted by persons having an understanding of reliability, validity, measurement error, and appropriate norms is standard testing practice for most commonly used educational and vocational tests. However, even these qualifications may not be sufficient for examiners using some of the instruments in the social-emotional category. Two of the most frequently used social-emotional assessment instruments, after the Meadow-Kendall, were the Bender-Gestalt and the House-Tree-Person. Both of these tests may be used as projective techniques to assess personality. When the Bender-Gestalt is used to assess perceptual-motor ability or visual-motor coordination, the interpretation of test performance is relatively objective and is likely to receive little criticism. However, the use of this test as a projective technique to assess personality has been likened by Benton (1953) to "the crudest sort of crystal gazing" (p. 145), for it places great demands on the person interpreting the results. The Koppitz developmental scoring system (Koppitz, 1964–1975) has been recognized as providing objectivity and quantification of Bender-Gestalt scores. Still, reliable scores are not necessarily valid; the test's validity and usefulness as a diagnostic instrument has not been demonstrated to the satisfaction of experts in the field of psychological assessment (e.g., Blakemore, 1965; Kitay, 1972).

Several such experts distinguish between projective score interpretations by naive examiners and experienced clinical psychologists (Kitay, 1972). Score interpretation, particularly for projective tests such as the Bender-Gestalt and the House-Tree-Person, requires that the person conducting the score interpretation be skilled in clinical psychological procedures, especially in projective drawing techniques. Whether the examiners using these tests with deaf students meet these stringent criteria has not been investigated.

Timely and Appropriate Norms

Test score interpretation for a student or group of students commonly benefits from the availability of normative information for students similar to those whose abilities and attitudes are being assessed. For most of the instruments administered to deaf students, only little or no normative information based on deaf students is available. This situation greatly decreases the interpretability of results from those tests. Although small-scale studies using deaf students have been reported for some of the instruments, for only a handful have adequate norms been made available.

If test users respond to this situation by reducing the number of tests given to deaf students to only those tests that have deaf norms, they will then have available a narrow range of assessment information on these students. In cases where test users desire broader scope assessment—that is, assessment of skills and attitudes outside those addressed by the few tests having deaf norms—the assessment results may be less than ideally useful for lack of appropriate normative information. There remains a challenge to researchers and practitioners working with hearing impaired students to collect, maintain, and disseminate well-documented validity and normative information on instruments used to assess these students' abilities and interests.

Cautious score interpretation should always be advised for persons working with deaf students. For example, the following questions should be asked: Has the test provided a valid assessment of the abilities or attitudes of interest? And is there an appropriate context of normative information in which the assessment results may be interpreted?

REFERENCES

Allen, T.E. (1986a). Patterns of academic achievement among hearing impaired students: 1974 and 1983. In A.N. Schildroth & M.A. Karchmer (Eds.), *Deaf children in America* (pp. 161–206). San Diego: College-Hill Press.

Allen, T.E. (1986b). *Understanding the scores: Hearing-impaired students and the Stanford Achievement Test (7th edition)*. Washington, DC: Center for Assessment and Demographic Studies.

Allen, T.E., Holt, J.A., Bloomquist, C.A., & Starke, M.C. (1987). *Item analysis* for the Stanford Achievement Test, 7th edition, 1983 standardization with hearing-impaired students. Washington, DC: Center for Assessment and Demographic Studies.

Allen, T.E., Holt, J.A., Hotto, S.A., & Bloomquist, C.A. (1987). Differential item difficulty—Comparisons of P values on the Stanford Achievement Test, 7th edition, between hearing and hearing-impaired standardization samples. Washington, DC: Center for Assessment and Demographic Studies.

Allen, T.E., White, C., & Karchmer, M.A. (1983). Issues in the development of a special edition for hearing impaired students of the seventh edition of the Stanford Achievement Test. American Annals of the Deaf, 128, 34–39.

Anastasi, A. (1982). Psychological testing (5th ed.). New York: Macmillan.

Benton, A.L. (1953). Visual Motor Gestalt Test. In O.K. Buros (Ed.), The fourth mental measurements yearbook (pp. 144–146, Ms. No. 144). Highland Park, NJ: Gryphon Press.

Blakemore, C.B. (1965). Bender-Gestalt Test. In O.K. Buros (Ed.), The sixth mental measurements yearbook (pp. 414–415, Ms. No. 203). Highland Park, NJ: Gryphon Press.

Bloomquist, C.A., & Allen, T.E. (1987, April). Comparison of Stanford Achievement Test reading comprehension item responses by hearing and hearing impaired students. Paper presented at the meeting of the American Educational Research Association, Washington, DC.

Bloomquist, C.A., & Allen, T.E. (1988, April). Comparison of mathematics test item performance by hearing and hearing impaired students. Paper presented at the meeting of the American Educational Research Association, New Orleans, LA.

Botterbusch, K.F. (1976). The use of psychological tests with individuals who are severely disabled. Menomonie: University of Wisconsin–Stout, Stout Vocational Rehabilitation Institute, Materials Development Center.

Bull, B., Bullis, M., & Sendelbaugh, J. (no date). Research on the school-to-community transition of adolescents and adults with hearing impairments: An annotated bibliography. Monmouth: Oregon State System of Higher Education and Regional Resource Center on Deafness, Teaching Research Division.

Buros, O.K. (Ed.). (1953). The fourth mental measurements yearbook. Highland Park, NJ: Gryphon Press.

Buros, O.K. (Ed.). (1959). The fifth mental measurements yearbook. Highland Park, NJ: Gryphon Press.

Buros, O.K. (Ed.). (1965). The sixth mental measurements yearbook. Highland Park, NJ: Gryphon Press.

Buros, O.K. (Ed.). (1972). The seventh mental measurements yearbook. Highland Park, NJ: Gryphon Press.

Buros, O.K. (Ed.). (1978). The eighth mental measurements yearbook. Highland Park, NJ: Gryphon Press.

Chun, K.-T., Cobb, S., & French, J.R.P., Jr. (1975). Measures for psychological assessment: A guide to 3,000 original sources and their applications. Ann Arbor, MI: Survey Research Center, Institute for Social Research.

Cobb, R.B., & Larkin, D. (1985). Assessment and placement of handicapped pupils into secondary vocational education programs. Focus on Exceptional Children, 17(7), 1-14. (ERIC Document Reproduction Service No. EJ 318 413)

DeStefano, L., Linn, R., & Markward, M. (1987). Review of student assessment instruments and practices in use in secondary/transition projects. Champaign: University of Illinois, Transition Institute at Illinois.

Holm, C.S. (1987). Testing for values with the deaf: The language/cultural effect. *Journal of Rehabilitation of the Deaf, 20*(4), 7–19.

Kitay, P.M. (1972). Bender-Gestalt Test. In O.K. Buros (Ed.), *The seventh mental measurements yearbook* (pp. 394–395, Ms. No. 161). Highland Park, NJ: Gryphon Press.

Koppitz, E.M. (1964–1975). *The Bender-Gestalt Test for young children*. New York: Grune & Stratton.

Levine, E.S. (1974). Psychological tests and practices with the deaf: A survey of the state of the art. *Volta Review, 76*, 298–319.

Meadow, K.P. (1983). *Manual: Meadow-Kendall Social-Emotional Assessment Inventories for deaf and hearing impaired students*. Washington, DC: Gallaudet University, Outreach.

Mental Measurements Yearbooks (MMY): Online database. (1988). Lincoln, NE: Buros Institute of Mental Measurement (Producer). Scotia, NY: Bibliographic Retrieval Services Information Technologies (Distributor).

Mitchell, J.V., Jr. (Ed.). (1985). *The ninth mental measurements yearbook* (2 vols.). Lincoln, NE: Buros Institute of Mental Measurement.

Reiman, J.W., & Bullis, M. (no date). *Research on measurement procedures with individuals with severe hearing impairments: An annotated bibliography*. Monmouth: Oregon State System of Higher Education and Regional Resource Center on Deafness, Teaching Research Division.

Sherman, S.W., & Robinson, N.M. (1982). *Ability testing of handicapped people: Dilemma for government, science, and the public*. Washington, DC: National Academy Press.

Spragins, A.B., Blennerhassett, L., & Mullen, Y. (1987, March). *Reviews of five types of assessment instruments used with hearing impaired students*. Paper presented at the annual convention of the National Association of School Psychologists, New Orleans, LA.

Sue, D.W. (1978). Dimensions of world views: Cultural identity. *Journal of Counseling Psychology, 25*, 419–428.

Sweetland, R.C., & Keyser, D.J. (1986). *Tests: A comprehensive reference for assessment in psychology, education, and business*. Kansas City, MO: Test Corporation of America.

Vernon, M., & Brown, D.W. (1964). A guide to psychological tests and testing procedures in the evaluation of deaf and hard-of-hearing children. *Journal of Speech and Hearing Disorders, 29*, 414–423.

Watson, D. (1979). Guidelines for the psychological and vocational assessment of deaf rehabilitation clients. *Journal of Rehabilitation of the Deaf, 13*(1), 29–57.

Zieziula, F.R. (Ed.). (1982). *Assessment of hearing-impaired people*. Washington, DC: Gallaudet College Press.

Appendix

TEST REVIEW 1

Bender Visual-Motor Gestalt Test

Koppitz Scoring System for the Bender Gestalt Test for Young Children

Publisher   Grune & Stratton, Inc.
111 Fifth Avenue
New York, NY 10003

Cost   (1982) $14.50 for 100 scoring sheets; $23.50 for manual; $25.00 for supplement.

Date of Publication   1938–1977 (Bender Visual-Motor Gestalt Test); 1963–1975 (Koppitz Scoring System).

Competencies Assessed   Level of perceptual motor development, which is intended to parallel cognitive development.

Population Characteristics   Children and adults; age 5–10 for Koppitz scoring system.

Recommended Uses   Clinical assessment of specific handicapping conditions; screening for problems of perceptual motor integration; and as part of a comprehensive diagnostic battery.

Test Content and Format   The Bender is administered by asking the individual to copy, on a blank sheet of paper, the abstract designs on each of the nine test cards.

Administration Time   The test is untimed, but average administration time is 10–20 minutes.

Skills/Materials Required   9 test cards; blank paper, pencil, administration guide in manual; (for projective use) interviewer/interpreter experienced in clinical psychological procedures, particularly in projective drawing techniques.

Derived Scores/Information   Several scoring systems are available. The Koppitz Scoring System was used with deaf students in a study sample (Levine, 1974).

Norming/Standardization Practices   A scoring system for use with children, developed by Elizabeth M. Koppitz, is based on a 1974 standardization that included a representative sample of children age 5–11 years, drawn from rural-urban communities, 14% of whom were minority children. Research by Levine (1974) indicated no significant difference on scores for hearing impaired children based on the hearing impairment alone. A scoring system for older children and adults, developed by Gerald E. Pascal and Barbara J. Suttell (1951), is standardized on a sample including high school students, college students, and adults—age 15–50. Berger, Holdt, and LaForge (1972) reported normative data based on 399 deaf adults using the Pascal and Suttell scoring system.

Reliability Varies depending on scoring system used. The Koppitz Scoring System has produced criteria that are considered objective and reliable (e.g., Wallbrown & Fremont, 1980).

Validity Several studies have examined the utility of the Bender for differentiating between normal and handicapped populations and for determining developmental level. The validity of the Bender has not yet been satisfactorily demonstrated, yet low predictive validities reported for the Bender as a projective test are in the general range typical for projective techniques (Kitay, 1972).

Comments Although the Bender is widely used in the identification of specific learning disabilities, its usefulness in the transition process is not clear. Koppitz's scoring system and scoring manual provide useful aids in application of the Bender to the study of children's problems. Several reviewers have warned against the use of this test as a projective technique to assess personality; at the least, performance should be interpreted by a person with the skills of an expert clinical psychologist (e.g., Blakemore, 1965; Kitay, 1972). Levine (1974) also qualifies the effectiveness of projective tests with deaf subjects.

References and Suggested Readings

Bender, L.A. (1938). *A visual motor Gestalt test and its clinical use*. New York: American Orthopsychiatric Association.
Benton, A.L. (1953). Visual Motor Gestalt Test. In O.K. Buros (Ed.), *The fourth mental measurements yearbook* (pp. 144–146, Ms. No. 144). Highland Park, NJ: Gryphon Press.
Berger, D.G., Holdt, T.J., & LaForge, R.A. (Eds.). (1972). *Effective guidance of the adult deaf*. The Oregon Vocational Research Project, June 1, 1966–August 31, 1970. Final Report. Salem: Oregon State Board of Control. (ERIC Document Reproduction Service No. ED 078 231)
Blakemore, C.B. (1965). Bender-Gestalt Test. In O.K. Buros (Ed.), *The sixth mental measurements yearbook* (pp. 414–415, Ms. No. 203). Highland Park, NJ: Gryphon Press.
Bolton, B. (1972). Quantification of two projective tests for deaf clients. *Journal of Clinical Psychology, 28*, 554–556.

Bolton, B., Donoghue, R., & Langbauer, W. (1973). Quantification of two projective tests for deaf clients: A large sample validation study. *Journal of Clinical Psychology*, *29*, 249–259.

Choynowski, M. (1970). Curve-fitting as a method of statistical correction of developmental norms, shown on the example of the Bender-Koppitz Test. *Journal of Clinical Psychology*, *26*, 135–141. (ERIC Document Reproduction Service No. EJ 017 740)

Clark, B.R., & Leslie, P.T. (1971). Visual-motor skills and reading ability of deaf children. *Perceptual and Motor Skills*, *33*, 263–269.

Foster, G.G., Boeck, D.G., & Reese, J. (1976). A comparison of special education teacher and psychologist scoring of the Bender Visual Motor Gestalt Test. *Psychology in the Schools*, *13*, 146–148. (ERIC Document Reproduction Service No. EJ 137 623)

Furr, K.D. (1970). Standard scores for the Koppitz Developmental Scoring System. *Journal of Clinical Psychology*, *26*, 78–79. (ERIC Document Reproduction Service No. EJ 017 258)

Gilbert, J.G., & Levee, R.T. (1967). Performance of deaf and normally hearing children on the Bender-Gestalt and the Archimedes Spiral Test. *Perceptual and Motor Skills*, *24*, 1059–1066.

Goff, A.F., & Parker, A.W. (1969). Reliability of the Koppitz Scoring System for the Bender-Gestalt Test. *Journal of Clinical Psychology*, *25*, 407–409.

Gregory, M.K. (1977). Emotional indicators on the Bender-Gestalt and the Devereux Child Behavior Rating Scale. *Psychology in the Schools*, *14*, 433–436. (ERIC Document Reproduction Service No. EJ 169 378)

Johnson, C.W., & Lanak, B. (1985). Comparison of the Koppitz and Watkins Scoring Systems for the Bender-Gestalt Test. *Journal of Learning Disabilities*, *18*, 377–378.

Johnson, K.A. (1975). *The relationship between emotional indicator scores on the Bender-Gestalt Test and teacher ratings on a behavior scale with young hearing impaired children*. Doctoral thesis, University of Utah, Salt Lake City. (University Microfilms No. 76-9817)

Kelly, T.J., & Amble, B.R. (1970). IQ and perceptual motor scores as predictors of achievement among retarded children. *Journal of School Psychology*, *8*, 99–102. (ERIC Document Reproduction Service No. EJ 022 266)

Keogh, B.K., Vernon, M., & Smith, C.E. (1970). Deafness and visuo-motor functioning. *Journal of Special Education*, *4*, 41–47.

Kitay, P.M. (1972). Bender Gestalt Test. In O.K. Buros (Ed.), *The seventh mental measurements yearbook* (pp. 394–395, Ms. No. 161). Highland Park, NJ: Gryphon Press.

Koppitz, E.M. (1958). The Bender Gestalt Test and learning disturbances in young children. *Journal of Clinical Psychology*, *14*, 292–295.

Koppitz, E.M. (1964–1975). *The Bender-Gestalt Test for young children*. New York: Grune & Stratton.

Koppitz, E.M. (1975). Bender-Gestalt Test, Visual Aural Digit Span Test and reading achievement. *Journal of Learning Disabilities*, *8*, 154–158. (ERIC Document Reproduction Service No. EJ 119 475)

Levine, E.S. (1974). Psychological tests and practices with the deaf: A survey. *Volta Review*, *76*, 298–319.

Master, I. (1962). *Bender-Gestalt responses of normal and deaf children*. Unpublished master's thesis, Brooklyn College, Brooklyn, NY.

Mordock, J.B., Terrill, P., & Novik, E. (1968–1969). The Bender-Gestalt Test in differential diagnosis of adolescents with learning difficulties. *Journal of School Psychology, 7*, 11–13. (ERIC Document Reproduction Service No. EJ 011 674)

Mykelbust, H.R., & Brutten, M. (1963). A study of the visual perception of deaf children. *ACTA Otolaryngological Supplement, 105*, 1–126.

Obrzut, J., Taylor, H.D., & Thweatt, R.C. (1972). Re-examination of Koppitz' Developmental Bender Scoring System. *Perceptual and Motor Skills, 34*, 279–282. (ERIC Document Reproduction Service No. EJ 057 444)

Pascal, G.R., & Suttell, B.J. (1951). *The Bender-Gestalt Test*. New York: Grune & Stratton.

Redfering, D.L., & Collins, J. (1982). A comparison of the Koppitz and Hutt techniques of Bender-Gestalt administration correlated with WISC-R performance scores. *Educational and Psychological Measurement, 42*, 41–47.

Rogers, D.L. (1980). Bender Test recall in children: An unreliable test. *Perceptual and Motor Skills, 50*, 859–862. (ERIC Document Reproduction Service No. EJ 229 427)

Spragins, A.B., Blennerhassett, L., & Mullen, Y. (1987, March). *Reviews of five types of assessment instruments used with hearing impaired students*. Paper presented at the annual convention of the National Association of School Psychologists, New Orleans, LA.

Taylor, R.L., Kauffman, D., & Partenio, I. (1984). The Koppitz Developmental Scoring System for the Bender-Gestalt: Is it developmental? *Psychology in the Schools, 21*, 425–428.

Wallbrown, F.H., & Fremont, T. (1980). The stability of Koppitz scores on the Bender-Gestalt for reading disabled children. *Psychology in the Schools, 17*, 181–184.

TEST REVIEW 2

Brigance Diagnostic Inventory of Essential Skills

Publisher   Curriculum Associates, Inc.
North Bellerica, MA 01862

Cost   (1983) $99.95 for examiner's tests and 10 student record books; $16.95 for 10 record books; free preview excerpts are available.

Date of Publication   1981.

Competencies Assessed   Reading (word recognition, grade placement, oral reading, reading comprehension, functional word recognition, word analysis), language arts (reference skills, schedules and graphs, writing, forms, spelling), mathematics (grade placement, numbers, number facts, computation, fractions, decimals, percents, measurement, metrics, math vocabulary), life skills (health and safety, vocational, money and finance, travel and transportation, food and clothing, oral communication and telephone).

Population Characteristics Grades 4–12; primarily for individuals who have minimum survival skills as their educational goal; special needs students.

Recommended Uses Useful as part of an individualized education program (IEP) when the student's education is focused on acquiring basic skills. The broad scope of the test also enables educators to select certain areas relevant to the student in question.

Test Content and Format 191 tests in four broad areas—some require that the examiner know the individual. Designed to assess the basic skills required for successful functioning as an adult.

Administration Time Some tests are timed, others have no time limit —cannot be used as part of a single assessment session, overall administration time is many hours.

Skills/Materials Required Response booklet, teacher's manual, tests; for some sections the instructor is required to know the student well.

Derived Scores/Information Manual provides suggestions for use, IEP objectives, and references.

Norming/Standardization Practices Lacks any kind of national norms.

Reliability No data available.

Validity High content validity; most questionable were those requiring the part rate skills—however, this is acknowledged by the author.

Comments Criterion referenced; manual emphasizes that local expectations and standards are more important than the grade levels provided in the manual.

References and Suggested Readings

Brigance, A. (1981). *Brigance Diagnostic Inventory of Essential Skills*. Newton, MA: Curriculum Associates.
Matuszek, P. (1985). Brigance Diagnostic Inventory of Essential Skills. In J.V. Mitchell, Jr. (Ed.), *The ninth mental measurements yearbook* (pp. 221–223, Ms. No. 165). Lincoln, NE: Buros Institute of Mental Measurement.

TEST REVIEW 3

Gates-MacGinitie Reading Test: Survey F

Publisher Houghton Mifflin Co.
1 Beacon Street
Boston, MA 02107

Cost $6.24 for 35 tests, $1.50 for specimen set of either edition, postage extra; separate answer sheet edition: answer sheets—$5.10 for 35 Digitek or IBM 1230, $2.70 for 35 IBM 805, $2.85 for 35 MRC, $10.00 for 100 NCS; hand-scoring stencil—$2.00 for set IBM 805, $1.00 for set NCS; MRC scoring service—.35 and over for test; NCS scoring service—.20 and over for test; NCS materials and scoring service available from National Computer Systems (NCS), 2510 North Dodge Street, Iowa City, IA 52245.

Date of Publication 1969–1972.

Competencies Assessed Measures reading achievement: speed and accuracy (number attempted, number correct), vocabulary, and comprehension.

Population Characteristics Grades 10–12.

Recommended Uses Used to identify those students who would benefit from remedial or accelerated programs, to evaluate instructional programs, to counsel students, and to report progress to parents.

Test Content and Format 4 scores, 2 forms, 2 editions: consumable booklet edition and separate answer sheet edition. Multiple item paper-pencil test.

Administration Time 50–60 minutes.

Skills/Materials Required Technical supplement, grade score norms, manual, separate answer sheets. There are two equivalent answer sheet forms: Forms 1 and 2 for hand scoring, and 1M and 2M for use with machine-scorable answer sheets.

Derived Scores/Information Scores can be interpreted in the form of raw scores, percentile ranks, or standardized scores.

Norming/Standardization Practices Norms were developed in 1969 by administering Survey F tests to a nationwide sample of more than 5,000 students in grades 9–12 in 35 communities. Students were also administered the Verbal section of the Large-Thorndike Intelligence Tests (1964 Multi-Level Edition). No norms for deaf students have been established.

Reliability Alternate form reliabilities for Grade 10 were .90 for vocabulary, .91 for comprehension, .73 for speed (number attempted), and .78 for accuracy (number correct); for Grade 11 they were .92, .88, .64, and .81 for the respective subtests above; and for Grade 12 they were .88, .85, .78, and .80. Average split-half reliabilities were reported only for vocabulary and comprehension at each of the grade levels: for Grade 10 they were .92 and .93; for Grade 11, .95 and .94; and for Grade 12, .93 and .93.

Validity Validity not reported in test's technical supplement.

Comments Important comprehension skills not (or slightly) assessed in this instrument include interpretative comprehension abilities such as making inferences, separating fact and opinion, and determining the writer's fairness and objectivity (Kingston, 1978); recognizing a writer's purpose, attitude, tone, and mood (Millman, 1972). The manual and technical supplement are considered well done, with the latter providing tables and explanations for further statistical interpretation. Survey F may not be appropriate for some deaf students because it requires an advanced reading level. Additional practice items may be required for deaf students, and time limits for deaf students need to be thoroughly investigated (Botterbusch, 1976, p. 25).

References and Suggested Readings

Botterbusch, K.F. (1976). *The use of psychological tests with individuals who are severely disabled*. Menomonie: University of Wisconsin–Stout, Stout Vocational Rehabilitation Institute, Materials Development Center.

Davis, W.Q. (1968). *A study of test score compatability among five widely used reading survey-tests*. Unpublished doctoral dissertation, Southern Illinois University, Carbondale.

Furth, H.G. (1966). A comparison of reading test norms of deaf and hearing children. *American Annals of the Deaf, 111*, 461–462.

Gates, A.I. (1947). *The improvement of reading: A program of diagnostic and remedial methods* (3rd ed.). New York: Macmillan.

Giangreco, C.J. (1966). The Hiskey-Nebraska Test of Learning Aptitude (Revised) compared to several achievement tests. *American Annals of the Deaf, 111*, 566–577.

Kingston, A.J. (1978). Gates-MacGinitie Reading Tests: Survey F. In O.K. Buros (Ed.), *The eighth mental measurements yearbook* (pp. 1192-1193, Ms. No. 727). Highland Park, NJ: Gryphon Press.

Millman, J. (1972). Gates-MacGinitie Reading Tests: Survey F. In O.K. Buros (Ed.), *The seventh mental measurements yearbook* (pp. 1083–1085, Ms. No. 690). Highland Park, NJ: Gryphon Press.

TEST REVIEW 4

Geist Picture Interest Inventory

Publisher Western Psychological Services
12031 Wilshire Boulevard
Los Angeles, CA 90025

Cost (1988) $21.00 for 20 test booklets, male; $18.50 for 20 test booklets, female; $21.00 for manual; motivation questionnaires also available for male ($7.00 for 20) or female ($5.40 for 20).

Date of Publication 1975.

Competencies Assessed Interest/motivation/vocational interests.

Population Characteristics Grades 8–16 and adults with reading disabilities.

Recommended Uses Counseling, career counseling, identifying employability; to determine occupations most preferred.

Test Content and Format 11 to 12 interest scores (11 for males, 12 for females): persuasiveness, clerical, mechanical, musical, scientific, outdoor, literacy, computational, artistic, social service, traumatic, social service; 7 motivational scores: family, prestige, financial, intrinsic, environmental, past experience. Identification of drawings that represent occupational interest. A special edition of the Geist for deaf males is available. Directions are simplified to fourth-grade reading level. The inventory may be self-administered or directions may be presented in any mode of communication.

Administration Time 30–50 minutes.

Skills/Materials Required Separate answer sheet, record booklet.

Derived Scores/Information Raw scores converted into T scores, assuming that the measured interests are normally distributed.

Norming/Standardization Practices The 1971 standardization sample included students in grades 9–12, two remedial groups, trade school sample, and university group. There are also norms for hearing impaired persons, in four groups (total $N = 2,171$), but these norms are more than 20 years old.

Reliability Test-retest reliability (6 month) fluctuates between .13 and .94, with median in the .60s. For the deaf form, median test-retest reliability for 15 groups of males ranged from .58 to .57 and for 6 groups of females from .67 to .81.

Validity Content validity questionable, concurrent validity not clearly demonstrated, construct validity assumed in comparison to Kuder, and no predictive validity established in terms of environmental criteria. Almost all scales correlate highly with parents' ratings of their children's interests.

Comments May be useful with students who have expressive language difficulties. Bolton (1971) suggests that the deaf male form restricts the occupational awareness of deaf persons and limits opportunities for choice to traditional deaf occupations. He suggests that deaf norms could supplement general norms, but not replace them.

References and Suggested Readings

Bolton, B. (1971). A critical review of the Geist Picture Interest Inventory: Deaf form: Male. *Journal of Rehabilitation of the Deaf, 5*(2), 21–29.
Bolton, B. (1972). A note on the Geist Picture Interest Inventory: Deaf Form: Male. *Rehabilitation Research and Practice Review, 3,* 43–44. (ERIC Document Reproduction Service No. EJ 069 068)
Geist, H. (1962). Occupational interest profiles of the deaf. *Personnel and Guidance Journal, 41,* 50–55.
Geist, H. (1962). *The Geist Picture Interest Inventory: Deaf Form: Male.* Los Angeles: Western Psychological Services.
Geist, H. (1963). Work satisfaction and scores on a picture interest inventory. *Journal of Applied Psychology, 47,* 369–373.
Geist, H. (1975). *The Geist Picture Interest Inventory: Revised manual.* Los Angeles: Western Psychological Services.
Montesano, N., & Geist, H. (1964). Differences in reasons for occupational choices between 9th and 12th grade boys. *Personnel and Guidance Journal, 43,* 127–134.
Tiedeman, D.U. (1960). Testing the test: Geist Picture Interest Inventory. *Personnel and Guidance Journal, 38,* 506–507.

TEST REVIEW 5

General Aptitude Test Battery (GATB)

Publisher   U.S. Government Printing Office
Washington, DC 20402

Cost   No fee if obtained from state Employment Service: $2.10 for Section I; $2.75 for Section II; $3.95 for Section III; $3.20 for Section IV; $2.50 for 100 record blanks; $7.50 for 100 profile-record cards.

Date of Publication   1977.

Competencies Assessed   Aptitudes measured include intelligence, verbal skills, numerical skills, spatial, form perception, clerical perception, motor coordination, finger dexterity, and manual dexterity.

Population Characteristics   Grades 9–12 and adults.

Recommended Uses   Occupational counseling.

Test Content and Format   Test format includes subtests in the following: three-dimensional space, vocabulary, arithmetic reasoning, computation, tool matching, form matching, name comparison, mark making, place, turn, assemble, and disassemble. Tests 9 and 10 require the use of USES Pegboard apparatus, tests 11 and 12 require the use of USES Finger Dexterity Board apparatus, and all other tests are multiple choice. Forms A and B differ only in specific sampling of items in tests 1–7.

Botterbusch and Droege (1972) describe special administration procedures for hearing impaired people.

Administration Time 1) screening device: 15–20 minutes; 2) pretest orientation: 90 minutes; 3) GATB: 150 minutes.

Skills/Materials Required Manual, handbook, tests, record blank, answer sheet; respondent, pegboard apparatus, and finger dexterity board.

Derived Scores/Information Raw scores converted to standard scores representing occupational aptitude patterns. Weighted raw scores are combined to form weighted composite scores.

Norming/Standardization Practices Longitudinal study involving 36,000 high school students as of 1965. Large samples have been utilized. Norms are not separated for male and female. Norms for hearing impaired people are not very recent; deaf norms are provided in the manual (1970), based on 403 students from schools in five states, and Botterbusch and Droege (1972) present GATB data on 408 deaf subjects. Berger, Holdt, and LaForge (1972) report normative data based on 399 deaf adults.

Reliability Coefficients of stability (i.e., test-retest coefficients for periods from 1 week to 1 year) = .80 to .90.

Validity Longitudinal study determined validity as predictor of occupational success; 317 tetrachoric correlations ranging from .24 to .96 (median = 65).

Comments Practice effect occurs. Reliability and validity high enough to be useful in hands of employer and guidance counselor. Age factor shows up in most categories. The U.S. Department of Labor's *Guide for Occupational Exploration* (1979), which, with the GATB forms an occupational guidance system, uses occupational titles and skill requirements for listed occupations that are 10 years old.

References and Suggested Readings

Berger, D.G., Holdt, T.J., & LaForge, R.A. (Eds.). (1972). *Effective vocational guidance of the adult deaf. The Oregon vocational research project June 1, 1966–August 31, 1970*. Final Report. Salem: Oregon State Board of Control. (ERIC Document Reproduction Service No. ED 078 231)

Botterbusch, K.F., & Droege, R.C. (1972). GATB aptitude testing of the deaf: Problems and possibilities. *Journal of Employment Counseling, 9*(1), 14–19.

General Aptitude Test Battery. (1958). Washington, DC: United States Department of Labor, Bureau of Employment Security.

Harlow, M.J.P., Moores, D.F., & Fisher, S.D. (1974). *Post-secondary programs for the deaf: IV: Empirical Data Analysis* (Research Report No. 75). Minneapolis: University of Minnesota, Research, Development and Demonstration Center in Education of Handicapped Children. (ERIC Document Reproduction Service No. ED 107 009)

Hourihan, J.P. (1974). A study of students entering Gallaudet College 1966 and 1971 (Doctoral thesis, Columbia University, New York). *Dissertation Abstracts International*, *35*, 2082A.

Sanderson, R.G. (1973). Preparation of the hearing impaired for an adult vocational life. *Journal of Rehabilitation of the Deaf*, 6(3), 12–18.

Sanderson, R.G. (1974). The effect of educational backgrounds of deaf children on their General Aptitude Test Battery performance scores (Doctoral thesis, Brigham Young University, Provo, UT). *Dissertation Abstracts International*, *35*, 828A.

Seitz, M.J. (1949). *A follow-up study of the use of the General Aptitude Test Battery of the United States Employment Service in the placement of high school seniors*. Unpublished master's thesis, University of Delaware, Newark.

Southern Test Development Field Center. (1979). *The development of GATB administration procedures for the deaf*. Raleigh, NC: U.S. Department of Labor, Employment and Training Administration.

U.S. Department of Labor. (1979). *Guide for occupational exploration*. Washington, DC: U.S. Government Printing Office.

TEST REVIEW 6

H-T-P: House-Tree-Person Projective Technique

Publisher   Western Psychological Services
12031 Wilshire Boulevard
Los Angeles, CA 90025

Cost   (1988) $6.90 for 25 drawing forms; $8.70 for 25 postdrawing interrogation folders; $8.70 for 25 children's revision postdrawing interrogation folders; $52.50 for manual.

Date of Publication   1946–1964.

Competencies Assessed   Personality (projective technique).

Population Characteristics   Age 3 and older.

Recommended Uses   Personality assessment.

Test Content and Format   The first part of the test is nonverbal: The individual makes a freehand drawing of a house, a tree, and a person. The second step is verbal and formally structured with a long set of standardized questions. Designed for individual administration, the test may also be group administered (Ellis, 1953). There are no standardized instructions for administration to deaf individuals.

Administration Time   60–90 minutes.

Skills/Materials Required Paper; interviewer/interpreter experienced in clinical psychological procedures, particularly in projective drawing techniques.

Derived Score/Information Qualitative scoring and interpretation are subjective. (Quantitative scoring of the H-T-P as a test of intelligence—one of its original purposes—is complex and time-consuming, and the test is infrequently used for this purpose today; there is no reliability or validity evidence for intelligence scores.)

Norming/Standardization Practices Norms for adults are provided by Buck (1978), but there are currently no available norms for deaf populations.

Reliability No data available. Difficult to judge because of the projective nature of the test.

Validity Inadequate evidence of validity. Difficult to judge because of the projective nature of the test.

Comments May be useful as an "icebreaker," in reducing anxiety and facilitating a transition to more verbal tasks. The amount of meaningful projective data to be derived from the drawings (and from the interview, if used) depends on the experience and orientation of the examiner (Haworth, 1965). It may be a valuable addition to the skilled clinical psychologist's battery of projective tests of personality evaluation (Ellis, 1953). The absence of published normative data on deaf individuals may limit the test's usefulness in many situations.

References and Suggested Readings

Bieliauskas, V.J. (1980). *The House-Tree-Person (H-T-P) Research Review, 1980 edition*. Los Angeles: Western Psychological Services.

Bieliauskas, V.J., & Moens, J.F. (1961). An investigation of the validity of the H-T-P as an intelligence test for children. *Journal of Clinical Psychology, 17*, 178–180.

Buck, J.N. (1948a). H-T-P technique: A qualitative and quantitative scoring manual. *Journal of Clinical Psychology*, Monograph Supplement No. 5.

Buck, J.N. (1948b). *H-T-P technique: A qualitative and quantitative scoring manual*. Los Angeles: Clinical Psychology Publishing Co.

Buck, J.N. (1978). *The House-Tree-Person technique: Revised manual*. Los Angeles: Western Psychological Services.

Davis, C.J. (1974). Comparison of House-Tree-Person drawings of deaf and hearing children ages seven through ten years. *Dissertation Abstracts International, 34*(10-B), 5186.

Davis, C.J., & Hoopes, J.L. (1976). Comparison of House-Tree-Person drawings of young deaf and hearing children. *Journal of Personality Assessment, 39*, 28–33.

Davis, E.E., & Ekwall, E.E. (1976). Mode of perception and frustration in reading. *Journal of Learning Disabilities*, *9*, 448–454. (ERIC Document Reproduction Service No. EJ 148 147)

DeVore, J.E. (1985). *A comparative study of the House-Tree-Person drawings of young hearing-impaired and normal children*. Doctoral dissertation, Memphis State University, TN.

DeVore, J.E., & Fryrear, J.L. (1976). Analysis of juvenile delinquents' hole drawing responses on the tree figure of the House-Tree-Person technique. *Journal of Clinical Psychology*, *32*, 731–736.

Donoghue, R.J. (1975). Personality development in deaf children as measured by the House-Tree-Person and Bender-Gestalt tests (Doctoral thesis, Northwestern University, Evanston, IL, 1974). *Dissertation Abstracts International*, *35*(10), 5106B.

Ellis, A. (1953). H-T-P: A projective device and a measure of adult intelligence. In O.K. Buros (Ed.), *The fourth mental measurements yearbook* (pp. 591–594, Ms. No. 108). Highland Park, NJ: Gryphon Press.

Eyal, C., & Lindgren, H.C. (1977). The House-Tree-Person test as a measure of intelligence and creativity. *Perceptual and Motor Skills*, *44*, 359–362.

Hammer, E.F. (1955). *The House-Tree-Person (H-T-P) clinical research manual*. Los Angeles: Western Psychological Services.

Haworth, M.R. (1965). H-T-P: House-Tree-Person projective technique. In O.K. Buros (Ed.), *The sixth mental measurements yearbook* (pp. 1240–1241, Ms. No. 215). Highland Park, NJ: Gryphon Press.

Jollis, I. (1952). *A catalog for the qualitative interpretation of the House-Tree-Person (H-T-P)*. Los Angeles: Western Psychological Services.

Spragins, A.B., Blennerhassett, L., & Mullen, Y. (1987, March). *Reviews of five types of assessment instruments used with hearing impaired students*. Paper presented at the annual convention of the National Association of School Psychologists, New Orleans, LA.

Stavrianos, B.K. (1971). Can projective test measures aid in the detection and differential diagnosis of reading deficit? *Journal of Personality Assessment*, *35*, 80–91.

Vernon, M., & Brown, D.W. (1964). A guide to psychological tests and testing procedures in the evaluation of deaf and hard-of-hearing children. *Journal of Speech and Hearing Disorders*, *29*, 414–423.

Zieziula, F.R. (Ed.). (1982). *Assessment of hearing-impaired people*. Washington, DC: Gallaudet College Press.

TEST REVIEW 7

Jewish Employment Vocational Service Work Sample System (JEVS)

Publisher Vocational Research Institute
Jewish Employment & Vocational Service
1700 Sansom Street
Philadelphia, PA 19103

Cost Specimen set $7,975—includes 28 work samples (hardware and consumables), training for one evaluator, and a 2-day consultation visit.

Date of Publication 1969–1976 (also called Philadelphia JEVS Work Sample Battery). (Although new sales have been discontinued, replacement parts are still available from Vocational Research Institute. JEVS has been replaced with VITAS Battery.)

Competencies Assessed Worker characteristics, functional abilities, time and quality scores, and vocational training/placement recommendations. Ratings by evaluator of behavior in interpersonal situations, worker characteristics, learning and comprehension, discriminations, manipulative skills, and significant worker characteristics. Time and quality ratings of each of 28 tests (work samples), including nut-bolt-washer assembly, telephone assembly, filing by letters, computing postage, and vest making.

Population Characteristics Unemployed/underemployed, physically and mentally handicapped populations (higher functioning educable mentally retarded [EMR] and above).

Recommended Uses Gives descriptive evaluation and quantitative results for use in constructing vocational placement and training plans.

Test Content and Format 28 work samples designed to assess vocational skills, work-related behaviors, and interests. Individually administered. Includes ratings by evaluator.

Administration Time Five to seven 6-hour days for 15 examinees to complete battery of 28 tests.

Skills/Materials Required 95% of all work sample materials are nonconsumable "machines," tools, hardware. Consumables average $3.50 per examinee. Administration should be standardized in an atmosphere resembling industry rather than a classroom.

Derived Scores/Information Raw scores for production time and "product" errors. A 10-page narrative report is produced on each evaluee.

Norming/Standardization Practices Normed on 1,200 educationally or economically disadvantaged, physically or mentally handicapped individuals served by vocational rehabilitation and Manpower installations—predominantly young black males with no work history. Norms were updated in 1975 based on 880 individuals from 32 facilities in 15 states representing all regions of the country. No norms for hearing impaired people have been established, but the publisher is willing to develop norms for specific populations if raw data are provided.

Reliability No studies regarding reliability of JEVS are available. There is no evidence that the JEVS system is either better or poorer than most other work sample systems regarding reliability.

Validity No validity data presented. Results indirectly support the validity of the JEVS in that intelligence scores as measured by the Revised Beta are related to the work sample overall performance.

Comments JEVS is tied into the U.S. Department of Labor's 1977 *Dictionary of Occupational Titles* and 1979 *Guide for Occupational Exploration*. Because of this direct relationship, the system provides information regarding clients' strengths and weaknesses for work. Both experience and research have identified difficulties in using it with moderately and severely mentally retarded persons. Because JEVS work samples do not rely heavily on speech or reading skills, many of the work samples may be suitable for hearing impaired examinees.

References and Suggested Readings

Botterbusch, K.F. (1980). *A comparison of commercial vocational evaluation systems*. Menomonie: University of Wisconsin–Stout, Stout Vocational Rehabilitation Institute, Materials Development Center.

Hurwitz, S.K., & DiFrancesca, S. (1968). Behavioral modification of the emotionally retarded deaf. *Rehabilitation Literature, 29*, 258–264.

JEVS Work Sample Evaluation System. (1973). Philadelphia: Jewish Employment and Vocational Service, Vocational Research Institute.

Kapes, J.T., & Mastie, M.M. (Eds.). (1983). *A counselor's guide to vocational guidance instruments*. Falls Church, VA: American Personnel and Guidance Association.

Nadolsky, J.M. (1973). *Vocational evaluation of the culturally disadvantaged: A comparative investigation of JEVS (Jewish Employment Vocational Service) system and a model-based system (final report)*. Auburn, AL: Auburn University. (ERIC Document Reproduction Service No. 101 203)

Tryjankowski, E.M. (1986, April). *Convergent-discriminant validity of the Jewish Employment Vocational System (JEVS)*. Paper presented at the meeting of the American Educational Research Association, San Francisco. (ERIC Document Reproduction Service No. ED 271 491)

U.S. Department of Labor. (1977). *Dictionary of occupational titles* (4th ed.). Washington, DC: U.S. Government Printing Office.

U.S. Department of Labor. (1979). *Guide for occupational exploration*. Washington, DC: U.S. Government Printing Office.

VITAS Battery. (1979). Philadelphia: Jewish Employment and Vocational Service, Vocational Research Institute.

TEST REVIEW 8

Meadow-Kendall Social-Emotional Assessment Inventory (SEAI) for Deaf and Hearing Impaired Students

Publisher Outreach
Pre-College Programs
Gallaudet University
KDES PAS #6
Washington, DC 20002

Cost (1988) $15.00 for manual; $5.00 for 10 forms.

Date of Publication 1983.

Competencies Assessed Social adjustment, self-image, and emotional adjustment. Identifies positive classroom and school behaviors as well as problem behaviors of hearing impaired children and adolescents.

Population Characteristics Hearing impaired children and adolescents age 7 to 21 years (school-age form) (3 to 6 years preschool form also available).

Recommended Uses Identifying a student's social and emotional strengths and weaknesses, IEP planning, communicating with parents.

Test Content and Format 59-item behavior checklist to be completed by adult informant. Items use a four-point response scale ranging from Very True to Very False.

Administration Time 20–30 minutes.

Skills/Materials Required Checklist, manual, adult informant familiar with the student's behavior by way of contact for at least 8 weeks.

Derived Scores/Information Scores on Scale 1, Social Adjustment; Scale 2, Self-Image; Scale 3, Emotional Adjustment. Raw scores can be converted to deciles based on normative data broken down by age group and sex.

Validity Construct validity is supported by factor analysis and inspection of items appropriate to hearing impaired students and the relationships between SEAI scores and the presence of other handicapping conditions in the norm sample.

Reliability The internal consistency reliabilities (Cronbach's alpha) of the three scales are .96 for Scale 1, .94 for Scale 2, and .91 for Scale 3, based on the norming sample. Interrater reliabilities and test-retest reliabilities are reported for another sample of only six children; interrater reliabilities and correlations with other variables are reported for larger samples, but little information is given about the samples and the data collection conditions.

Norms for Hearing Impaired People Norms for the SEAI are based on hearing impaired children from both residential schools and day programs in the Northeast, Midwest, Southwest, and South United States. Three variables were accounted for in the norming sample selection: sex, type of education program, and age group. Participating sites were voluntary and not randomly selected. There were 2,071 students available for establishing norms for Scale 1; 1,757 students for Scale 2; and 2,042 students for Scale 3. There are separate norms for girls and boys, ages 7 to 15 and 16 to 21 for Scales 1 and 2; norms are by age group only for Scale 3. Normative information includes means, standard deviations, and deciles.

Comments   The SEAI is useful in developing IEPs for hearing impaired children. Its use in the transition process warrants future study. Systematic, large-scale reliability (interrater, test-retest), and validity studies of the scale are needed (Demorest, in press; Sheldon, in press).

References and Suggested Readings

Demorest, M.E. (in press). Meadow-Kendall Social-Emotional Assessment Inventory for Deaf and Hearing Impaired Students. In J.V. Mitchell, Jr. (Ed.), *The tenth mental measurements yearbook*. Lincoln, NE: Buros Institute of Mental Measurement. (Mental Measurements Yearbooks online database Ms. No. 1012-91)

Levine, E.S. (1981). *The ecology of early deafness*. New York: Columbia University Press.

Meadow, K.P. (1976). Personality and social development of deaf persons. In B. Bolton (Ed.), *Psychology of deafness for rehabilitation counselors* (pp. 67–80). Baltimore: University Park Press.

Meadow, K.P. (1983). *Meadow-Kendall Social-Emotional Assessment Inventories for Deaf and Hearing-Impaired Students* (The revised SEAI manual, forms for school-age and preschool children). Washington, DC: Gallaudet University.

Meadow, K.P., & Dyssegaard, B. (1986). Teachers' ratings of deaf children: An American-Danish comparison. *American Annals of the Deaf, 28*, 900–908.

Mindel, E.D., & Vernon, M. (1971). *They grow in silence: The deaf child and his family*. Silver Spring, MD: National Association of the Deaf.

Schlesinger, H.S., & Meadow, K.P. (1972). *Sound and sign: Childhood deafness and mental health*. Berkeley: University of California Press.

Sheldon, K.L. (in press). Meadow-Kendall Social-Emotional Assessment Inventory for Deaf and Hearing Impaired Students. In J.V. Mitchell, Jr. (Ed.), *The tenth mental measurements yearbook*. Lincoln, NE: Buros Institute of Mental Measurement. (Mental Measurements Yearbooks online database Ms. No. 1012-91)

Zieziula, F.R. (Ed.). (1982). *Assessment of hearing-impaired people: A guide for selecting psychological, educational, and vocational tests*. Washington, DC: Gallaudet College Press.

Zwiebel, A., Meadow-Orlans, K.P., & Dyssegaard, B. (1986). A comparison of hearing-impaired students in Israel, Denmark, and the United States. *International Journal of Rehabilitation Research, 9*, 109–118.

TEST REVIEW 9

Stanford Achievement Test, 7th Edition

Publisher The Psychological Corporation
Harcourt Brace Jovanovich
Academic Court
San Antonio, TX 78204-0952

Special Stanford Materials for Hearing Impaired
Center for Assessment and Demographic Studies
Gallaudet University
800 Florida Avenue, N.E.
Washington, DC 20002

Cost (1988) $24.00–$29.00 for 100 practice tests; $3.00 for directions for administering practice test; $4.50 for directions for administering complete or basic battery; $10.00 for norms booklet; $3.00 for class record—content cluster analysis; $16.00 for examination kit of any one level; machine scoring service available. From Center for Assessment and Demographic Studies, individual copies of tests and of deafness-related materials (1988): $.10 for practice test; $.10 for directions for practice test; $4.50 for directions for administering complete battery, including special instructions; $4.25 for directions for administering mathematics test, including special instructions; $1.85–$2.50 for complete battery test booklet; $1.00–$2.00 for mathematics test booklet; $.35–$.40 for answer sheet; $40.00 for complete sample set; $3.00 for complete set hand-scoring materials; $10.00 for technical manual "Understanding the Scores"; machine-scoring service available including deaf norms; Student-Problem (S-P) Analysis reports available.

Date of Publication 1982 (1989, 8th edition, in development; 1973, 6th edition, still available).

Competencies Assessed 13 to 16 subtests per level: reading (word reading, reading comprehension, word reading plus reading comprehension), word study skills, mathematics (concepts of number, computation and applications, computation, applications, total), listening (vocabulary, comprehension, total), language (spelling, language, total), environment, science, social science, using information. Subtests with deaf norms available: reading comprehension, spelling, language, concepts of number, math computation, math applications.

Population Characteristics Children: Primary 1, grades 1.5–2.9; Primary 2, 2.5–3.9; Primary 3, 3.5–4.9; Intermediate 1, 4.5–5.9; Intermediate 2, 5.5–7.9; Advanced, 7.0–9.9; screening tests for hearing impaired children and adolescents ages 7 through 19 can be used to assign test levels.

Recommended Uses Achievement testing. The test focuses on those subject and skill areas that are generally considered basic for most elementary, middle, and junior high school students.

Test Content and Format 6 levels, 2 forms (3 forms for grades 1.5–2.9), number of tests in the various levels ranges from 13 to 16. Group administration. Paper-and-pencil test.

Administration Time Grades 1.5–2.9: 250 minutes in 4 sessions; Grades 2.5–3.9: 275 minutes in 6 sessions; Grades 3.5–4.9: 350 minutes in 6 sessions; Grades 4.5–5.9: 370 minutes in 7 sessions; Grades 5.5–7.9: 370 minutes in 7 sessions; Grades 7.0–9.9: 330 minutes in 6 sessions.

Skills/Materials Required Administrator's guide; technical manual (or norms booklet); practice test and directions for primary levels 1, 2, 3, and intermediate levels 1–2; separate answer sheets may be used in grades 4.5–9.9.

Derived Scores/Information Four types of norms are provided: percentiles, stanines, grade equivalents, and scaled scores; deciles for each age 8 through 18 by region, school type, degree of hearing loss, additional handicap status, and ethnic group are provided for the hearing impaired norming population.

Norming/Standardization Practices Norms are based on 485,000 hearing students from 300 school districts, with separate norms for fall, mid-year, and spring testings. Separate norms by sex, ethnic group, or urban, suburban, and rural schools are not provided. Norms for hearing impaired students are based on 7,700 students (Allen, 1986) and include scaled scores by decile for each age 8 through 18 by region, school type, degree of hearing loss, additional handicap status, and ethnic group.

Reliability Internal consistency KR 20 reliabilities are high for the national sample (from .92 to .97 for the Total Mathematics Test), as are alternate form reliabilities for the national sample (from .88 to .95 for the Total Mathematics Test). For the hearing impaired sample, reported KR 20 reliabilities range from .76 to .91 for commonly given subtests. Alternate form reliabilities for those subtests range from .56 to .91.

Validity The test was carefully constructed to measure what is commonly taught in most elementary, middle, and junior high schools. The *Stanford Achievement Test Index of Instructional Objectives* (Madden, Gardner, Rudman, Karlsen, & Merwin, 1983) provides the test user a means for local content validation of subtests and of content clusters. The reading test has been criticized for failing to measure what it purports to measure rather than "what is commonly taught" (Smith, 1985). For the hearing impaired students, construct validity and criterion-related validity evidence was briefly summarized, and detailed evidence of content validity was presented (Allen, 1986). Based on a random subsample of 2,500 students from the larger norming sample, evidence of curriculum coverage and actual performance information presented for the Mathematics Computation and Reading Comprehension content categories showed that, in general, these two subtests have good content validity for hearing impaired students (Allen, 1986).

Comments The Stanford is judged to be one of the best available achievement batteries (e.g., Davison, 1985; Subkoviak & Farley, 1985). The availability of deaf norms greatly enhances its utility with hearing impaired students. Criterion-related validity evidence for the test's use in transition is needed. Subkoviak and Farley recommend that achievement test selection should involve comparing competing tests with respect to: 1) how well a test mirrors school curriculum, 2) usefulness of the test scores for the intended purpose, 3) comparability of the school's population to the test's norm groups, and 4) amount of time and money available for testing.

References and Suggested Readings

Allen, T.E. (1984a). Interpreting the new Stanford Achievement Test for hearing-impaired students. *Perspectives*, *2*, 21–23.

Allen, T.E. (1984b). *Out-of-level testing with the Stanford Achievement Test (7th edition): A procedure for assigning students to the correct battery level.* Washington, DC: Gallaudet Research Institute Monograph Series 1. (ERIC Document Reproduction Service No. ED 250 368)

Allen, T.E. (1986). *Understanding the scores: Hearing-impaired students and the Stanford Achievement Test (7th edition).* Washington, DC: Gallaudet Research Institute, Center for Assessment and Demographic Studies. (ERIC Document Reproduction Service No. ED 280 247)

Allen, T.E., Holt, J.A., Bloomquist, C.A., & Starke, M.C. (1987). *Item analysis for the Stanford Achievement Test, 7th edition, 1983 standardization with hearing-impaired students.* Washington, DC: Center for Assessment and Demographic Studies.

Allen, T.E., Holt, J.A., Hotto, S.A., & Bloomquist, C.A. (1987). *Differential item difficulty—Comparisons of P-values on the Stanford Achievement Test, 7th edition, between hearing and hearing-impaired standardization samples.* Washington, DC: Center for Assessment and Demographic Studies.

Allen, T.E., White, C.S., & Karchmer, M.A. (1983). Issues in the development of a special edition for hearing-impaired students of the seventh edition of the Stanford Achievement Test. *American Annals of the Deaf*, *128*, 34–39. (ERIC Document Reproduction Service No. EJ 281 124)

Bloomquist, C.A., & Allen, T.E. (1987, April). *Comparison of Stanford*

Achievement Test item responses by hearing and hearing impaired students. Paper presented at the meeting of the American Educational Research Association, Washington, DC.

Bloomquist, C.A., & Allen, T.E. (1988, April). *Comparison of mathematics test item performance by hearing and hearing impaired students.* Paper presented at the meeting of the American Educational Research Association, New Orleans, LA.

Center for Assessment and Demographic Studies. (1983). *Administering the 1982 Stanford Achievement Test (seventh edition) to hearing-impaired students.* Washington, DC: Gallaudet Research Institute.

Center for Assessment and Demographic Studies. (1986). *Beyond the grade equivalent: The student-problem analysis.* Washington, DC: Gallaudet Research Institute.

Davison, M.L. (1985). Stanford Achievement Test, 1982 Edition. In J.V. Mitchell, Jr. (Ed.), *The ninth mental measurements yearbook* (pp. 1449–1450, Ms. No. 1172). Lincoln, NE: Buros Institute of Mental Measurement.

Holt, J.A., & Allen, T.E. (in press). Alterable school variables influencing reading and mathematics achievement of hearing impaired students. *International Journal of Educational Research.*

Hotto, G., & Schildroth, A. (1984). *A resource for educators and parents of hearing-impaired students: Seventh edition Stanford Achievement Test for use with hearing-impaired students.* Washington, DC: Center for Assessment and Demographic Studies.

Karchmer, M.A., & Allen, T.E. (1984). *Adaptation and standardization, Stanford Achievement Test (seventh edition) for use with hearing impaired students* (final report). Washington, DC: Gallaudet Research Institute. (ERIC Document Reproduction Service No. ED 257 237)

Madden, R., Gardner, E.F., Rudman, H.C., Karlsen, B., & Merwin, J.C. (1983). *Stanford Achievement Test Index of Instructional Objectives.* New York: Harcourt Brace Jovanovich.

Rawlings, B.W., & Allen, T.E. (1987, June). *Response patterns on the Stanford: A new means of assessing student performance.* Paper presented at the biennial meeting of the Conference of American Instructors of the Deaf, Santa Fe, NM.

Smith, K.J. (1985). Stanford Achievement Test: Reading Tests, 1982 Edition. In J.V. Mitchell, Jr. (Ed.), *The ninth mental measurements yearbook* (pp. 1455–1456, Ms. No. 1175). Lincoln, NE: Buros Institute of Mental Measurement.

Subkoviak, M.J., & Farley, F.H. (1985). Stanford Achievement Test, 1982 Edition. In J.V. Mitchell, Jr. (Ed.), *The ninth mental measurements yearbook* (pp. 1450–1452, Ms. No. 1172). Lincoln, NE: Buros Institute of Mental Measurement.

TEST REVIEW 10

Street Survival Skills Questionnaire (SSSQ)

Publisher McCarron-Dial Systems—Common Market Press
P.O. Box 45628
Dallas, TX 75245

Cost $137.50 plus shipping/handling; $9.00 for 50 score forms; $5.00 for 50 planning charts.

Date of Publication 1979.

Competencies Assessed Survival skills; work potential of neuro-psychologically disabled adults; fundamental community living and pre-vocational skills.

Population Characteristics Mentally disabled adolescents and adults.

Recommended Uses To provide basic information in specific content areas that, in conjunction with additional measures of sensorimotor skills, emotional adjustment, information processing skills, and vocational, educational, and social skills, may provide guidelines for selection, training, and placement of mentally disabled individuals into the community. Can serve as baseline for training; can be curriculum blueprint.

Test Content and Format Content includes: basic concepts, functional signs, tools, domestic management, health/safety/first aid, public service, time, money, measurement. Multiple-choice pictorial format that permits sampling of several aspects of adaptive behavior. Orally presented. Individually presented. Examinee responds by pointing to picture, large print, graphic presentation. Each of 24 items that constitute a content area is identified on the chart by a word that corresponds to the content of the item. Scoring procedure provides item-by-item analysis.

Administration Time 30–45 minutes.

Skills/Materials Required Nine volumes of picture plates, manual, scoring sheet, planning chart, examiner, examinee. McCarron and Stall (1981) recommend adaptations for administering the SSSQ to deaf individuals.

Derived Scores/Information Raw scores obtained by summing correct responses within each section. Raw scores can be converted to standardized scores. Results can be converted into scale scores enabling comparison within specific norm group. Scores can be plotted on a profile. Raw scores can be converted into Survival Skills Quotient (SSQ) that allows direct comparison to intelligence quotient. Scores are by age and sex.

Norming/Standardization Practices Norms are available for mentally disabled adults (based on a norm group of 500, ages 15–55) and normal adolescents (based on a norm group of 200, ages 14–18).

Reliability Reliability coefficient on the total test is .97; the standard error of measurement is 3.00.

Validity Construct validity—similar to Peabody Picture Vocabulary Test (PPVT). Used as a component to predict work behavior/potential of neuropsychologically disabled adults.

Comments SSSQ does not assess maladaptive behavior.

References and Suggested Readings

Dunn, L.M. (1981). Peabody Picture Vocabulary Test (rev. ed.). Circle Pines, MN: American Guidance Service.

Giller, V.L., Dial, J.G., & Chan, F. (1986). The Street Survival Skills Questionnaire: A correlational study. *American Journal of Mental Deficiency*, *91*, 67–71.

Linkenhoker, D., & McCarron, L. (1979). *Street Survival Skills Questionnaire*. Dallas: McCarron-Dial Systems.

McCarron, L.T., Cobb, G., Smith, C., & Barron, P. (1982). *Curriculum guides for the SSSQ*. Lubbock: Texas Tech University, Research and Training Center in Mental Retardation. (ERIC Document Reproduction Service No. ED 248 684)

McCarron, L.T., & Stall, C.H. (1981). *Street Survival Skills Questionnaire for the deaf*. Lubbock: Texas Tech University, Research and Training Center in Mental Retardation.

TEST REVIEW 11

VALPAR Component Work Sample Series

Publisher Valpar Corporation
3801 E. 34th Street
Tucson, AZ 85713

Cost Individual samples range from $495 to $990 per unit. $1,125 for complete set of 15 videotapes for hearing impaired people. (Work samples and videotapes may be purchased separately.)

Date of Publication Updated continually—dates vary from work sample to work sample—latest is 1988.

Competencies Assessed Vocational and functional skills.

Population Characteristics Disabled and nondisabled; all age groups appropriate for work skills evaluation.

Recommended Uses Produces scores and clinical observations useful for job placement, selection of training programs, and design of education and rehabilitation plans. Designed to measure certain universal worker characteristics (e.g., a person's ability to use eyes, hands, and feet simultaneously and in a coordinated manner).

Test Content and Format Most samples focus on general work characteristics; some are related to specific job areas. Each sample involves hands-on tasks.

Administration Time Varies from 10 minutes to 6 hours per work sample.

Skills/Materials Required Training is not required for purchase, but is highly suggested for those using the work samples. Answer sheets are essentially the only consumable materials necessary.

Derived Scores/Information Worker qualifications profiles and Method-Times-Measurement (MTM) percents. Evaluators write and summarize their own results.

Norming/Standardization Practices Standardization sample included: deaf–congenitally deaf; severely to profoundly deaf; institutional retarded–sheltered living; institutional retarded–independent/community living; Seminole Community College–disadvantaged population; Air Force; San Diego employed workers; skill center–low income, unemployed; employed workers—unselected; congenitally and adventitiously blind; exceptional youth. Sample size for each group was about 50. All groups are clearly described.

Reliability Test-retest reliability coefficients for the work sample components range from .80 to .97.

Validity Minimal data available. Some degree of content validity information is provided by relating measured characteristics to specific jobs and worker trait groups in the *Dictionary of Occupational Titles* (U.S. Department of Labor, 1977). Even though face validity is fairly high, the abstract nature of some of the tasks makes it difficult to associate them with actual job skills.

Comments VALPAR work samples are well designed, appealing to clients, and relatively easy to administer and score. Components may be added to as program needs change. There is a tendency for the components to focus on physical skills, making them especially useful for physically and industrially disabled individuals. Because little information is available concerning reliability and validity, the use of VALPAR work samples must be approached with caution.

References and Suggested Readings

Backman, M.E. (1977, December). *The feasibility of group evaluation in reha-bilitation agencies.* Paper presented at a meeting of the Michigan Association of Rehabilitation Facilities, Kalamazoo. (ERIC Document Reproduction Service No. ED 152 831)

Botterbusch, K.F. (1976). *A comparison of seven vocational evaluation systems*. Menomonie: University of Wisconsin–Stout, Stout Vocational Rehabilitation Institute, Materials Development Center. (ERIC Document Reproduction Service No. ED 186 738)

Botterbusch, K.F. (1982). *A comparison of commercial vocational evaluation systems* (2nd ed.). Menomonie: University of Wisconsin–Stout, Stout Vocational Rehabilitation Institute, Materials Development Center. (ERIC Document Reproduction Service No. ED 273 803)

Botterbusch, K.F. (1987). *Vocational assessment and evaluation systems: A comparison*. Menomonie: University of Wisconsin–Stout, Stout Vocational Rehabilitation Institute, Materials Development Center. (ERIC Document Reproduction Service No. ED 289 079)

Brandon, T.L., Button, W.L., Rastatter, C.J., & Ross, D.R. (1975). Valpar Component Work Sample system. In A. Sax (Ed.), Innovations in vocational evaluation and work adjustment. *Vocational Evaluation and Work Adjustment Bulletin, 8*(2), 59–63.

Dickson, M.B. (1976). *Work sample evaluation of blind clients: Criteria for administration and development*. Master's thesis, University of Wisconsin–Stout, Stout Vocational Rehabilitation Institute, Materials Development Center. (ERIC Document Reproduction Service No. ED 186 756)

Growick, B., Kaliope, G., & Jones, C. (1983). Sample norms for the hearing-impaired on select components of the VALPAR Work Sample Series. *Vocational Evaluation and Work Adjustment Bulletin, 16*(2), 56–57.

Kapes, J.T., & Mastie, M.M. (Eds.). (1983). *A counselor's guide to vocational guidance instruments*. Falls Church, VA: American Personnel and Guidance Association.

Kimmel, D.S, Honig, J., & Jonas, J. (1981). *Vocational assessment of deaf adults* (final report, July 1, 1980–June 30, 1981). Fair Lawn, NJ: Fair Lawn Community School. (ERIC Document Reproduction Service No. ED 206 905)

Rastatter, C.J., & Ross, D.R. (1985). Vocational and educational evaluation— The Valpar philosophy. *Valparspective, 3*(2), 1–4. (Newsletter available from Valpar Corporation, Tucson, AZ.)

Ross, D.R. (1981). *VALPAR Component Work Sample Series: Research Data*. Tucson, AZ: Valpar Corporation.

Ross, D.R., & Rastatter, C.J. (1988). *Test validation*. Tucson, AZ: Valpar Corporation.

Sligar, S. (1976). The use of commercial work samples with a hearing-impaired population. In D. Watson (Ed.), *Deaf evaluation and adjustment feasibility* (pp. 59–88). New York: New York University, Deafness Research and Training Center.

Smith, C., & Fry, R. (Eds.). (1985). *National forum on issues in vocational assessment: The issues papers*. Menomonie: University of Wisconson–Stout, Stout Vocational Rehabilitation Institute, Materials Development Center. (ERIC Document Reproduction Service No. ED 278 781)

U.S. Department of Labor. (1977). *Dictionary of occupational titles* (4th ed.). Washington, DC: U.S. Government Printing Office.

VALPAR Component Work Sample Series: #1–13. (1974). Tucson, AZ: Valpar Corporation.

VALPAR Component Work Sample Series: #14–16. (1977). Tucson, AZ: Valpar Corporation.

VALPAR Component Work Sample Series: #17. (1978). Tucson, AZ: Valpar Corporation.

VALPAR Component Work Sample Series: #18. (1979). Tucson, AZ: Valpar Corporation.
VALPAR Component Work Sample Series: #19. (1987). Tucson, AZ: Valpar Corporation.
VALPAR Component Work Sample Series: #201–205. (1988). Tucson, AZ: Valpar Corporation.

TEST REVIEW 12

Vineland Adaptive Behavior Scales

Publisher American Guidance Service, Inc.
Publishers Building
Circle Pines, MN 55014

Cost (1984) $11.50 for 25 record booklets; $14.50 for manual.

Date of Publication 1984 (revision of the 1965 Vineland Social Maturity Scale) (Interview Edition Survey Form contains 297 items; other editions available are 577-item Expanded Form and 244-item Classroom Edition).

Competencies Assessed Communication (expressive, receptive, written); daily living skills (personal, domestic, community); socialization (interpersonal relations, play and leisure time, coping skills); motor skills (gross, fine); adaptive behavior composite.

Population Characteristics All children from birth to 18 years, 11 months; also appropriate for a wide age range of handicapped and nonhandicapped individuals.

Recommended Uses Useful for identification and placement, program planning, and program evaluation purposes.

Test Content and Format Semistructured interview (requires a respondent who is familiar with the individual). Items are statements about what the individual does (e.g., "sets table with assistance"). Respondents answer "yes, usually"; "sometimes or partially"; "no, never"; "no opportunity"; or "don't know."

Administration Time 20–60 minutes.

Skills/Materials Required Interview form; respondent who is familiar with the individual being assessed; trained professional interviewer.

Derived Scores/Information Standard scores (normalized with mean 100 and standard deviation 15, by age); national percentile ranks; stanines; adaptive level; age equivalents; and percentile ranks for supplementary norms groups, including hearing impaired. Raw score conversions for the hearing impaired group are by percentile rank and ranges only, and not by ages or standard scores.

Norming/Standardization Practices National sample of 4,800 handicapped and nonhandicapped individuals stratified by 15 age groups—birth to 18 years, 11 months. Supplementary norms based on 323 hearing impaired children ages 6 years to 12 years, 11 months in residential facilities; 1,050 ambulatory and nonambulatory mentally retarded adults in residential facilities; 134 emotionally disturbed residents ages 9 years to 15 years, 6 months; and 185 visually impaired residents ages 6 years to 12 years, 11 months.

Reliability 1) Split-half: typically in mid-80s to low 90s for each age group and scale combination, 2) test-retest: typically in 80s for composite score, 3) interrater: range from .62 to .78 for five adaptive scales.

Validity Evidence of construct validity includes developmental progression of scores, factor analytic results, and comparisons of supplementary norms groups. Correlations with the Kaufman Assessment Battery for Children are highest for communication (.32 to .52); correlations with a variety of other measures are also provided.

Comments The Vineland has good documentation, clear directions for administration and scoring, and a good discussion of the interpretation of the results. Additional illustrations of interpretation in the context of transition programs would be useful, as would norms for hearing impaired adolescents and adults.

References and Suggested Readings

Avery, G. (1948). Social competence of pre-school acoustically handicapped children. *Exceptional Children*, *15*, 71–73. [Used Vineland Social Maturity Scale.]

Bradway, K.P. (1937). Social competence of exceptional children: The deaf, the blind, and the crippled. *Exceptional Children*, *4*, 64–69. [Used Vineland Social Maturity Scale.]

Britton, W.H., & Eaves, R.C. (1986). Relationship between the Vineland Adaptive Behavior Scales–Classroom Edition and the Vineland Social Maturity Scales. *American Journal of Mental Deficiency*, *91*, 105–107.

Burchard, E.M.L., & Myklebust, H.R. (1942). A comparison of congenital and adventitious deafness with respect to its effect on intelligence, personality, and social maturity: Part II, social maturity. *American Annals of the Deaf*, *87*, 140–154. [Used Vineland Social Maturity Scale.]

Campbell, I.A. (1985). Vineland Adaptive Behavior Scales. In J.V. Mitchell, Jr., (Ed.), *The ninth mental measurements yearbook* (pp. 1660–1662, Ms. No. 1327). Lincoln, NE: Buros Institute of Mental Measurement.

Doll, E.A. (1953). *Measurement of social competence*. Circle Pines, MN: American Guidance Service.

Doll, E.A. (1965). *Vineland Social Maturity Scale: Condensed manual of directions.* Circle Pines, MN: American Guidance Service.

Kaufman, A., & Kaufman, N. (1983). *Kaufman Assessment Battery for Children (K-ABC).* Circle Pines, MN: American Guidance Service.

Myklebust, H.R., & Burchard, E.M.L. (1945). A study of the effects of congenital and adventitious deafness on the intelligence, personality and social maturity of school children. *Journal of Educational Psychology, 36,* 321.

Quarrington, B., & Solomon, B. (1975). A current study of the social maturity of deaf students. *Canadian Journal of Behavioral Sciences, 7,* 70–77. [Used Vineland Social Maturity Scale.]

Roszkowski, M.J. (1980). Concurrent validity of the Adaptive Behavior Scale as assessed by the Vineland Social Maturity Scale. *American Journal of Mental Deficiency, 85,* 86–89.

Snyder, M.M. (1985). Review of the Vineland Adaptive Behavior Scales. *Diagnostique, 11,* 40–51.

Sparrow, S.S., Balla, D.A., & Cichette, D.V. (1984). *Vineland Adaptive Behavior Scales: Survey form manual.* Circle Pines, MN: American Guidance Service.

Streng, A., & Kirk, S. (1938). The social competence of deaf and hard of hearing children in public day-school. *American Annals of the Deaf, 83,* 244. [Used Vineland Social Maturity Scale.]

TEST REVIEW 13

Wide Range Achievement Test, Revised Edition (WRAT-R)

Publisher   Jastak Associates, Inc.
P.O. Box 4460
Wilmington, DE 19807

Cost   (1989) $12.00 for 25 tests, $20.00 for manual, $2.00 for monograph on content validity; cash orders postpaid.

Date of Publication   1984.

Competencies Assessed   Measures basic educational skills of reading, spelling, and arithmetic. Reading includes recognizing and naming letters and pronouncing printed words; spelling includes copying marks resembling letters, writing name, and printing words; arithmetic includes counting, reading number symbols, and oral and written computation.

Population Characteristics   Ages 5–11, 12 and over.

Recommended Uses   Can be used for educational placement, measuring school achievement, vocational assessment, job training and placement.

Test Content and Format   3 scores: spelling, arithmetic, reading; 2 levels: Level 1 for ages 5–11 and Level 2 for ages 12 and over; individual administration in part with provision for group administration of some parts under specific conditions. In order to address those young or mentally retarded individuals for whom even the easier items of the regular test would be too difficult, an oral section is provided, to be used below a specified age or for examinees who do poorly on the regular test. Subtests may be administered in any order.

Administration Time 15–30 minutes, 10 minutes for each subtest.

Skills/Materials Required Record booklet for both levels; manual; test. Optional word lists for both levels of the reading and spelling tests are offered on plastic cards, and a recorded pronunciation of the lists is provided on cassette tape. The tape itself can be used to administer the spelling section. A one-level edition is available for clinicians and teachers who are willing to spend more time in testing in order to be able to analyze error patterns. A large print edition is available for those who require magnification of reading material.

Derived Scores/Information Grade equivalents, standard scores, and percentiles are available.

Norming/Standardization Practices The WRAT-R was standardized using a stratified national sample technique; 5,600 individuals were included in the norms, including 200 people in each of the 28 age groups from 5 years, 0 months to 74 years, 11 months. No deaf norms have been established.

Reliability Both internal consistency and test-retest reliabilities appear to be adequate. Test-retest reliability coefficients were determined on a selected number of individuals from the normative sample. Test-retest reliabilities for Level 1 (ages 7.0 to 7.5 and 10.0 to 10.5) were .96 for reading, .97 for spelling, and .94 for arithmetic. For Level 2 (ages 13.0 to 13.5 and 16.0 to 16.5) they were .90, .89, and .79 for the areas above, respectively.

Validity Content, construct, and concurrent validity are reported. In terms of concurrent validity, correlations of the WRAT with the Peabody Individual Achievement Test (PIAT), the California Achievement Test, and the Stanford Achievement Test are reported. However, no validity studies are reported employing the WRAT-R, but it is very similar in content to previous editions of the test, and results of previous studies may still be applicable. Some comparisons of the WRAT-R and earlier editions of the WRAT are provided, but on close reading these appear to be of questionable appropriateness.

Comments The WRAT-R should be used only as a screening instrument for the determination of a global achievement level. Restricted item content and high intercorrelations among the subtests render it unsuitable for use as a diagnostic tool in the identification of specific skill deficits. Its desirable features are that it can be administered and scored easily and quickly, and it is an acceptable alternative to group administered achievement tests. The WRAT-R is an age normed test, meaning that each individual taking the WRAT-R can have his or her score compared with an age group of individuals who are representative of the national population. The WRAT-R may be inappropriate for many hearing impaired persons. Most subtests are administered orally and therefore discriminate against hearing impaired people who rely on sign language or other visual cues. In addition, the lack of hearing impaired norms limits comparison and interpretation of individual results (Zieziula, 1982, p.19).

References and Suggested Readings

Bonham, S.J., Jr. (1963). *Predicting achievement for deaf children (Dayton City School District)*. Columbus: Ohio State Department of Education.

Covin, T.M., & Lubimiv, A.J. (1976). Concurrent validity of the WRAT. *Perceptual and motor skills*, *43*(2), 573–574.

Dillon, J.E. (1973). Performance characteristics of four special education subgroups on the WISC, BVMGT, HFD, WRAT, and experimental scales (Doctoral thesis, University of Northern Colorado, Greeley). *Dissertation Abstracts International*, *34*, 189A.

Washington, E.D., & Teska, J.A. (1970). Relations between the Wide Range Achievement Test, the California Achievement Test, the Stanford-Binet, and the Illinois Test of Psycholinguistic Abilities. *Psychological Reports*, *26*, 291–294.

Woodward, C.A., Santa-Barbara, J., & Roberts, R. (1975). Test-retest reliability of the Wide Range Achievement Test. *Journal of Clinical Psychology*, *31*(1), 81–84.

Zieziula, F.R. (Ed.). (1982). *Assessment of hearing-impaired people*. Washington, DC: Gallaudet College Press.

TEST REVIEW 14

Wide Range Interest-Opinion Test (WRIOT), 1979 Edition

Publisher Jastak Associates, Inc.
P.O. Box 4460
Wilmington, DE 19807

Cost (1989) $27.00 for manual, $15.00 for picture book, $15.00 for 50 answer sheets, $45.00 for set of answer keys.

Date of Publication 1979.

Competencies Assessed   Vocational interests and attitudes.

Population Characteristics   Grades K–12 and adults, unskilled labor to the highest levels of technical, managerial, and professional training.

Recommended Uses   Designed to be used with learning disabled, mentally retarded, deaf and other special populations. Does not require reading ability.

Test Content and Format   WRIOT is a pictorial interest test that is designed to be culturally and sexually unbiased. It does not require reading or language understanding. Pictorial presentation reduces the confusion of mental images and multiple meanings that words evoke. It contains a reusable booklet containing 150 sets of 3 pictures each, from which likes and dislikes are picked by forced choice and recorded by the test taker on an answer sheet. The test can be individually or group administered, but individual administration is necessary for persons who are too limited by age, mental ability, or physical limitations to complete the answer sheet with written responses.

Administration Time   40 minutes (individual), 50–60 minutes (group).

Skills/Materials Required   Test booklet, answer sheet, scoring stencils. D.A. Farrugia (1981) is developing administration procedures for hearing impaired people.

Derived Scores/Information   Results are presented on a report form that graphically shows an individual's strength of interest in each of the 18 interest clusters as well as 8 more general attitude clusters. This report form can be given to the client for vocational counseling purposes.

Norming/Standardization Practices   Normed on 9,184 persons divided into seven age groups from age 5 through adulthood, separate for males and females. No deaf norms have been reported.

Reliability   Grade/age levels are not reported. Split-half reliabilities for the 26 scales reported for 150 males and 150 females (other sample characteristics unreported) ranged from .82 to .95. Test-retest reliability is not reported.

Validity   Authors report limited evidence (interscale correlations with the Geist) based on 55 males and 45 females to support the construct validity of the WRIOT. Predictive validity is not reported.

Comments   Deaf students, according to Botterbusch (1976, p. 63), should be able to take the WRIOT with little or no change in test materials. For students who have problems reading the directions on the answer sheet, the method of giving directions would have to be changed, and additional practice exercises may be needed. The WRIOT has received much criticism from test reviewers (e.g., Zytowski, 1978, for the 1972 edition; Hsu [1985] and Manuele [1985] for the 1979 revised edition). Hsu (1985) found the WRIOT "unacceptable for any but research uses because of (1) ambiguity of constructs and [nonindependent] T scores resulting from the presence of extensive item overlap of the different clusters, (2) possible ambiguity of stimulus materials, especially for members of the targeted 'special' populations, (3) virtual absence of evidence of reliability and validity, especially for members of the special populations, (4) inadequacy of norms for the special populations, and (5) absence of objective methods of matching profiles with occupations" (p. 1738).

References and Suggested Readings

Botterbusch, K.F. (1976). *The use of psychological tests with individuals who are severely disabled.* Menomonie: University of Wisconsin-Stout, Stout Vocational Rehabilitation Institute, Materials Development Center.

Farrugia, D.A. (1981). *A study of deaf high school students' vocational interests and attitudes.* Unpublished doctoral dissertation, Northern Illinois University, De Kalb.

Farrugia, D.L. (1982). Deaf high school students' vocational interests and attitudes. *American Annals of the Deaf, 127,* 753–762. (ERIC Document Reproduction Service No. EJ 274 382)

Hsu, L.M. (1985). Wide Range Interest-Opinion Test. In J.V. Mitchell, Jr. (Ed.), *The ninth mental measurements yearbook* (pp. 1737–1739, Ms. No. 1366). Lincoln, NE: Buros Institute of Mental Measurement.

Jastak, J.F., & Jastak, S. (1979). *Wide Range Interest-Opinion Test.* Wilmington, DE: Jastak Associates.

Manuele, C.A. (1985). Wide Range Interest-Opinion Test. In J.V. Mitchell, Jr. (Ed.), *The ninth mental measurements yearbook* (pp. 1739–1740, Ms. No. 1366). Lincoln, NE: Buros Institute of Mental Measurement.

Zytowski, D.G. (1978). Wide Range Interest-Opinion Test. In O.K. Buros (Ed.), *The eighth mental measurements yearbook* (pp. 1641–1643, Ms. No. 1029). Highland Park, NJ: Gryphon Press.

Rehabilitation and Special Education Programs Enrolling Deaf High School Students

9

The focus of this chapter is the relationship of state rehabilitation agencies and special education programs enrolling severely and profoundly hearing impaired high school students in grades 9 through 12. The information reported in this chapter was collected in a survey of these programs during the 1986–1987 school year and describes the relationship from their viewpoint at that particular time. Although the data do not represent all the programs from which the student and counselor data described elsewhere in this book (Chapters 4, 5, 6, and 7) were gathered, there is a large overlap between these data sources: 68% of the programs sending in student/counselor information to the survey office also responded to the survey questionnaire whose results are described in this chapter.

After a brief description of the historical relationship of vocational rehabilitation (VR) agencies to special schools educating deaf students and of the survey instrument and methodology, the remainder of the chapter presents the results of the survey and discusses their relevance to the transition of deaf students from high school into their postsecondary careers. (Although "rehabilitation" is a much broader process than the strictly vocational, in this chapter "vocational rehabilitation," "rehabilitation," and "rehabilitation agencies or offices" are used interchangeably.)

HISTORICAL PERSPECTIVE

No study of the relationship between state rehabilitation agencies and education for deaf students would be complete without at least a brief mention of the role vocational education has played in the special schools for deaf students. There has been a long history of systematic vocational training in these residential and day schools in the United States. (References in the early literature to the vocational training of deaf students being educated outside the special school system—in what are called "local programs" in this chapter—are more difficult to find.) The involvement of state rehabilitation agencies with these special schools is a much more recent phenomenon.

Special Schools and Vocational Training

From their beginnings in the early 19th century, special schools for deaf students have been steadily committed to what they variously called "vocational or industrial education," "manual training," "prevocational education," or "technical training." The large number of references to these subjects in the early indices of the *American Annals of the Deaf* makes abundantly clear the major role vocational education played in the minds of educators of these students. In a 1917 *Annals* the claim is made that schools for deaf students have been "pioneers" in "the most prominent trend in modern educational thought, industrial training," and that officials from the regular or "common-school system" have visited these special schools to study the vocational curriculum being taught there (Fay, 1917, p. 101). A 1922 issue of *Annals* (Fay, 1922, p. 13) lists 96 separate "industries" being taught in American schools for deaf students at that time, a catalog that includes "auto-repairing," "lace-making," and "photography." For the most part, training in specific trades or skills was what early special school educators of deaf students meant by "vocational education."

Nineteenth-century educators clearly recognized the need for their deaf students to be trained in vocational areas that would allow them to become independent and productive citizens (Carr, 1941). Quoting a 19th century school official, a history of the North Carolina School for the Deaf at Morganton indicates the purpose of vocational education: ". . . to give them [students] much instruction along industrial lines as will fit them to earn an independent living for themselves and families" (Betts, 1945, p. 52). The concern of these educators was more acute because of their keen realization of the severe communication difficulties and misunderstandings experienced by large numbers of deaf men and women in workplaces populated and supervised by hearing individuals.

Beginning especially in the early 20th century, there is a troubling contradiction in the relationship between vocational education in the special schools and the employment of deaf persons. Through much of the 19th century, the vocational curricula within residential and day schools for deaf students appear to have kept reasonably abreast of the industries and technologies developing during that period (Moores, 1969). Nevertheless, although accurate national employment results for the students of these schools are not readily available, there is some indication that unemployment among deaf persons was high and that the specific training given to many of these students had tenuous relationships to the occupations they acquired after leaving school. At the 1919 conference of superintendents and principals of American schools for the deaf, J. Stuart Morrison, superintendent of the Missouri School for the Deaf, asked: ". . . why teach trades to our deaf boys and girls when not more than ten per cent of them follow after leaving school the trades they are taught in school?" (1920, pp. 214–215). A 1934 Civil Works Administration Survey reported that only 55.6% of the 19,580 deaf and hard of hearing survey respondents who were seeking work were actually employed (Fusfeld, 1937). (This particular period in American history was, of course, one of high unemployment generally.) This survey also revealed a "wide discrepancy" for many hearing impaired workers between the vocational training in the school and the occupation obtained after school. A similar discrepancy was found in a Franklin County, Ohio, survey in the early 1940s; the survey concluded: " . . . the vocational training of the adult deaf has been inadequate" (Flood, 1943, p. 327). Certain vocational subject areas—printing, for one—seem to have had a better record in terms of matching the school's training with later employment after school (Betts, 1945).

As 20th century technology accelerated and diversified, it became increasingly difficult for the special schools to provide qualified staff and modern, state-of-the-art equipment to educate deaf high school youth in the technical fields and trades (Boatner, 1969; Moores, 1969), a condition noted almost 35 years earlier at a meeting of American instructors of deaf students (Fusfeld, 1933). This growing inability to adapt to the latest changes in technology and industry led many schools to experiment with other types of vocational education. Work-study or work-experience programs and on-the-job training were, in part, responses to the need to place deaf high school students in actual work positions in industry and business, where the latest technological advances and equipment could be utilized (Vernon, 1969).

Another vocational education model introduced into these schools was "career education," a concept stressed by former U.S. Commissioner of Education Sidney Marland, Jr., in the 1970s, but with roots in the early 20th century (Kett, 1982; Marland, 1971). As envisioned by its proponents, career education begins in the elementary grades and emphasizes general vocational preparation rather than specific occupational skills, with the latter training usually initiated in high school (Brolin, 1982; Rusch, Mithaug, & Flexer, 1986). Career education has been endorsed by the Conference of Educational Administrators Serving the Deaf who recommended that it be a "comprehensive . . . part of every educational program serving hearing-impaired students" (Lauritsen et al., 1985, p. 74). Work habits and the general attitude toward a career were to be "infused" throughout a school's curriculum rather than limited to a single class or subject area.

Thus, the traditional "industrial training" of specific skills, though still much in evidence in the special schools, has been supplemented and in some cases replaced by newer models of vocational and prevocational education. Chapter 6 discusses in more detail the specific vocational areas taught in the special schools in recent years.

Special Schools and Rehabilitation

Serious and systematic federal involvement in the rehabilitation movement began in the 20th century, receiving much of its momentum from the government's response to military casualties of two world wars and from the Great Society efforts and civil rights movement of the 1960s (Lassiter, 1972; Obermann, 1965; Whitten, 1957). Although the vocational or technical education taught in the special schools, discussed in the previous section, is not the same phenomenon as 20th century "vocational rehabilitation," the early 19th century introduction of a vocational emphasis in these schools was a harbinger of what would later become a collaboration between state rehabilitation agencies and schools educating deaf students.

The transition was not always a smooth one. A problem surfaced with an early 20th century ruling by the Federal Board for Vocational Education " . . . which in effect classifies the deaf with defectives and delinquents" ("*Resolutions,*" 1920, p. 271). The linking of "defectives and delinquents" reflected widespread popular opinion of the period associating deafness and other disabilities with potential criminality and including deaf persons among the "socially inadequate classes" (Walter, 1987, p. 10; see also Obermann, 1965, p. 8). Since early rehabilitation thinking within the federal government emphasized the potential outcome of "paid employment" as one of the criteria for offering services to a client, the board, by classifying deaf persons as "defectives," was effectively excluding them from rehabilitative assistance. As a more enlightened attitude toward disabilities emerged in society and as federal rehabilitation efforts broadened to include a wider range of disabled clients, this major obstacle impeding the relationship of the special schools to vocational rehabilitation gradually diminished.

A second problem in the relationship of these schools and rehabilitation involved the governmental policy of strict separation of education from rehabilitation. This policy was enunciated by J.W. Studebaker, former U.S. Commissioner of Education, in a 1936 statement citing federal rehabilitation legislation: " . . . the education of exceptional children should not be confused with vocational rehabilitation . . . This [federal legislation] precludes its use [i.e., funding] for the education of exceptional children or for the supervision of such education" (Fusfeld, 1936, p. 277). Since, as has been seen, the special schools had a long history of vocational training embedded in their educational curricula, this strict separation of school from rehabilitation created administrative and legal problems for some schools.

Although the concept of rehabilitation as an eligibility program and education as an entitlement program persists, the rigid wall erected between these two concepts has, to some extent, been eroded. There has been a broadening of the concept of rehabilitation beyond the strictly "vocational" and, under the prodding of federal legislation and legal strategies designed to secure entitlement to rehabilitation services, an extension of these services to a wider group of clients (Laski, 1979). This has happened to such an extent over the past 50 years that special schools in some areas have been able to locate state rehabilitation counselors on their campuses. It is not so clear whether this lowering of the wall between special education and rehabilitation has extended to all special schools or to the education programs for disabled students in the local school systems. (Perhaps because the organizational lines of authority in the special schools are sharper and have a longer tradition than those in the local programs, there appears to be greater freedom in arriving at accommodations among special education staff and vocational educators within these special schools and the rehabilitation counselors providing services to their students.)

Although these early issues regarding the relationship between the schools educating deaf students and VR were eventually resolved, a more general malaise set in and has clouded the relationship between special education and rehabilitation, affecting not only schools for deaf students but other educational institutions for disabled individuals. The high hopes for the collaboration of special education and rehabilitation agencies inaugurated by federal legislation for previously underserved segments of the American population and by various reform movements were gradually tempered during the period following 1950 (Tooman, 1986). Inflated expectations, turf battles, administrative boondoggles, and plain incompetency often led to antagonism between educators and rehabilitation staff and counselors.

Tooman (1986) captures this mood of mutual antagonism and suspicion by quoting a teacher in special education and a VR counselor:

> Special education personnel have built in the past and continue to build tremendous . . . anger [toward VR] as they see the fruits of their labors essentially going down the tubes . . . .

> Vocational rehabilitation counselors and administrators talk about the inappropriate expectations of school personnel . . . that special education people haven't equipped their students for the real world . . . schools only refer to vocational rehabilitation those that they can't place themselves. (p. 13)

Although the pessimistic picture just sketched relates to the overall relationship between rehabilitation and special education, a very similar situation has been noted between these two agencies serving deaf individuals in both the special schools and in local programs. The 1967 Las Cruces National Conference for Coordinating Rehabilitation and Education Services for the Deaf (Ott, 1967) detailed many of the problems confronting educators and rehabilitation counselors and their relationships with one another. Garretson (1969) quotes Boyce Williams, a distinguished leader in the deaf community and formerly an official in the Rehabilitation Services Administration:

> The fact is that neither . . . education nor rehabilitation work for the deaf can be proud . . . The persistent failure of both education and rehabilitation to mount dynamic developmental and corrective action . . . must . . . be a cause for deep anguish among all true professionals. (pp. 7, 9)

It is within this larger historical context of the relationships among the special schools and vocational education and rehabilitation that the present survey was conducted.

SURVEY METHODOLOGY AND INSTRUMENT

Annual Survey of Hearing Impaired Children and Youth

The data reported in this chapter are based on a survey of special education programs enrolling deaf students during the 1986–1987 school year. A list of these programs has been compiled since 1968 by the Center for Assessment and Demographic Studies in its Annual Survey of Hearing Impaired Children and Youth. Each year the center contacts all special education programs known to enroll hearing impaired students at the preschool, elementary, and high school levels and asks them to complete a questionnaire on the demographic, audiological, and education-related characteristics of each of their students. These programs may be a single special school entirely devoted to the education of deaf students, a school district with hearing impaired students dispersed in special education programs at regular schools with hearing students, or a single regular/local school educating both hearing and hearing impaired students. The Annual Survey list of programs is updated each year through contact with the special education directors in each state who are asked to eliminate defunct programs and add newly established ones to the list. (Since the Annual Survey is completely voluntary, its data file does not include *all* hearing impaired students receiving special education services in the United States.)

Chapter 4 in this book discusses in detail how representative Annual Survey data are of the total population of hearing impaired children and youth receiving special education services in the United States. A quotation from that chapter summarizes the argument for the representative quality of the Annual Survey data:

> . . . although there is not a complete overlap of the Annual Survey and the 'child count' numbers [reported to the federal government each year by the states] . . . the Annual Survey data file represents a sizable majority of the hearing impaired students receiving special education services in the United States. (this volume, Chapter 4, p. 59)

The reader is referred to Chapter 4 for a fuller description of the Annual Survey of Hearing Impaired Children and Youth.

Program Survey

The Program Survey was drafted by center staff after discussion with vocational and rehabilitation personnel at Gallaudet University and at high school programs for deaf students. The survey form resulting from these discussions was reviewed by staff in several schools, and a final form was then developed (see Appendix A at the end of this book).

In January, 1987, the Center for Assessment and Demographic Studies sent this questionnaire to all Annual Survey programs, requesting information on their enrollment of severely and profoundly hearing impaired students in grades 9 through 12 and on the services provided by the state rehabilitation agencies to these students. Of the 1,452 programs on the Annual Survey list, 881 responded to this survey. Of these 881 programs, 518 indicated they had deaf (i.e., severely and profoundly hearing impaired) students enrolled during the 1986–1987 school year in grades 9 through 12.

The 518 programs represent 49 states, the District of Columbia, and the territory of Guam. The total high school enrollment of deaf youth reported by these 518 programs was 8,534: 5,203 in 75 special schools, either residential or day, for deaf students; and 3,331 in 443 special education programs at the local level. These latter students were either in self-contained classrooms full time with other deaf students or in partially integrated classes with hearing students for some of their schoolwork. Thus, although the special schools accounted for only 14% of the 518 programs in this study, they reported 61% of the total high school enrollment of deaf students in these programs. Implications of this difference in the enrollment of the two program types and limitations of this survey are delineated in the "Discussion" and "Summary" sections of this chapter.

Table 9.1. Relationship between state rehabilitation agencies (VR) and 518 programs enrolling severely and profoundly hearing impaired high school students as reported by programs: By type of program and by number of students enrolled, 1986–1987 school year

Relationship	% of programs by program type[a]		% of local programs by number of students enrolled[a]		
	Special schools	Local programs	1	2–10	11 or more
VR provides services	(N=75) 89%	(N=432) 74%	(N=96) 57%	(N=211) 74%	(N=98) 89%
VR initiates contact with program	(N=75) 75%	(N=419) 47%	(N=92) 38%	(N=206) 44%	(N=95) 61%
If VR initiates contact, *when?*	(N=59)	(N=206)	(N=32)	(N=95)	(N=65)
Grade 9	31%	14%	22%	12%	9%
Grade 10	20%	24%	25%	27%	20%
Grade 11	27%	36%	25%	37%	43%
Grade 12	22%	26%	28%	24%	28%
No contact or unknown	(N=15)	(N=238)			
VR visited program in 1986–1987 school year	(N=74) 89%	(N=428) 52%	(N=91) 31%	(N=212) 49%	(N=98) 80%
VR counselor signs and students sign[b]	(N=64) 95%	(N=180) 70%	(N=17) 41%	(N=86) 65%	(N=70) 83%
VR has formal written arrangement with program	(N=72) 39%	(N=396) 17%	(N=88) 8%	(N=191) 20%	(N=94) 17%

[a]Enrollment of severely and profoundly hearing impaired high school students in the 75 *special schools* represented in this table was 5,203 for the 1986–1987 school year; the 443 *local programs* enrolled 3,331 students. Four special schools and 17 local programs did not report enrollment. *N*s vary due to missing data.

[b]Programs in which students do not sign are excluded from the calculations.

SURVEY RESULTS

Table 9.1 presents the results of the Program Survey, giving an overall picture of the schools' relationship to the state rehabilitation agencies. This picture sketches only a general outline of the relationship, presenting it, as indicated earlier, from the schools' perspectives. Furthermore, this picture does not include information on the work of other critical agencies and participants in the rehabilitation process (e.g., departments of mental health, family services, family members, friends, and employers) (Halpern, 1985; Sanderson, 1982; Szymanski & Danek, 1985). For deaf persons, the deaf community—what Halpern, in the general context of transition, calls the "social and interpersonal networks" (p. 481)—can be an extremely important source of support in the transition process.

Table 9.1 displays percentage responses to the survey questions for those programs indicating they enrolled deaf high school students. In columns 1 and 2 these programs are grouped according to two types: the special schools, residential or day, in column 1; and the local programs in column 2. A second classification of the 443 local programs—in columns 3, 4, and 5—groups the programs by number of deaf students enrolled, beginning in column 3 with those enrolling only one deaf student to the last category in column 5, those enrolling 11 or more deaf students. (Only three local programs in this survey reported a high school enrollment of over 40 deaf students.) Since program type may be a surrogate for program size in this study (i.e., special schools tend to have larger student enrollments than local programs), the second classification by enrollment in Table 9.1 (columns 3, 4, and 5) does not include the special schools. The analyses by program type and size of enrollment are based on previous studies indicating an apparent relationship between these two variables and the provision of services to handicapped students (e.g., Fairweather, 1988; Spragins, Karchmer, & Schildroth, 1981).

Provision of VR Services

The Program Survey asked the special education program if vocational rehabilitation provided services to its deaf students to prepare them for the transition from high school to work or to postsecondary education. As Table 9.1 shows, a large majority of both the special schools (89%) and the local programs (74%) answered affirmatively to this question. These percentages represent a total of 388 programs with an enrollment of almost 7,500 deaf students for whom vocational rehabilitation was providing some transition services.

An examination of those programs for whom VR did *not* provide transition services is also instructive. There were 119 programs in this category, with a total high school enrollment of 839 deaf students: 8 special schools and 111 local programs. Although this is almost one quarter of the 518 programs participating in the survey, it represents only 10% of deaf student enrollment in these programs, an indication that the programs reporting no VR services tended to be those with small deaf student enrollments in high school.

The data in Table 9.1 support this conclusion. Only 57% of the local programs enrolling one deaf high school student reported VR provision of services, compared to 89% for programs with 11 or more of these students. The eight special schools reporting no rehabilitation services had a deaf high school enrollment of 286, with one large special school accounting for 81% of this total.

Regionally, the Midwest reported the highest percentage of VR services (83%) for their deaf high school students, regardless of program type or size of enrollment. VR availability was lowest in the West (68%), due largely to the higher percentage of local programs reporting no rehabilitation services than in the other three regions of the country. In the South only 1 of 24 special schools reported no VR services for its deaf high school students.

Initiation of VR Services

A follow-up question to that regarding provision of VR services for deaf high school students asked about the initiation of these services by vocational rehabilitation. Responses were quite different for the special schools and for the local programs; 75% of the former reported VR initiated contact, compared to only 47% of the latter. Just over 5% of both the special schools and the local programs answered this question by a write-in response, indicating that the school had to initiate the contact with VR.

When information reported by the local programs on this question is analyzed in terms of deaf student enrollment, the larger programs appear to have an advantage over smaller programs. Only 38% of the local programs enrolling one deaf high school student reported VR initiation of services; the percentage rises to 44% for schools enrolling 2–10 deaf students, and to 61% for schools with 11 or more deaf students.

For those schools indicating an initiation of contact by VR, a second question was asked regarding the time of this initial contact. In general, the special schools indicated an earlier time of contact than did the local programs. Thirty-one percent of the residential and day schools reported VR contact in grade 9, compared to only 14% of the local programs. Freshman year was most often cited by the special schools for contact with VR; for the local programs, junior year was most frequently reported.

When program size is examined—columns 3, 4, and 5 of Table

9.1—the two smaller enrollment categories within the local programs, somewhat surprisingly, reported an earlier initiation of these services than did the larger schools. Forty-seven percent of local programs with only one deaf student indicated initiation of rehabilitation services in grades 9 or 10, compared to only 29% of the programs with 11 or more deaf students. Nevertheless, grade 12 was the typical year for initiation of VR services in the programs with only one deaf student; for the two larger student enrollment categories grade 11 was the most frequently reported.

Campus Visits by VR

The schools were asked about VR visits or plans to visit the school campus during the 1986–1987 school year. The results of this question, classified by type of school and enrollment size, are displayed in Table 9.1. (One distinct advantage of some special schools, especially of the residential type, is that they have a rehabilitation counselor located at the school.)

Almost 90% of the special schools reported a visit or a planned visit by the rehabilitation counselor to the school during the 1986–1987 school year. Fifty-two percent of the local programs indicated this type of VR contact. Viewed from an enrollment perspective, the larger local programs reported a better record of VR school visitation than did the smaller programs: only 31% of the programs with one deaf student reported a VR visit to the school, compared to 80% for the large programs enrolling 11 or more deaf students.

Communication with Students by VR

As indicated earlier, communication is a critical factor in the provision of services to deaf students (Schein, 1980). Lack of communication and misunderstandings can undermine the best of intentions and frustrate the efforts of both counselors and their clients. The Program Survey requested information on the rehabilitation counselor's ability to communicate by the use of sign language. If a program's deaf students did not sign, the program was asked to indicate that fact in its response to this question. Those programs indicating no need for a rehabilitation counselor who signed are excluded from the calculations in Table 9.1. The questionnaire did not inquire about the quality of the signing or of other equally important communicative qualities of the counselor.

A large majority of the special schools in the United States have adopted a "total communication" system in educating their deaf students (i.e., a system using both speech and sign) (Schildroth, 1988). It is not surprising, therefore, to find that almost all special schools in this survey have been assigned a rehabilitation counselor able to use sign language.

Over 95% of these special schools fell into this category. A large majority of local programs (70%) with signing students also had a rehabilitation counselor able to communicate through sign language.

Those local programs enrolling smaller numbers of deaf students were the least likely to have a counselor with signing ability. Only 61% of the 103 programs enrolling between 1 and 10 deaf students able to sign reported a counselor also able to sign.

Formal Written Arrangement with VR

The need for cooperative agreements between VR and other agencies serving deaf persons, including special education, has long been recognized. The report from the 1967 Las Cruces conference of rehabilitation and education professionals (Ott, 1967) and the *Model State Plan for Rehabilitation of Deaf Clients: Second Revision* (Schein, 1980) call for the establishment of such agreements. In order to ascertain the extent of these arrangements in programs for deaf high school students, programs were asked about the existence of a "formal WRITTEN cooperative arrangement" between the program and vocational rehabilitation "for providing services to deaf high school students in the transition from high school to work or . . . to postsecondary education" (Appendix A, this volume, p. 237). Survey results for this question are displayed in Table 9.1.

The percentage of affirmative answers to this question was much lower for all program types and enrollment categories in Table 9.1 than to the other questions on the survey form. The special schools, at 39%, reported this arrangement more frequently than did the local programs (17%); the two larger local program categories had such agreements more often than did programs with only one student. Regionally, special schools in the South reported this arrangement more frequently (46%) than did the residential and day schools of the other three regions. Less than 20% of the local programs in all four regions indicated involvement in such formal collaboration with VR.

Specific Services Provided by VR

The programs also were asked about specific services provided by the state rehabilitation agency to their deaf students. Eleven services were listed on the survey form, with an additional option for the program to write in "other" services. (See Appendix A, "Program Survey," item 7). (Only 30 programs reported the "other" service category, with "provision of interpreter services" being the most frequently cited.) Local tradition and interpretation of the law may have considerable influence on provision of these specific services.

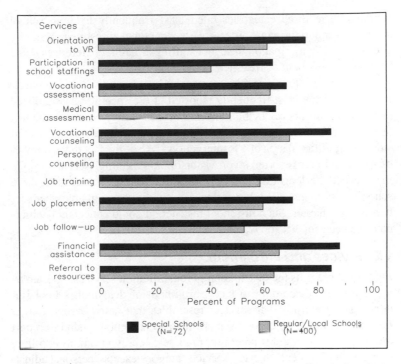

Figure 9.1. Rehabilitation services reported by programs enrolling deaf students, 1986–1987 school year.

VR Services in Special Schools and Local Programs

Figure 9.1 shows the response pattern to this question for the special schools and the local programs. In each of the specific service categories (in Figure 9.1, these appear in abbreviated form as compared to the actual Program Survey) the special residential and day schools for deaf students reported a higher rate of assistance from state rehabilitation agencies than did the local programs. The widest discrepancies in the reporting of specific rehabilitation services between the two program types involved "participation in school staffings, parent conferences," "financial assistance for postsecondary education," and "referral to appropriate community resources." In these three service categories, the special schools were 21 to 23 percentage points higher than the local programs.

The three services cited most frequently as being provided by VR were the same for both the special schools and the local programs: "financial assistance for postsecondary education," "individual career/vocational counseling," and "referral to appropriate community resources." The three categories cited least frequently by both school systems—and in the same order—were: "personal adjustment or family counseling," "participation in school staffings, parent conferences," and "medical assessment or treatment."

Failure of VR to provide "personal adjustment or family counseling"—by far the least frequently reported of the specific services listed on the Program Survey by both program types—may be due to the fact that this service, although obviously important, has not always been considered a traditional area of VR intervention. Also, the fact that a number of special schools reported no provision of "job training" services by VR may reflect the long tradition of vocational/technical training in these schools prior to any VR intervention, a topic discussed in an earlier section of this chapter. Such in-school instruction could conceivably eliminate the need for VR job training services.

VR Services and Enrollment

Figure 9.2 presents the distribution of rehabilitation services reported by local programs according to their enrollment of deaf high school students. The pattern of VR services resembles that noted earlier: Larger programs (i.e., those enrolling more than 10 students) tended to report more services than did smaller programs, especially programs enrolling only one deaf student. In every service category except "personal adjustment or family counseling," programs enrolling more than 10 deaf students reported VR assistance more often than did those enrolling only one deaf student, with an average difference of 23 percentage points in favor of the larger programs. However, the pattern is not as pronounced in regard to programs enrolling between 2 and 10 students, and in several service categories ("participation in school staffings, parent conferences" and "vocational assessment through performance tests, work samples") programs enrolling between 2 and 10 deaf high school students reported slightly higher percentages than did the larger local programs.

For programs enrolling under 11 deaf students, "individual career/vocational counseling" and "vocational assessment through performance tests, work samples" were the two rehabilitation services most frequently specified. For the larger programs, "financial assistance for postsecondary education" and "referral to appropriate community resources" were most frequently reported. As illustrated in Figure 9.1, "personal adjustment or family counseling" and "participation in school staffings, parent conferences" were the services cited least frequently for all three enrollment categories. The largest discrepancy between the larger programs and the two smaller program types occurred for "financial assistance for postsecondary education"; 87% of the programs enrolling 11 or more deaf high school students reported this service, compared to 46% for those

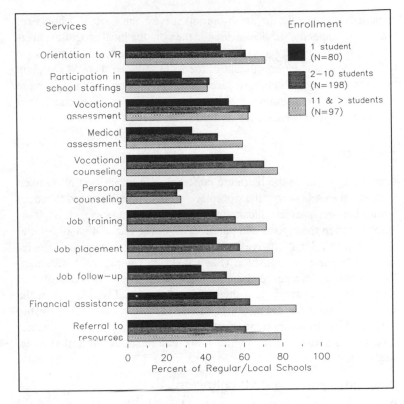

Figure 9.2. Rehabilitation services reported by regular/local programs enrolling deaf students, 1986–1987 school year.

with only one student and 63% for those enrolling between 2 and 10 students.

Number of VR Services Provided

Although the number of services provided is no assurance of the quality of those services, it can give some indication of the extent of VR involvement in the school system. In the 1988 report by the U.S. Department of Education on the number of anticipated services required by handicapped youth leaving the secondary schools, the hard of hearing and deaf group —including deaf-blind—are second only to multihandicapped students in the average number of services needed per student, services that include transitional employment assistance, vocational training and placement, and postemployment services (Office of Special Education and Rehabilitative Services, 1988). Since the department lumps together anticipated services for deaf *and* hard of hearing youth, the estimate of services needed is undoubtedly conservative in regard to deaf students considered separately. In the Program Survey, the special schools reported more specific services available than did the local programs, averaging 8.6 services, compared to 7.1 services for the local programs. In terms of deaf student enrollment in the local schools, there is a slightly higher rate of rehabilitation services within the schools with 11 or more students. The average number of services available for these schools was 7.6, compared to 6.9 for each of the two smaller enrollment categories.

DISCUSSION

A recurring topic in the literature concerning the transition of disabled students from school into the workplace is the compelling need for cooperation between special education and rehabilitation agencies. It is a topic emphasized in the reports and publications of the U.S. Office of Special Education and Rehabilitative Services (1986, 1987), as well as in the research literature on transition (Szymanski & Danek, 1985; Tooman, 1986; Wehman, Kregel, & Barcus, 1985; Will, 1985). In terms of deaf high school students, it is a theme played over and over again in the periodic conferences and meetings convened to examine the relationship between these two important agencies. The data reported in this chapter reflect this relationship in the mid-1980s and raise several important issues for the transition of deaf students.

Program Type and Rehabilitation

Perhaps the most important issue raised by the data reported here is that concerning program type. The responses to certain questions in this survey indicate that there is widespread collaboration between special education programs—both the special schools and the local programs—and rehabilitation agencies in the transition experience of their deaf high school students. A large majority of both types of education programs in this survey reported that VR provides transitional services to their students. A majority of both program types—though less so for the local programs—also indicated that a rehabilitation counselor visited or planned to visit them during the school year. Over 90% of the special schools and 70% of the local programs reported that the counselor assigned to their signing deaf students was able to sign. Job placement and job follow-up after placement, two of the more important and exacting duties of the rehabilitation counselor, were offered in over 50% of both program types.

However, if it is true that a more active participation and involvement by rehabilitation with the special education program can facilitate the transition of disabled students, then the picture captured in the data presented here appears to favor the special school setting: greater provision of rehabilitation services, more frequent and earlier initiation by VR in providing transition services, more visits by VR to special schools, a higher percentage of signing rehabilitation counselors for students using this method of communication, more specific services offered, and a greater percentage of special schools having formal agreements with VR. In several important specific service areas—shown in Figure 9.1—a substantially higher percentage of special schools reported VR provision of such services than did the local programs.

It is difficult to say why this advantage for the special schools exists. But whatever the reasons—their long history of vocational education, their ties to the deaf community, perhaps even their stable roots in a single geographic location for a long time—the conclusion from the data presented here confirms that of another recent study of state special education and rehabilitation coordinators by Sendelbaugh and Bullis (1988): " . . . more transition planning with VR occurs in residential schools [for deaf students] than in mainstreamed programs" (p. 19).

This finding takes on greater significance in light of an important ongoing shift in the educational placement of deaf students. Schildroth (1988) has documented this change over the past decade: the steep decline in enrollment in special schools for deaf students, especially in the residential schools where enrollment has dropped by one third between 1978 and 1987, and a corresponding increase in enrollment of these students in local programs. Through a variety of causes—including social and philosophical changes in thinking about the education of disabled students; demographic changes within the United States; and legislative enactment, especially PL 94-142 with its mandate for placement of handicapped children in the "least restrictive environment"—the century-and-a-half dominance of special residential and day schools as the primary educational environment for deaf students appears to be waning in favor of local school education in mainstream settings. At some point a "critical enrollment mass" will almost certainly be reached in a number of these special schools, and economic realities will dictate their closing or a change in their operation; the latter situation has already occurred in at least one long-established school, the Pennsylvania School for the Deaf, whose high school department has been closed.

The special schools have traditionally enrolled students with more severe hearing impairments than have the local programs. They also enroll large numbers of minority and multihandicapped children and youth and many students with academic deficits, especially in reading (Allen, 1986; Schildroth, 1988)—precisely those students in greatest need of educational and rehabilitative transition services.

If the changing placement pattern just described continues and there is an influx of deaf students into local school systems, then careful attention must be given toward strengthening the relationship of the local programs with rehabilitation agencies. This will be a difficult task, since the dispersion of these students into the local programs will often mean the assignment of rehabilitation counselors to multiple school locations instead of a single special school location. Much of the relationship of rehabilitation to the local programs will depend on how the local school system structures its education of deaf high school students, which in turn may depend on the urban/rural make-up of the school district. (More is said of this point in the next section of this chapter.) Perhaps even more, it will also depend on the quality of the training given to the rehabilitation counselors working with these students. The fact that 30% of the local programs with students using sign language did not have a signing counselor is not an encouraging indication of the communication training of these counselors.

There is one more point to be emphasized in regard to program type. As indicated earlier, although the special schools represent only 14% of the 518 programs in this study, they enrolled 61% of the deaf high school students reported by the 518 programs. Since one finding of this study indicates a better relationship between the special schools and rehabilitation, the reader may conclude that a large majority of deaf high school students are in these special schools where such a relationship exists. This conclusion would not be accurate.

Special school participation in the Annual Survey of Hearing Impaired Children and Youth has always been high. Local program participation, however, has been more difficult to achieve. These latter programs are more geographically dispersed than the long-established special schools; they change addresses and come in and out of existence, with the consequence that their participation in the Annual Survey is less extensive and more irregular than the special schools. Thus, in the Program Survey described in this chapter, which used the Annual Survey program list, there is also a more complete representation of the special schools than of the local programs. In the total deaf high school enrollment across the nation, there is a larger number of deaf high school students enrolled in these local programs than this Program Survey would lead one to believe. During the 1986–1987 school year, for example, there were 4,506 severely and profoundly hearing impaired students in the 14 through 21 age bracket reported to the Annual Survey from the local programs (compared to 5,761 of these students reported from the special schools). If more of the local programs had participated in the Program Survey, the larger number of deaf high school students in such programs would be evident.

Enrollment Size of Local Programs and VR

The data according to the number of deaf students enrolled in the local programs participating in the Program Survey were also examined. (Special schools, generally larger programs, were discussed in the previous section and are excluded from the analysis here.) The local programs were placed into one of three categories: those enrolling only one deaf student, those with 2 through 10 deaf students, and those with 11 or more deaf students.

In general, the data present a more favorable picture for the larger local programs in their relationship with VR than for those with smaller deaf student enrollments, especially those with only one deaf student. In each of the following areas, schools enrolling 11 or more deaf students reported higher percentages than the two smaller program categories: provision of rehabilitation transition services, VR initiation of contact with the school, VR visits to the school, rehabilitation counselor ability to sign with students who sign, and average number of specific services provided by rehabilitation. (Programs with one deaf student reported an earlier intervention by VR, but the frequencies for these programs tend to be small; the resulting percentages, therefore, may not represent an accurate picture of the situation in these schools.)

The issue raised by this finding is connected to the previous discussion of changes occurring in the educational placement of deaf students. With the decline in enrollment in the special schools, these students are more often being placed in local programs. Because deafness is a low-incidence disability, many of these local programs, especially in more rural areas of the country, enroll few deaf youth, sometimes only one student. (In the 1986–1987 Annual Survey of Hearing Impaired Children and Youth, there were 4,387 individual schools enrolling a single hearing impaired student; almost 1,000 of these students had a severe or profound hearing loss.)

In light of the data presented here regarding enrollment size and provision of rehabilitation services, a question arises about the quantity and quality of rehabilitative services that can be provided deaf students in small programs, who require, as the Office of Special Education and Rehabilitative Services (1988) has reported, a large number of these services. This presents a challenge to all programs involved in the transition of deaf students into the workplace. In a special way the programs with small deaf student enrollments are challenged to take the initiative in ensuring that these students receive the services they need to make this transition. In some cases, this may require the local program or school district to consider enrollment at the state residential program or in a larger nearby central program that is better adapted and staffed to provide such services. In either case, the cost to the local program or school district may be considerably higher than strictly local school enrollment. It is a cost, however, that is not only justified by long-range benefits to the individual and to society as a whole but is also required by the law.

Thus, the data reported here bring to the fore a fundamental question beyond that of special education and rehabilitation. It is a question of how education of deaf students will be structured; because of the qualities associated with prelingual deafness and the special services required, this structure must differ from that for other disabilities. If deaf students are to be educated at the local level, then the structure of that education must take into consideration the distinctive needs and abilities of these students.

SUMMARY

There is a tension inherent to the relationship between special education and state rehabilitation agencies. On the one hand, special education staff wish to see an earlier participation of VR in high school transition planning for their deaf students. Of the 89 comments written in on the Program Survey forms, over one half in some way or other indicated that more timely VR intervention would benefit the transition process. The 1967 Las Cruces conference, mentioned previously in this chapter, called for this earlier contact: "It is felt that the deaf child would benefit if the cooperative effort [between the school and rehabilitation] was initiated at an earlier stage" (Ott, 1967, p. 19). A more recent conference on postsecondary education for hearing impaired students made the same plea (White, 1986). It would be strange, indeed, to find any disagreement in the literature on transition with such an obviously sound recommendation.

On the other hand, evidence from the written "Comments" section of the Program Survey indicates that high school programs for deaf students perceive that lack of earlier VR intervention into the transition process is due to a number of factors: legal or administrative limitations to this early involvement, VR budgetary restrictions, and/or rehabilitation counselor case overload. On many of the survey forms, schools indicated that VR could not or would not intervene in the transition process until after the students graduated from high school. There appears to be much latitude in this regard in various parts of the United States. In some special schools, because the school and VR belong to the same state department, there is a broad interpretation of the laws, the result being a close cooperation between the two service agencies. In other areas of the country, a much stricter separation of special education and rehabilitation is in evidence.

This tension between special education and rehabilitation makes one finding of this study—the widespread absence of a formal, written arrangement for transition services between the two agencies—especially regrettable. This formal arrangement relates to the cooperation between special education and rehabilitation in a way similar to the Individualized Written Rehabilitation Programs guiding the relationship between rehabilitation counselors and their clients. It is only through such an agreement that the services legally available to deaf persons can be clarified, specific objectives spelled out, and misunderstandings avoided. The *Model State Plan for Rehabilitation of Deaf Clients: Second Revision* (Schein, 1980) strongly supports this type of document. The advantages of such a formal arrangement have been confirmed in other studies (e.g., Hasazi et al., 1985). The confusion regarding transition responsibilities between special education and rehabilitation personnel noted in the Sendelbaugh and Bullis study (1988) is one result of the lack of such an agreement. The fact that considerably more than one half of the 518 programs participating in the Program Survey, both special schools and local programs, reported that such a plan did not exist or that they were unsure of its existence or had no knowledge of its existence will almost certainly ensure confusion and uncertainty in transition planning for deaf students.

The reader must be careful about drawing too many conclusions from a survey such as this that raises more questions than it answers. The limitations of this study have been discussed earlier but bear a brief repetition. The data presented here have been reported from programs educating deaf high school students. Other information—from rehabilitation administrators and counselors, from parents and other social agencies—needs to be collected and analyzed to provide a more complete picture of the transition of deaf students from school to work. Further, the survey questions analyzed in this chapter do not address the quality of rehabilitation services or any outcomes of these services (e.g., in terms of employment or independent living). It is possible, too, that the more complete reporting to the Program Survey by the special schools resulted in a more favorable picture of their relationship to rehabilitation than that of the local programs. It is also possible that because the special schools often enroll a somewhat different type of deaf student than do the local programs, the rehabilitative needs of the students in these two program types are somewhat different (e.g., financial assistance for postsecondary education versus job placement assistance).

Given these limitations, however, the data collected in this study reveal a consistent pattern for the variables included in this survey: The relationship between rehabilitation and special education for deaf high school students is better established and organized in the special schools than in the local programs, and in the larger local programs than in the smaller ones, especially those with only one deaf student. Whether this better relationship generally leads to more successful transitions for deaf students into their postsecondary careers needs further study.

REFERENCES

Allen, T. (1986). *Understanding the scores: Hearing-impaired students and the Stanford Achievement Test (7th Edition).* Washington, DC: Gallaudet College Press.

Betts, O.A. (1945). *The North Carolina School for the Deaf at Morganton, 1894–1944: The education of the deaf in North Carolina, 1845–1945.* Morganton: North Carolina School for the Deaf.

Boatner, E.B. (1969). The vocational rehabilitation program of the American School for the Deaf. *Journal of Rehabilitation of the Deaf, 3,* 69–79

Brolin, D.E. (1982). *Vocational preparation of persons with handicaps.* Columbus, OH: Charles E. Merrill.

Carr, M.T. (1941). *History of the Tennessee School for the Deaf.*

Fairweather, J.S. (1988). Comparing traditional and nontraditional approaches to preparing secondary level handicapped students for work and life after school. *The Journal for Vocational Special Needs Education, 10*(2), 23–27.

Fay, E.A. (1917). Miscellaneous. *American Annals of the Deaf, 62,* 99–106.

Fay, E.A. (1922). Industries taught in American schools for the deaf. *American Annals of the Deaf, 67,* 13.

Flood, J.T. (1943). The adult deaf of Franklin County, Ohio—their educational background and interests—III. *American Annals of the Deaf, 88,* 312–328.

Fusfeld, I.S. (1933). The International Congress on the Education of the Deaf. *American Annals of the Deaf, 78,* 275–341.

Fusfeld, I.S. (1936). Miscellaneous. *American Annals of the Deaf, 81,* 269–280.

Fusfeld, I.S. (1937). Miscellaneous. *American Annals of the Deaf, 82,* 97–101.

Garretson, M.D. (1969, October). *Education and rehabilitation of the deaf: A question of relevance.* Paper presented at the Region IV Conference for Coordinating Improved Rehabilitation and Educational Services for Deaf People, Knoxville, TN.

Halpern, A.S. (1985). Transition: A look at the foundations. *Exceptional Children, 51,* 479–486.

Hasazi, S.B., Gordon, L.R., Roe, C.A., Hull, M., Finck, K., & Salembier, G. (1985, December). A statewide follow-up on post high school employment and residential status of students labeled "mentally retarded." *Education and Training of the Mentally Retarded, 20,* 222–234.

Kett, J.F. (1982). The adolescence of vocational education. In H. Kantor & D.B. Tyack (Eds.), *Work, youth, and schooling: Historical perspectives on vocationalism in American education* (pp. 79–109). Stanford, CA: Stanford University Press.

Laski, F.J. (1979). Legal strategies to secure entitlement to services for severely handicapped persons. In G.T. Bellamy, G. O'Connor, & O.C. Karan (Eds.), *Vocational rehabilitation of severely handicapped persons: Contemporary service strategies* (pp. 1–32). Baltimore: University Park Press.

Lassiter, R.A. (1972). History of the rehabilitation movement in America. In J.G. Cull & R.E. Hardy (Eds.), *Vocational rehabilitation: Profession and process* (pp. 5–58). Springfield, IL: Charles C Thomas.

Lauritsen, R., Bishop, M.E., Galloway, V., Hicks, T.J., Updegraff, D.R., & Wyks, H.W. (1985). Career education: The position paper of the Conference of

Educational Administrators Serving the Deaf. *American Annals of the Deaf*, *130*, 74–78.

Marland, S.P., Jr. (1971). Career education now. In G.F. Law (Ed.), *Contemporary concepts in vocational education* (pp. 41–49). Washington, DC: American Vocational Association.

Moores, D.F. (1969). The vocational status of young deaf adults in New England. *Journal of Rehabilitation of the Deaf*, *2*(5), 29–41.

Morrison, J.S. (1920). Industrial training: What shall we subtract, and what shall we add, in the new century of the education of the deaf? *American Annals of the Deaf*, *65*, 213–224.

Obermann, C. (1965). *A history of vocational rehabilitation in America*. Minneapolis: T.S. Denison & Co.

Office of Special Education and Rehabilitative Services (1986). *Eighth annual report to Congress on the implementation of The Education of the Handicapped Act*. Washington, DC: U.S. Department of Education.

Office of Special Education and Rehabilitative Services. (1987). *Ninth annual report to Congress on the implementation of The Education of the Handicapped Act*. Washington, DC: U.S. Department of Education.

Office of Special Education and Rehabilitative Services. (1988). *Tenth annual report to Congress on the implementation of The Education of the Handicapped Act*. Washington, DC: U.S. Department of Education.

Ott, J.T. (Ed.). (1967). *Proceedings: National Conference for Coordinating Rehabilitation and Education Services for the Deaf*. New Mexico State University. Las Cruces.

Resolutions. (1920). *American Annals of the Deaf*, *65*, 271–272.

Rusch, F.R., Mithaug, D.E., & Flexer, R.W. (1986). Obstacles to competitive employment and traditional program options for overcoming them. In W.E. Kiernan & J.A. Stark (Eds.), *Pathways to employment for adults with developmental disabilities* (pp. 7–21). Baltimore: Paul H. Brookes Publishing Co.

Sanderson, R.G. (1982). *The impact of certain social services on the vocational rehabilitation of deaf clients*. Washington, DC: Gallaudet College.

Schein, J.D. (Ed.). (1980). *Model state plan for rehabilitation of deaf clients: Second revision*. Silver Spring, MD: National Association of the Deaf.

Schildroth, A. (1988). Recent changes in the educational placement of deaf students. *American Annals of the Deaf*, *133*, 61–67.

Sendelbaugh, J., & Bullis, M. (1988). Special education and rehabilitation policies for the school to community transition of students with hearing impairments. *Journal of the American Deafness and Rehabilitation Association*, *21*(4), 15–20.

Spragins, A., Karchmer, M., & Schildroth, A. (1981). Profile of psychological service providers to hearing impaired students. *American Annals of the Deaf*, *126*, 94–105.

Szymanski, E.M., & Danek, M.M. (1985). School-to-work transition for students with disabilities: Historical, current, and conceptual issues. *Rehabilitation Counseling Bulletin*, *29*, 81–89.

Tooman, M.L. (1986). An historical background of transitional employment programs and a perspective on the future. In L.G. Perlman & G.F. Austin (Eds.), *The transition to work and independence for youth with disabilities* (pp. 9–17). Alexandria, VA: National Rehabilitation Association.

Vernon, M. (1969). A work-study program for deaf and hard of hearing youth. *Journal of Rehabilitation of the Deaf*, *3*(2), 29–33.

Walter, V. (1987). In der nacht. *Gallaudet Today*, *18*(2), 6–11.

Wehman, P., Kregel, J., & Barcus, J.M. (1985). From school to work: A vocational transition model for handicapped students. *Exceptional Children, 52,* 25–37.

White, R.H. (1986). Collaboration between vocational rehabilitation and education: The making of dual winners. In D.H. Ashmore (Ed.), *1986 Proceedings: Regional Conference on Postsecondary Education for Hearing-Impaired Students* (pp. 53–63). Knoxville, TN: Postsecondary Education Consortium, The University of Tennessee.

Whitten, E.B. (1957). The state-federal program of vocational rehabilitation. In H.A. Pattison (Ed.), *The handicapped and their rehabilitation*. Springfield, IL: Charles C Thomas.

Will, M. (1985, Spring). OSERS programming for the transition of youth with disabilities: Bridges from school to working life. *Rehabilitation/WORLD, 9*(1), 4–7, 42–43.

Reality Reconsidered

10

Policy Implications of the Transition Study

Several chapters of this book reflect on the fact that educational and rehabilitation conferences and meetings regarding deafness-related issues often produce recommendations and resolutions made in previous meetings, recommendations sometimes made decades ago. This can be a discouraging prospect for deaf persons and for the professionals working with them. All of these individuals, like those engaged in other movements and reform efforts, would prefer to have the "myth" and the "reality", the "ideal" and the "practical"—described in Chapter 1 of this book—coincide, or at least eventually converge much more quickly than they do in a democratic society with its dissonant constituencies and prolonged debate.

One would wish, for example, that there were ideal support services for deaf students in their educational placements; at the same time, one also realizes that the pursuit of divergent goals by other groups in the educational environment—better funded or better organized or simply more numerous—will probably have the result of imposing financial limitations on the number and quality of these support services. While a parent in Chapter 2 regrets the inability of rehabilitation to assist a deaf daughter to explore various career options to find the one for which she is best suited, a rehabilitation professional in Chapter 3 emphasizes the reality: the limited funding available to rehabilitation agencies that precludes the type of career exploration available to many college students with private financial resources. It becomes obvious from these two examples that, rather than a merger of the ideal with the reality, there must be a compromise, a resolution of the two views.

Lasting progress, almost of necessity, comes gradually—with the education of the citizenry on the critical issues of society. One needs only

Scott Campbell Brown of the Center for Assessment and Demographic Studies contributed significantly to this chapter.

review the slow-moving history of racial integration in American society, a history not yet finished by any means, to realize this. The dilatory nature of much reform is not psychologically satisfying to the reformer; it is, however, often the only route to lasting change and improvement.

The fact that many recommendations for reform keep recurring in the history of education and rehabilitation of deaf students is, at once, an indication of the journey still to be traveled and, at the same time, a recognition of the reality of a society in which success often comes imperceptibly and only after much turmoil. It is incumbent on descriptive, practical research to recognize the progress made in education, to point to areas where progress is lacking, and to indicate possible ways of how that progress can be accomplished.

Chapter 1 has described some of the progress made in the area of transition for deaf students (e.g., the increased number of postsecondary programs for these students and the legislative progress regarding transition made in recent years). Other chapters have discussed the vocational training deaf students are receiving in special education programs across the country, the kinds of work in which these students are engaged, the assessment instruments used in the transition process, and the relationship of special education programs to state rehabilitation agencies in this process. These chapters have all noted the progress made in their respective areas.

Reviewing data reported to the "Study of Deaf Students in Transition from School to Work," the following sections of this last chapter summarize areas where progress still needs to be made and other issues need to be considered. It also suggests possible avenues of action that would encourage that progress.

LEVELS OF DISADVANTAGE

When individuals talk or write about "the deaf population," the discussion is often in terms of generalities. There may be an underlying assumption that, because these individuals share an inability to hear, they are somehow all the same. This is not necessarily true. Degrees of hearing loss, age at onset of loss, and causes of loss vary widely among deaf people, with the result that certain accommodations, such as hearing aids, may assist some deaf individuals but not others.

In Chapter 4 of this book, the deaf youth who are the focus of this transition study are described in terms of several key demographic variables: age, sex, ethnic background, cause and severity of hearing loss, additional handicapping conditions, and the educational setting where the student receives classroom instruction. When these characteristics are considered in their interaction with other factors associated in the transition from school to work, it becomes clear that some deaf youth are more disadvantaged than others.

The deaf youth described in Chapters 4 through 8 did not all have equal access to services or exit school on an equally qualified basis. Not all youth graduated with diplomas. Chapter 5 reports that only 52% of deaf youth in the study graduated with a diploma, while 19% received a certificate. The remaining 29% dropped out. Chapter 7 notes that some deaf youth were able to obtain more work experience than others. Males were more likely to hold jobs during the school year than females; deaf students with no or only one additional handicap were more likely to be working than those with two or more additional handicaps.

Some segments of the deaf student population received vocational and academic training at different rates than their peers (Chapter 6). White students and those without additional handicaps were more likely to receive academic training than were minority students or those with additional handicapping conditions. Discrepancies in the hourly earnings of deaf youth also were found, with males, whites, and those with no additional handicaps more likely to earn higher salaries than other groups (Chapter 7).

In planning effective transition services for deaf youth, the physical impairment cannot be viewed in isolation. The other characteristics of the individual and the community in which the individual functions, as well as the relative influence of a variety of factors that contribute to the disadvantage, must be evaluated. One way of looking at physical impairment and its association with disadvantages has been proposed by the World Health Organization (WHO, 1980) in the development of their International Classification of Impairments, Disabilities, and Handicaps (ICIDH). Under the ICIDH system, the concept of disablement is viewed in three ways: as impairment, as disability, and as handicap. These three concepts are not interchangeable.

Impairment is defined as any loss or abnormality of psychological, physiological, or anatomical function. An impairment is the actual condition of the organ and can be described medically. Disability is defined as any restriction or lack (resulting from an impairment) of ability to perform an activity in the manner or range considered normal for a human being. It is a measure of a person's performance and is important from a rehabilitation perspective.

The most relevant aspect of ICIDH to transition is the concept of handicap. " . . . Handicap is a disadvantage for a given individual . . . that limits or prevents fulfillment of a role that is normal (depending on age, sex, social, and cultural factors) for that individual" (WHO, 1980, p. 183). The concept of handicap is thus:

> . . . concerned with the value attached to an individual's situation or expe-
> rience when it departs from the norm. It is characterized by a discordance
> between the individual's performance or status and the expectations of
> the individual himself or of the particular group of which he is a member.
> Handicap thus reflects socialization of an impairment or disability, and as
> such it reflects the consequences for the individual—cultural, social, eco-
> nomic and environmental. . . . (WHO, 1980, p. 183)

It is possible to reduce or minimize the handicaps associated with
deafness. Implicit in the mandate for transition services for deaf students
is the conviction that, without such services, deaf youth will be disadvantaged. Transition interventions are designed specifically to reduce handicaps by increasing occupational and social skills with the ultimate goal of
integration into the labor force. Examples of interventions might include
intensified training in the area of communication skills—written, oral,
and sign—to aid in integration on the job. Family and friends may provide support for learning appropriate social skills needed in the workplace. Career training and work experience, two components of the transition process, offer the deaf student the opportunity to gain work skills
needed for employment.

This view of handicaps has not been fully developed or accepted by
persons working in the field of disablement. However, there are two important contributions of this view of handicaps. First, the scheme encour-
ages those planning a youth's transition plan to focus on the entire individual and not just on one or two characteristics. Second, it promotes
consideration of improvements in physical environments, social situations, and resources to reduce the handicap.

In the real world of assisting deaf youth in the transition process,
rehabilitation counselors share the heavy responsibility of making decisions that affect the lives of individuals. They must determine eligibility
for rehabilitation services and the types of services rehabilitation agencies can provide. Levels of disadvantage must be considered in making
these decisions. If the degree of service provided is commensurate with
the level of disadvantage, some of the gap between the "myth" and the
"reality" of transition may be reduced.

THE ROLE OF HIGH SCHOOLS IN PROVIDING VOCATIONAL TRAINING TO DEAF STUDENTS

There is little disagreement in the transition literature that high schools
should play an important role in the transition of deaf students from
school to work. However, there is less consensus about the specific activities in which schools should engage. In this section, the role of the
schools in providing specific job training for deaf students is considered.

The question addressed is: Should high schools be training deaf students to enter specific occupations?

This question has been debated for nonhandicapped students repeatedly throughout the history of the vocational education movement. On the one hand, vocational education proponents point to the obligation that schools have to society for preparing youth for the labor force. They also note the potential benefits to society when such preparation is provided. Opponents, on the other hand, contend that schools should aim to increase the general literacy levels of their students, particularly in a contemporary, technological society. Opponents also point to the lack of statistical evidence showing the association of high school vocational training with eventual career selections.

For deaf students, this difficult question becomes even more complex. If schools choose to defer vocational training for deaf students, then society must be willing to establish and support agencies that assume this responsibility for the deaf adult population. As documented in the 1988 report of the Commission on Education of the Deaf (COED), deaf adults are inadequately served by existing postsecondary vocational training centers.

Whatever the appropriate response to the question, it is evident from the data presented in this book that the large majority of deaf students in the United States *are* receiving coursework in specific vocational areas as part of their high school curricula. It is not clear whether the training received by these students is effective in helping them find and keep jobs after high school. Regardless of whether the endeavor is effective, the data indicate that considerable resources are devoted to it.

In considering the central question of this section, it is useful to review some of the findings of the research reported in this book, as well as some of the well-documented characteristics of the deaf student population revealed by the Annual Survey of Hearing Impaired Children and Youth. A review of these "findings" may contribute toward recommendations regarding the future role of vocational education in the schools.

Many deaf students stay in school beyond the age of 18, extending the "entitlement" period up to the age of 22.

As evidenced by the current study, many deaf students remain in high school up to the age of 22. This fact alone argues for strong vocational training programs for these older students who opt to remain in school. For some programs, this training would be provided by qualified vocational teachers working directly through the school curriculum. For others, it would involve networks of cooperative agreements with community agencies and industry.

One program reporting data to the current study noted that it had recently begun a special program for deaf students beyond the age of 18 who had failed to meet diploma requirements. In this program, students took vocational classes in the morning and were placed in either paid or unpaid jobs every afternoon with support from a career education specialist and a VR counselor.

Certainly, deferring specific job training for deaf youth until the age of 22 would place these youth at a competitive disadvantage to hearing students who have been out of high school for up to 4 years. Furthermore, once students are no longer in school, they must prove eligibility in order to obtain appropriate training and support from rehabilitation agencies. Strong vocational programs in the schools allow for providing appropriate job training for *all* students, whatever their level of handicap.

A large percentage of deaf students beyond the age of 18 (over 70%) attend special schools for deaf students.

This finding is significant because it underscores the importance of vocational education to deaf students attending the special schools. Students who remain in school until the age of 22 should be ready and trained to start work immediately. The special schools are currently viewed as having an important role in assuring this rapid transition to the world of work.

At the same time, one may question whether the special schools are able to fulfill this role adequately. The rapid technological changes that are taking place in industry make it very difficult for schools to continually upgrade their vocational training facilities to levels necessary for adequate training. Assuming that the special schools can offer a broad array of state-of-the-art vocational training experiences on their own, without extensive additional funding, is unrealistic.

A large number of deaf students drop out.

Students drop out of school for many reasons. It was not the purpose of the current study to examine reasons for the high drop-out rates among deaf students. Nonetheless, it might be proposed that stronger vocational training for deaf students in high school would encourage more students to stay in school. The research literature suggests that vocational training is often a positive educational experience for those who are not academically inclined.

There is a shortage of vocational training centers for deaf adults, as indicated by the COED report (1988).

The recommended solution to this shortage is the creation of regional training centers (COED, 1988). However, in the current federal budget climate of mounting deficits, it is unrealistic to expect federal support of new vocational centers. Given the current study's finding of increased vocational emphasis for students in the 18 to 22 age range in the special schools for the deaf, the federal government might do well to consider models in which the vocational offerings of currently existing residential or day facilities for deaf students are expanded, and mechanisms for offering training to deaf adults in the community are developed. Special facilities have staffs well qualified to work with deaf students, and they usually have long-established direct linkages with state rehabilitation agencies. This relationship is discussed more fully below. Expanding vocational training services through these already existing facilities might be an appropriate and cost-efficient alternative to establishing regional vocational training centers.

Deaf students have problems communicating in English, reading English, and writing English.

There are many implications of this fact for the provision of vocational training. First and foremost, it implies that whoever trains deaf individuals for jobs must be able to communicate effectively with them. Appropriate support services, including interpreters, should be available while deaf students are learning trades.

Aside from the need for training programs staffed with individuals who are skilled in communicating with deaf students, the English language deficit is more fundamental to the question of what role the schools should play in the vocational training of deaf students. Due to the increasing technological demands of the work force, the need for entry-level workers who have strong literacy and computational skills has never been greater. Thus, a radical point of view would hold that the entire vocational education endeavor for deaf students wastes precious instructional time and school resources. From this point of view, deaf high school students should spend all, or nearly all, of their instructional time learning to read, write, and compute.

During the Gallaudet student protest in the spring of 1988, a favorite expression among the protestors was, "Deaf people can do anything that hearing people can, except hear." Unfortunately, many research studies have documented the fact that a majority of deaf persons enter the work force handicapped by their limited skills in English. The juxtaposition of the rallying cry with the reality exemplifies the earlier discussion of considering aspects of impairment, disability, and handicap separately. True, deaf youth differ from hearing youth (biologically) only in their *impaired* hearing; however, this impairment, for many, has led to *disabled* receptive speech communication that, in turn, has resulted in delayed English language abilities. American society requires this ability for its high-status occupations; this societal requirement is the source of the *handicap*.

Whatever the level of their communication skills, it is nonetheless true that many deaf youth face impediments to a full integration into American working society because they lack the same level of English literacy as their hearing peers. If, therefore, the optimism of the Gallaudet protest is accepted, the inescapable conclusion is that the majority of deaf students leave school achieving far below their academic potential. Thus, it should be viewed as the school's primary responsibility to narrow the English literacy gap between deaf and hearing youth entering the workplace.

The opposing, and equally radical, point of view would be one that questions the possibility or likelihood of *ever* narrowing the English literacy gap between deaf and hearing youth. Such a viewpoint would note the persistence of the third to fourth grade median reading levels of deaf high school leavers throughout the past 2 decades, despite continuing educational reform and debate in the deaf educational community. Whether this point of view is overly pessimistic or simply realistic, the data are compelling. They argue for intensive vocational training that begins as early in a student's schooling as possible, in skill areas that require minimum English literacy skills. This point of view not only begins with a pessimistic premise, it implies a society in which the opportunities for many deaf individuals are limited to a given set of low-status occupations.

In summary, the philosophical debate over the appropriateness of vocational training for high school students is magnified for many deaf youth because of limitations in their levels of English literacy. This fact can be viewed as supporting both sides of the vocational education argument. It can be viewed as either emphasizing the need for more literacy training or emphasizing the need for a strong vocational component, depending upon one's philosophical point of view.

POSTSECONDARY EDUCATION

The discussion of transition has focused primarily on the preparation of students for entry into the labor force. Many deaf students graduating from high school extend this transition process by attending a postsecondary program to gain additional skills and training.

There are a number of reasons to be optimistic about the postsecondary educational opportunities now available to deaf students. These include increased availability of programs, enrollment rates of deaf students in postsecondary programs, provision of financial support from rehabilitation agencies, and data confirming the increased earning power that accompanies additional education. Each of these reasons for optimism, however, is tempered by the reality of what is encountered when deaf students attempt to avail themselves of these postsecondary options.

Increased Opportunities

There are currently more postsecondary educational opportunities for deaf students than ever before (Rawlings, Karchmer, & DeCaro, 1987; Rawlings & King, 1986). Mendelsohn and Brown, in Chapter 2 of this book, describe their children's decision-making process in selecting a college and the various options considered. Josh selected a college offering a program specifically designed for deaf students; Stephanie enrolled at a university for hearing students where she could get support services through an office for disabled students. Both parents describe the challenges of selecting an appropriate program and locating the needed support services.

For nearly 100 years since its establishment, Gallaudet College (now Gallaudet University) was the only postsecondary program specifically designed for deaf students in the world. Beginning in the 1960s, the number of options for deaf students increased dramatically. The National Technical Institute for the Deaf (NTID) at Rochester Institute of Technology was created by federal legislation to serve deaf students from across the nation. Also, four federally funded regional postsecondary education programs for the deaf (RPEPDs) were established. At the same time, a number of technical and vocational institutions, community colleges, and other postsecondary institutions set up specially designed programs for deaf students offering a wide range of centrally coordinated support services.

The directory *College and Career Programs for Deaf Students* (Rawlings, Karchmer, & DeCaro, 1988) lists over 150 postsecondary institutions providing programs specifically designed for deaf students. When the first edition of this book was published 15 years earlier, it contained descriptions of only 27 such programs (Stuckless & Delgado, 1973).

Recent federal legislation has also had an impact on the availability of postsecondary opportunities for deaf students. In Chapter 1 of this book, Danek and McCrone discuss the impact of Section 504 of the Rehabilitation Act of 1973 (PL 93-112) as it relates to postsecondary education for deaf students. This legislation requires institutions receiving federal funds to make their programs accessible to disabled persons. For deaf students, as well as other disabled students, this has meant that they cannot be discriminated against in applying to colleges and universities and that the institutions must provide equal access to the programs offered.

The report of the Commission on Education of the Deaf (1988), however, noted several concerns about postsecondary program availability. First, COED questioned whether many institutions were, in fact, in compliance with Section 504. Insufficient provision of support services at many of the institutions was the basis of this concern. A similar cautionary note was mentioned in a 1986 study of postsecondary programs, where it was shown that many of the programs recruiting deaf students offered only minimal support services (Rawlings et al., 1987).

Clearly, not all students with hearing impairments need the comprehensive services provided by programs such as Gallaudet, NTID, or the RPEPDs. Students themselves must determine what support services they require and carefully evaluate the quantity and quality of the services offered by the postsecondary program being considered. To be successful in the program, the student must make a good match between the services needed and those available.

Enrollment Rates

Several studies suggest that deaf high school graduates enroll in postsecondary programs at rates similar to those for hearing students (Armstrong & Schneidmiller, 1983; Kerstetter, 1985; White, Karchmer, Armstrong, & Bezozo, 1983). These studies report that from 30% to 53% of deaf high school graduates from special education programs continue their education.

Estimates of the total number of hearing impaired students in colleges and universities range from 8,000 to 11,000 (Armstrong & Schneidmiller, 1983; Wulfsberg & Petersen, 1979). The 1987 enrollments for the programs for deaf students included in the *College and Career Programs for Deaf Students* (Rawlings et al., 1988) total nearly 7,500 students; 82% of these deaf students were enrolled on a full-time basis. This figure underestimates the total number of deaf students attending college because it is limited to a study of institutions that have designated units offering support services to deaf students.

Although these figures are encouraging, other data reflect a less optimistic view of the situation. Chapter 5 in this book reports that a large number of deaf students do not complete high school. Only 5 out of every 10 deaf students leaving high school graduate with a diploma. The remaining school leavers either get a certificate of attendance or drop out, and are therefore not eligible for admission to most postsecondary programs. The higher drop-out rates for Hispanic deaf youth and deaf youth with two or more additional handicaps also suggest that these segments of the population will be underrepresented in college enrollment figures.

Another concern for colleges and universities is that of attrition. Although deaf youth appear to be enrolling in postsecondary programs at rates comparable to hearing youth, many never complete the program. While extensive data are not available, the attrition rates for deaf students at many postsecondary programs are high. A 1987 study by Walter, Foster, and Elliot reported an attrition rate of 70% for hearing impaired students attending postsecondary institutions that predominantly serve hearing students.

It is not sufficient to examine the rates at which deaf youth enroll in postsecondary programs. Their rates of graduation from these programs provide a better indication of their potential for future success in the labor market.

Financial Support

In Chapter 3 of this book Wright discusses the role rehabilitation plays when students seek postsecondary education; rehabilitation can provide financial support for postsecondary education when such training is necessary for the student to obtain employment. An indication of the extent of this important service is noted in Chapter 9; schools indicated the most frequently provided vocational rehabilitation service to deaf students was financial assistance for postsecondary education. In an age of ever-increasing costs for postsecondary education, these available funds may assist deaf youth who otherwise could not afford to continue their education. At the same time, it is somewhat ironic that this large outlay of rehabilitation funding for postsecondary education may be an indicator of disproportionate services for a select group of rehabilitation clients—those *able* to pursue a postsecondary education.

As described by Wright (Chapter 3) and Brown (Chapter 2), there are certain restrictions that accompany these rehabilitation funds. First, the educational training must be viewed as a means to an end—namely, employment. Education simply for the goal of acquiring learning in an area in which rehabilitation does not believe the student can gain employment may not be funded. Rehabilitation agencies may establish restrictions not only on the course of instruction but also on the postsecondary program selected. For example, some state rehabilitation agencies are reluctant to fund the education of deaf youth if they select a postsecondary program outside their home state or region.

Thus, while funding for postsecondary education is available, this financial support comes with strings attached. Students and their parents need to be made aware of the availability of these monies, and also that eligibility for the funds needs to be established. This is yet another reason to begin early collaboration with rehabilitation counselors in developing transition plans.

Increased Earning Power

A 1987 report from the U.S. Bureau of the Census found that:

> Most degrees beyond high school have significantly higher income and earnings values associated with them than the next lower degree . . . In addition, the mean income and earnings measures for persons with only a

high school diploma are in turn substantially larger than those for persons who did not complete high school. (p. 2)

In the United States in 1984, persons with degrees beyond high school, regardless of the degree, earned average monthly incomes of $865 more than those with only a high school diploma. Those with a high school diploma earned $352 more a month on average than those who did not graduate from high school (U.S. Bureau of the Census, 1987). A study of deaf students at the National Technical Institute for the Deaf showed similar findings. The earnings of graduates of NTID increased with the level of the degree earned (Walter, 1987).

In order to make the most appropriate choice of a postsecondary program and courses of study and to determine the financial resources required, students, families, educational counselors, and vocational rehabilitation personnel must be involved as early as possible in the decision making process (HEATH Resource Center & The Association on Handicapped Student Service Programs in Postsecondary Education, 1986). Postsecondary education is an option available to deaf high school graduates and can be an important step in the transition from school to work. As mentioned in the preface to this book, it is difficult to say exactly when the transition from school to work begins and ends. For many it is a lifelong process.

APPROPRIATE ROLE OF ASSESSMENT IN MAKING TRANSITION DECISIONS FOR DEAF YOUTH

The promise of standardized assessment instruments is that they will render educational or vocational decisions fairly because they enforce a common yardstick by which the abilities, interests, and attitudes of students will be measured. Ironically, the "common yardstick" feature of this argument may be precisely its source of "unfairness" when standardized tests are administered to deaf students. There are two primary reasons why this irony exists. First, because deaf students have had limited auditory input throughout their lives, they can be expected, in general, to have had different life experiences than their hearing peers. Therefore, the situations that are depicted in test or assessment items may be inappropriate. An obvious example of such an item would be a question on an interest inventory that asks students to state whether they prefer to "listen to records" or "go on a hike." A review of commercially available tests reveals many such auditory-based items.

Second, most tests require some proficiency with the English language; it may not be correct to assume that individual deaf students have mastered a level of English reading skill required by a given test. The verbal load of content-area achievement tests is especially problematic. For example, standardized science achievement tests are, in effect, reading tests for many deaf students. Thus, such tests will likely underestimate the science abilities of deaf students who understand scientific concepts but who have difficulty reading. If the results of a standardized science test are used to select which students are to be placed in courses designed to train laboratory technicians, it is likely that many deaf students will be unfairly excluded because of their limited reading ability, not because of deficits in their scientific knowledge.

In Chapter 8 of this book, Traxler notes the need to establish test validity when tests are administered to deaf students. "Validity" is an easy word to bandy about. Unfortunately, the term has as many meanings as there are contexts in which tests are used. This book has documented the widespread use of tests in a number of different contexts (e.g., for making tracking or course placement decisions), each requiring its own validity evaluation. In Chapter 2, Brown questions the appropriateness of particular tests in determining her daughter's postsecondary options. Chapter 5 notes the negative impact of requiring minimum competency tests for graduation on the likelihood that deaf students will graduate with diplomas. Recent court cases supporting states' rights to deny diplomas to handicapped students who fail to pass minimum competency tests emphasize this trend toward using test results to determine competence for graduation. (For example, see *Brookhart v. Illinois State Board of Education,* reported by Education Commission of the States, 1983.)

Clearly, assessment practices are widespread in transition endeavors. It is astounding, in the case of vocational assessment, that 54 separate commercially available instruments were reported as being administered to an average of 1% of those deaf students administered vocational instruments for the purpose of course placement or tracking. One must ask whether the proliferation of tests—many of questionable reliability and validity—negatively or unfairly influences the post–high school options available to deaf students.

To validate 54 vocational instruments with the deaf student population by using psychometrically appropriate methods would be impossible. In the case of achievement testing, the availability of norms and specialized scoring for the Stanford Achievement Test has led to a large-scale adoption of this test for deaf students. While this practice ensures the use of a test whose technical properties are known when it is administered to deaf students, there is danger that its status as the sole achievement test for use with deaf students might lead to its overuse and overinterpretation. Furthermore, the Stanford is not a perfect test; therefore, its widespread use also guarantees the widespread application of its imperfections. (It is interesting to note that of the 23 transition projects—

serving 307 hearing impaired youth—funded by the Office of Special Education and Rehabilitative Services during 1986–1987, not a single project used the Stanford Achievement Test and its special norms with their deaf clients [Dowling & Hartwell, 1987].)

The following recommendations are offered as starting points to a course that may lead to more judicious assessment policies:

- Consumers and interpreters of test information need to be educated regarding the meaning and limitations of the tests they use. In particular, test score users must know when tests have not been specifically validated with the deaf population. Also, they must be aware of the reported standard errors of obtained scores, which indicate the *range of confidence* around observed measures. These often can be quite wide for deaf students. (The wider the range of confidence, the lower the reliability.)

- Teachers and other users of test information should seek multiple indicators of the traits they desire to measure. No test score should be taken at face value as the sole indicator of an ability, preference, or attitude. In preparing Individualized Written Rehabilitation Programs (IWRPs) for individual students, placement decisions should never be made on the basis of a single test score. Sources of confirming evidence for the validity of a particular test result could come from other tests, from teacher or parent judgments, or from other behavioral measures.

- Test results should be evaluated at the item level, as well as at the score level. It is often easy to determine, through a review of student responses to individual items, which items may have been inappropriate or invalid. This practice also leads to a greater diagnostic value when shortcomings on specific skills can be articulated through examination of student performance on individual items.

- Finally, a low test score does not imply, as some might wish to say, an invalid test score. Low achievement levels among deaf students, especially in course areas dependent on English reading and writing skills, are a reality. However, when a low test score is used to make an important transitional decision, the agencies using the test result to make this decision have the responsibility for demonstrating that the particular test used and the manner in which the score contributed to the decision were both valid and defensible.

TRANSITION, SPECIAL EDUCATION, AND REHABILITATION

Chapter 1 of this book addresses the general issue of myth and reality in regard to the transition of deaf youth from high school into their postsecondary careers. In the relationship between special education and state rehabilitation agencies, this dichotomy is perhaps more appropriately described as the tension between the ideal and the practical, that is, between the world of the ideal proposed by the law or human aspirations and the world of the possible, of the very limited and gradual incorporation of that ideal into the structures and activities of human society.

A similar tension between the ideal and the reality may be found in the relationship between special education programs for deaf students— the special schools and the local programs—and state rehabilitation agencies. Chapter 9 documents the near unanimous declaration by government officials, educators, rehabilitation professionals, and researchers concerning the critical need for collaboration between these two agencies. The same chapter also discusses the distance and lack of cooperation that often seem to characterize their relationship.

An obvious question arises from this apparent contradiction. In the face of the general conviction that close cooperation between special education and rehabilitation agencies is essential to the transition process, why is there this dissonance and lack of cooperation, at least in some important areas?

Several explanations have been given for this situation. Tooman (1986), for example, has described the "disengagement" (p. 15) of the education and the rehabilitation agencies from an historical and legislative perspective. He advances an instructive review of how the goals of the two agencies, with different program constraints and different client criteria, can become entangled and then diverge, resulting in a " 'death knell' to local cooperative efforts" (1986, p. 12). Elsewhere, Brolin (1982, pp. 20–21) lists six major "barriers" to interagency cooperation (see also Fenton & Keller, 1981). There are undoubtedly other explanations for this collaboration problem. However, the following discussion of the relationship between special education and rehabilitation focuses only on issues arising from the data and presentations advanced in this book.

From the material reported in Chapter 2 (the parents' viewpoint), Chapter 3 (the rehabilitation perspective), and Chapter 9 (data from a 1987 survey about the schools' relationship to rehabilitation), certain pivotal issues emerge regarding this relationship. The areas discussed here are not all-encompassing—there are other issues in the relationship between special education and rehabilitation that are of equal importance. Nor is it a question of assigning blame to either of the two agencies. As Chapter 9 has pointed out in its "Discussion" section, there are indications that progress has been made in the relationship, that the conferences and workshop recommendations and resolutions over the past 20 years—cited by Danek and McCrone in Chapter 1—have not gone completely unheeded.

Nevertheless, there are several important practical issues raised by the chapters in this book regarding special education programs for deaf high school students and state rehabilitation agencies. These are discussed in the following sections.

Whose Invitation, Whose Initiative?

In Chapter 3 of this book, Wright, writing from a rehabilitation perspective, cites ways in which rehabilitation agencies and special education programs can cooperate:

> Collaboration between rehabilitation, education, and parents can begin as early as the 9th or 10th grade by inviting the rehabilitation counselor to participate in IEP staffings, by conducting joint training sessions, or through other activities that encourage vocational exploration and increased knowledge about the world of work and rehabilitation. (p. 54)

The statement implies that the invitation to collaborate comes from special education. The school survey data of Chapter 9 regarding the "initiation" of services to the schools by rehabilitation indicates that 25% of the special schools and 53% of the local programs reported no initiation of contact *by rehabilitation agencies* with their deaf students. (Thirty-eight special education programs in the survey specified that the school had to initiate the contact.) At best, there appears to be some confusion over whose responsibility it is for taking the initiative regarding contact between special education and rehabilitation.

The school survey question implied that rehabilitation has the responsibility to initiate contact with the school. However, unless a particular state or local jurisdiction has adopted regulations ordering such contact by rehabilitation, there does not appear to be a clear responsibility on either side to initiate such contact. Given the probability of counselor and school staff involvement with more pressing work and the lack of incentives for such time-consuming activity, the likelihood of neither rehabilitation agencies nor special education programs taking this initiative seems high. This likelihood would be further increased by the large turnover of rehabilitation counselors and by counselor unfamiliarity with deafness found in some areas of the country; both situations are cited in the school survey results analyzed in Chapter 9 of this book.

When Does Rehabilitation Become Involved?

A related finding in Chapter 9 in this book concerns the grade in school in which rehabilitation made contact with deaf students. The 1987 school survey indicated that almost 50% of the special schools in which rehabilitation initiated contact with deaf students reported this contact in either

11th or 12th grade; 62% of the local special education programs indicated contact in these last 2 years of high school.

From the several workshops and national meetings cited in Chapter 9—including the 1967 Las Cruces meeting, the first national meeting jointly sponsored by the U.S. Office of Education and the Rehabilitation Services Administration—it is clear that earlier involvement by rehabilitation in high school postsecondary planning is considered more appropriate involvement. The Las Cruces meeting reached consensus on its recommendation for rehabilitation contact with the schools "at a much earlier age and grade level" (Ott, 1967, p. 10). Although a definite time was not specified, it seems obvious that the "much earlier age and grade level" recommended there are not those of the student's junior or senior year.

Wright, in Chapter 3 of this volume, also refers to a time for rehabilitation contact:

> Because preparation for employment begins early for most individuals through incidental learning, time of referral for the deaf student is critical. If referral is postponed until the student is near graduation or has graduated, opportunities for career preparation are lessened. (p. 54)

She then proceeds, as noted above, to cite participation by rehabilitation in school staffings as early as 9th or 10th grade, presumably opportune times for rehabilitation contact.

The question regarding time of involvement by rehabilitation is related to the "Whose Invitation, Whose Initiative?" problem discussed above. In the absence of state or local regulations governing the time of rehabilitation contact with schools, it is likely that such contact will occur later rather than sooner, that it will gravitate, imperceptibly and without any clear decision being made about it, toward the end of the student's high school career—especially if the student's family is unaware of rehabilitation service availability or the range of such services. The data from the school survey reported in Chapter 9 seem to support this view, especially for the regular/local mainstream programs.

This is the "reality." The "ideal"—myth is perhaps the wrong word here—is "the earlier the involvement, the better." The ideal or rhetoric is pulling in one direction—toward involvement of rehabilitation in 9th or 10th grade; the reality—when the contact is actually made—is inching in the opposite direction, toward 11th or 12th grade and graduation.

At first glance, it might seem that responsibility for making this earlier contact lies with the rehabilitation agency. However, there is another "reality" involved here, and that reality is the immediate contact and control that the special education programs exercise with their deaf students. The 1967 Las Cruces conference recognized this when it recommended that, "schools should involve rehabilitation personnel with the deaf child at a much earlier age and grade level for participation in the planning process for the child and in the total evaluation procedure (Ott, 1967, p. 10). The emphasis here is on the *schools* and their responsibility to involve rehabilitation in the collaborative transition process with deaf students.

In light of the schools' ongoing and immediate contact with their deaf students, it seems more appropriate that the initiative for making contact with rehabilitation should rest with the school. This is especially true at the present time when deaf students are being placed in local programs more frequently than in the past; that is, deaf students are being placed in special education programs in local schools that may lack the ongoing contact with rehabilitation often found in many residential and day schools for deaf students. (Obviously, it is easier for a rehabilitation agency to make or maintain contact with a long-established school enrolling a relatively large deaf student body grouped together than with numerous local special education programs enrolling deaf students scattered over a school district and enrolling one or only a few such students.)

It is perhaps appropriate here to recall what was said in Chapter 9 regarding the educational placement of deaf students. In view of the different characteristics of these students in the various types of educational settings (Schildroth, 1988), the school, through its ongoing experience with deaf students, should have an earlier and more comprehensive insight into the transition services needed by an individual student and should, therefore, take the initiative in contacting the rehabilitation agency.

What Agreement?

The discrepancy between the ideal of early transition involvement by the rehabilitation agency and the reality—that transition contact often occurs in junior or senior year or even after graduation—has been noted in both Chapter 9 of this book and in this chapter. Can one assign a cause for this gap between the support for rehabilitation contact "at a much earlier age and grade level," on the one hand, and, on the other hand, the actual later intervention documented in Chapter 9?

At least one major cause for this gap is the lack of formal cooperative agreements between state rehabilitation agencies and special education programs that spell out in detail the responsibilities and duties of both parties in serving the transition needs of deaf youth. As reported in Chapter 9, only 39% of the special schools and 17% of the local programs for deaf students reported the existence of such a formal contract between rehabilitation and special education. The widespread lack of such a formal plan for transition is confirmed in the study of Sendelbaugh and

Bullis (1988). (A parallel situation is noted in Chapter 6 in this book, which reported that only 25% of deaf students in the transition study had Individualized Written Rehabilitation Programs prepared jointly by school and rehabilitation agency personnel.)

The irony here is that the basis for establishing such an agreement has been available since 1973. The second revision of the *Model State Plan for Rehabilitation of Deaf Clients: Second Revision* (Schein, 1980), developed by rehabilitation professionals, educators, and researchers after the initial publication of the plan in 1973, is meant to serve not as a model to be taken over *in toto* by individual states, but as a blueprint to guide them in developing cooperative plans suitable for their own particular circumstances. (A third revision of the *Model State Plan for Rehabilitation of Deaf Clients* is being developed and should appear in late 1988 or early 1989.) Such state plans would be the result of collaborative efforts of rehabilitation and special education professionals and presumably would spell out responsibilities of the two agencies in regard to the initiation of rehabilitation contact with deaf students, the timelines for this initial contact, and the kinds of services available before and after graduation.

Translation of any formal agreement or legislation into local situations involving unique circumstances is always difficult. However, without such a legal and procedural framework, formally drawn up and agreed upon by the two agencies, the results can only be confusion, misunderstanding, arbitrary provision of services, and disillusionment on all sides—including that of the student and the student's family. Such a formal agreement runs the risk of excessive legalism, but there seems no other way to avoid the arbitrariness of a relationship not founded on this kind of arrangement.

Participation in School Staffings?

A corollary of the early involvement by rehabilitation agencies in the transition process concerns the type of intervention this will be. In which area of the overall special education/rehabilitation system will this contact take place? As Wright has indicated in Chapter 3 of this book, there is a difference between the entitlement aspect of education and the eligibility criterion of rehabilitation. It is a difference that is perhaps not clearly understood by those seeking rehabilitation services, but it is obviously a critical difference.

If there are criteria for, and limits to, the kinds of services available from rehabilitation agencies—specified in Chapter 3—then the basis for those criteria and limits should be made clear to all the parties involved, including the student, the parents, and the special education staff involved with that student. This is perhaps the most significant point made by Wright in Chapter 3: the need for communication between all the parties in the transition process in order to eliminate misunderstandings and to establish, as clearly as possible, the ground rules for the services, if any, to be provided by rehabilitation agencies.

In light of this need for dialogue and communication, the data reported in Chapter 9 regarding participation by rehabilitation personnel in school staffings and conferences are not encouraging. This service was one of three cited least frequently by special education programs—both special schools and local programs for deaf students—as being provided by rehabilitation. It is important to recall here what was said in a previous section regarding involvement by rehabilitation agencies in the transition process: In the absence of a specific plan detailing the responsibilities of special education and rehabilitation in this process, there is a good chance that such rehabilitation agency participation in school staffings and conferences will be sporadic and dependent on the workload and/or enthusiasm of individual personnel, either in the school or in the rehabilitation agency.

Thus, three problem areas raised by the school survey discussed in Chapter 9—initiation of rehabilitation services, time of this intervention, and kind of intervention—could be greatly clarified by the existence of a formal, written agreement between special education and rehabilitation detailing the responsibilities of each agency—and of the student and family also—in the transition of deaf students from school to work.

Communication

Another issue, related more loosely to those just discussed but equally important, involves the qualifications of rehabilitation counselors in their communication with deaf students. It is, of course, a broader issue than signing; but the question on the survey form was limited to those schools with deaf students who signed and their contact with a counselor who also signed.

A critical component of the transition process is the communication between the rehabilitation counselor and the deaf client. It is a component, like so much of the discussion about transition, that surfaces at every convention, workshop, or meeting concerned with rehabilitation and education. The need for counselors trained in communication skills with deaf persons is obvious. The 1978 Amendments to the Rehabilitation Act of 1973 (PL 95-602) recognized this need by requiring minimum standards of training for rehabilitation personnel to enable them to communicate in the client's native language or mode of communication (Kemp, 1988).

In light of this need, the fact that 95% of the special schools and 70% of the local programs reported a rehabilitation counselor able to sign with their signing students is an encouraging fact. However, three special schools with a total enrollment of 190 students who used sign reported a rehabilitation counselor unable to sign; 30% of local programs reported a nonsigning rehabilitation counselor with their signing students. The latter schools generally were programs with small deaf student enrollments (i.e., programs enrolling less than 11 deaf high school students).

The *Model State Plan for Rehabilitation of Deaf Clients: Second Revision* is clear in its insistence on communicative abilities for both the Statewide Coordinator for Deafness (SCD) and the Rehabilitation Counselor for Deaf Clients (RCDC), listing the ability to communicate as the first qualification for both these positions (Schein, 1980). Although a single survey question cannot provide much information on the quality of the communication between counselor and client, it seems clear from the data reported in Chapter 9 in this book that there is room for improvement in communication training and qualifications of counselors, especially within the regular/local program setting. Here again, a formal agreement between rehabilitation and special education should make clear the need for a counselor with special knowledge of deafness and special communication abilities—not just the ability to sign—in dealing with deaf persons. However, the "ideal" embodied in any agreement may very well give way to the "reality" of limited funds to provide the training for these special abilities and the very real scarcity of this kind of specialist in many areas of the country.

CONCLUSION

A 1987 report of the Hudson Institute makes several important points relevant to any study of deaf youth and their transition from school to work (Johnston & Packer, 1987). The first point concerns the level of skills required for *existing* jobs in the U.S. economy and the level required for *new* jobs. Basing their findings on skill level criteria of the U.S. Bureau of Labor, Johnston and Packer found that 40% of existing jobs require limited skills of language, mathematics, and reasoning abilities (i.e., competencies at a minimum or close to minimum level). This compares to only 27% of new jobs requiring this lower level of abilities. At the other end of the skills scale, 24% of existing jobs require skills at the upper three levels (e.g., ability to read journals and technical manuals), compared to 41% for existing or soon-to-be-created jobs in the economy. Put simply, new jobs in the United States will require significantly higher skill levels.

Johnston and Packer (1987) make a second point relevant to this discussion of transition: the shift in the U.S. economy from production of goods to production of services, a shift that is confirmed by the Bureau of

Labor Statistics (Kutscher, 1987) and that is likely to continue into the near future. The four largest of these "service industries" are retail trade, education, health care, and general government—areas that may present special problems to deaf persons entering the labor market. (This is especially true if special schools for deaf students—a traditional area of employment for deaf professionals—continue their enrollment decline, as noted earlier in this chapter.)

A third point made by Johnston and Packer (1987) concerns minorities and the employment picture. "By almost every measure of employment, labor force participation, earnings, and education, black and Hispanic minorities suffer much greater disadvantages than white . . . " (p. 90). These minorities face the greatest difficulties in the emerging labor market. The irony here is that according to Bureau of Labor estimates, the labor force will increasingly comprise minority and female workers (Fullerton, 1987; Kutscher, 1987). (Deaf students of minority ethnic background, it should be noted, generally have scored below white, non-Hispanic students on standardized achievement tests [Allen, 1986]).

If one believes these data and the projections accompanying them to be an accurate picture of what is and will be occurring on the U.S. labor scene, then they present special challenges to the individuals and agencies assisting deaf youth in the transition process. To the educators, they present the challenge of bringing the reading, mathematics, and reasoning skills of their deaf students to a level sufficient for competing in the job market. To rehabilitation personnel, the data challenge them to provide adequate vocational counseling, job training, placement, and follow-up—even the development of job areas—for their deaf clients. To employers, they present the challenge of keeping their minds and businesses open to the possibility of hiring qualified deaf workers. To deaf students, these data challenge them to achieve their maximum potential and to plan for their postsecondary careers. For all of these individuals and agencies, these data present a rigorous test of their *willingness to cooperate* in the transition of deaf youth from school to work.

REFERENCES

Allen, T.E. (1986). *Understanding the scores: Hearing-impaired students and the Stanford Achievement Test (7th edition).* Washington, DC: Gallaudet College Press.

Armstrong, D., & Schneidmiller, K. (1983). *Hearing impaired students enrolled in U.S. higher education institutions: Current status of enrollments and services* (Institutional Studies Report 83-3). Washington, DC: Gallaudet College.

Brolin, D.E. (1982). *Vocational preparation of persons with handicaps.* Columbus, OH: Charles E. Merrill.

Commission on Education of the Deaf. (1988). *Toward equality: Education of the deaf.* Washington, DC: U.S. Government Printing Office.

Dowling, J., & Hartwell, C. (1987). *Compendium of project profiles 1987.* Champaign: Transition Institute at Illinois, University of Illinois.

Education Commission of the States. (1983). Testing and the handicapped. *State Education Review, 1.*

Fenton, J., & Keller, R.A. (1981). Special education—vocational rehabilitation: Let's get the act together. *American Rehabilitation, 6*(5), 26–30.

Fullerton, H.N., Jr. (1987, September). Labor force projections: 1986 to 2000. *Monthly Labor Review,* pp. 19–29.

HEATH Resource Center & The Association on Handicapped Student Service Programs in Postsecondary Education. (1986). *How to choose a college: Guide for the student with a disability.* Washington, DC: Author.

Johnston, W.B., & Packer, A.H. (1987). *Workforce 2000: Work and workers for the 21st century.* Indianapolis, IN: Hudson Institute.

Kemp, G. (1988, January/February). News and notes. *American Deafness and Rehabilitation Association Newsletter, 1.*

Kerstetter, P. (1985). *Demographic predictors of postsecondary program choice of hearing impaired secondary school students.* Unpublished doctoral dissertation, Gallaudet College, Washington, DC.

Kutscher, R.E. (1987, September). Overview and implications of the projections to 2000. *Monthly Labor Review,* pp. 3–9.

Ott, J.T. (Ed.). (1967). *Proceedings: National Conference for Coordinating Rehabilitation and Education Services for the Deaf.* Las Cruces: New Mexico State University.

Rawlings, B., Karchmer, M., & DeCaro, J. (1987). Postsecondary programs for deaf students at the peak of the "rubella bulge." *American Annals of the Deaf, 132,* 36–42.

Rawlings, B., Karchmer, M., & DeCaro, J. (1988). *College and career programs for deaf students.* Washington, DC: Gallaudet University.

Rawlings, B., & King, S. (1986). Postsecondary education opportunities for deaf students. In A. Schildroth & M. Karchmer (Eds.), *Deaf children in America* (pp. 231–257). San Diego: College-Hill Press.

Schein, J.D. (Ed.). (1980). *Model state plan for rehabilitation of deaf clients: Second revision.* Silver Spring, MD: National Association of the Deaf.

Schildroth, A. (1988). Recent changes in the educational placement of deaf students. *American Annals of the Deaf, 133,* 61–67.

Sendelbaugh, J., & Bullis, M. (1988). Special education and rehabilitation policies for the school to community transition of students with hearing impairments. *Journal of the American Deafness and Rehabilitation Association, 21*(4), 15–20.

Stuckless, E.R., & Delgado, G. (1973). *A guide to college/career programs for deaf students.* Washington, DC: Gallaudet College.

Tooman, M.L. (1986). An historical background of transitional employment programs and a perspective on the future. In L.G. Perlman & G.F. Austin (Eds.), *The transition to work and independence for youth with disabilities* (pp. 9–17). Alexandria, VA: National Rehabilitation Association.

U.S. Bureau of the Census. (1987). *What's it worth? Educational background and economic status: Spring 1984.* Washington, DC: U.S. Government Printing Office. (Current Population Reports, Series P-70, No. 11)

Walter, G. (1987). *Outcomes of increased access to postsecondary education by deaf persons*. Unpublished manuscript, National Technical Institute for the Deaf, Rochester Institute of Technology, Rochester, NY.

Walter, G., Foster, S., & Elliot, L. (1987, July). *Attrition and accommodation of hearing-impaired college students in the U.S.* Paper presented at the Tenth National Conference of the Association on Handicapped Student Service Programs in Postsecondary Education, Washington, DC.

White, C., Karchmer, M., Armstrong, D., & Bezozo, C. (1983). Current trends in high school graduation and college enrollment of hearing impaired students attending residential schools. *American Annals of the Deaf, 128,* 125–131.

World Health Organization. (1980). *International classification of impairments, disabilities and handicaps: A manual of classification relating to the consequences of disease.* Geneva: Author.

Wulfsberg, R., & Petersen, R. (1979). *The impact of Section 504 of the Rehabilitation Act of 1973 on American colleges and universities.* Washington, DC: National Center for Education Statistics.

Appendix A

Survey Forms and Questionnaires

Annual Survey of Hearing Impaired
Children and Youth
1985–1986 Survey Form

Program Survey

Student Questionnaire

Counselor Questionnaire

ANNUAL SURVEY OF HEARING IMPAIRED CHILDREN & YOUTH
1985-1986 SCHOOL YEAR
FOR FURTHER INSTRUCTIONS, SEE BACK OF PAGE
PLEASE DO NOT FOLD THIS FORM

I. This form is for new students and for previously reported students. N.B.: For previously reported students IT IS NOT NECESSARY TO FILL IN BUBBLES IF THE PREVIOUSLY REPORTED INFORMATION, INDICATED BY AN "X", IS CORRECT AND UP-TO-DATE.

II. For items marked with an asterisk (*), please try to complete, as they were left blank in the previous survey.

III. Questions 7 B-1 and 11 are new for this year's survey and should be completed for all students.

IV. Please use a NO. 2 PENCIL to complete this form, NOT ink, ballpoint, or felt-tip pen.

1. STUDENT NAME or SCHOOL-ASSIGNED CODE

MAXIMUM SCHOOL-ASSIGNED CODE

2. PRESENT PROGRAM, SCHOOL OR AGENCY

A. School _____
NAME

Location _____
(city/state)

B. (OPTIONAL) Actual location where services are received, if different from 2A:

Name of school _____

3. FOR PREVIOUSLY REPORTED STUDENTS

Is this student still enrolled in the program named in 2A?

○ NO (If "NO," there is no need to complete remainder of this form, **but return it to Survey office**)

○ YES (If "YES," please complete remainder of this form)

○ TRANSFERRED TO ANOTHER SCHOOL WITHIN OUR SYSTEM (Complete remainder of this form):

NAME OF SCHOOL IN YOUR SYSTEM TO WHICH THIS STUDENT TRANSFERRED

4. DATE OF BIRTH

	MO.	○①②③ ○①②④⑤⑥⑦⑧⑨⑩⑪
DAY	○①②④⑤⑥⑦⑧⑨ ④⑤⑥⑦⑧
YR.	○①②④⑤⑥⑦⑧⑨

Previously reported

5. SEX

Previously reported   ○ Male   ○ Female

8. CAUSE OF HEARING LOSS (Complete only one section, either A or B or C or D)

A. If onset at birth, what was the probable cause(s)?

○ MATERNAL RUBELLA
○ TRAUMA AT BIRTH
○ HEREDITY
○ PREMATURITY
○ Rh INCOMPATIBILITY
○ OTHER COMPLICATIONS OF PREGNANCY
○ CYTOMEGALOVIRUS
○ OTHER (Specify) _____

B. If onset after birth, what was the probable cause(s)?

○ MENINGITIS
○ HIGH FEVER
○ MUMPS
○ INFECTION
○ MEASLES
○ OTITIS MEDIA
○ TRAUMA
○ OTHER (Specify) _____

C. ○ CAUSE CANNOT BE DETERMINED (though attempt was made)

D. ○ DATA NOT AVAILABLE IN STUDENT'S RECORD

9. UNAIDED AUDIOLOGICAL FINDINGS

A. AUDIOLOGICAL RESULTS

PREVIOUSLY REPORTED DATA				NEW STUDENT OR UPDATED			
	500	1000	2000		500	1000	2000
RIGHT				RIGHT			
LEFT				LEFT			

B. (If unaided air conduction results are not available, complete the category which describes student's hearing loss without amplification.)

○ NORMAL LIMITS (Less than 27 dB. ISO)
○ MILD (27-40 dB. ISO)
○ MODERATE (41-55 dB. ISO)
○ MODERATELY SEVERE (56-70 dB. ISO)
○ SEVERE (71-90 dB. ISO)
○ PROFOUND (91 dB plus, ISO)

6. ETHNIC BACKGROUND

PREVIOUS

- ○ White
- ○ Black
- ○ Hispanic
- ○ American Indian
- ○ Asian/Pacific
- ○ Other
- ○ Cannot Report
- ○ Unknown

7. PRESENT TYPE OF EDUCATIONAL PROGRAM (Please answer all items)

A. Does this hearing impaired student receive special education classroom instruction (e.g., residential or day school, full or part-time special ed classes, resource room, itinerant teacher, etc.)?

- ○ YES
- ○ NO

A-1. If YES, indicate the type of facility PRIMARILY providing this special education instruction. (PLEASE CHECK ONLY ONE)

- ○ Residential School for the Deaf
- ○ Day School for the Deaf
- ○ Speech & Hearing Clinic/Center
- ○ Regular Education facility for hearing students
- ○ Other (Specify) _____

B. Does this student receive regular ACADEMIC classroom instruction with hearing students, either full or part-time?

- ○ YES
- ○ NO

B-1. If YES, indicate total number of hours each week this student is integrated with hearing students for academic classroom instruction:

- ○ 1 to 5 hrs/wk
- ○ 6 to 10 hrs/wk
- ○ 11 to 15 hrs/wk
- ○ 16 or more hrs/wk

C. Does student live at school during week?

- ○ YES
- ○ NO

10. HEARING STATUS OF PARENTS

Are parents of the student deaf or hard-of-hearing?

Mother:	○ Normal Hearing	○ Hearing Impaired	○ Data not available
Father:	○ Normal Hearing	○ Hearing Impaired	○ Data not available

11. COMMUNICATION

Which of the following methods is PRIMARILY used to teach this student? (PLEASE CHECK ONLY ONE.)

- ○ Auditory/oral ONLY
- ○ Sign and speech
- ○ Other (Specify) _____

12. ADDITIONAL HANDICAPPING CONDITIONS

Does this student have an educationally significant handicapping condition in addition to hearing impairment?

- ○ YES
- ○ NO

If "YES," mark all educationally significant additional handicaps. (If you wish to add an additional handicap to one(s) previously reported, fill in bubbles for BOTH the new and the previously reported handicaps. If you wish to correct previously reported wrong information, fill in bubble for correct handicap, or for the "NO" bubble, only.)

GROUP 1

- ○ Legal Blindness
- ○ Uncorrected Visual Problem (but not Legally Blind)
- ○ Brain Damage or Injury
- ○ Epilepsy (Convulsive Disorder)
- ○ Orthopedic (other than cerebral palsy)
- ○ Cerebral Palsy
- ○ Heart Disorder
- ○ Other Health Impaired (Specify) _____

GROUP 2

- ○ Mental Retardation
- ○ Emotional/Behavioral Problem
- ○ Specific Learning Disability (includes perceptual-motor problem)
- ○ Other (Specify) _____

Thank You.

PROGRAM SURVEY

CAREER TRAINING OF DEAF STUDENTS

1. Does the school/program named on the label on the front enroll deaf (i.e., severely or profoundly hearing impaired) **high school** students (Grades 9-12)?

   ☐ Yes   ☐ No   (If "no," stop here and return the form in the envelope provided.)

2. If "yes," indicate the number of deaf **high school** students enrolled in the 1986-87 school year in the program named on the label on the front.

   _____ (number of deaf **high school** students)

3. Does the state office of Vocational Rehabilitation presently provide services to deaf students in your high school to prepare them to make the transition from school to work or from school to postsecondary education?

   ☐ Yes   ☐ No   (Proceed to Question 5)

4. If "yes" to Question 3, does a VR counselor usually INITIATE contact with your deaf **high school** students?

   ☐ Yes   ☐ No contact with our deaf high school students is initiated.

   If "yes,"   WHEN? ☐ Grade 9   ☐ Grade 11
                      ☐ Grade 10   ☐ Grade 12

5. Has a state VR counselor visited or made plans to visit your school to provide services to deaf students during the present 1986-87 school year?

   ☐ Yes   ☐ No   (Proceed to Question 7)

6. If "yes" to Question 5, is the VR counselor serving deaf students in your high school able to communicate by the use of sign language?

   ☐ Yes   ☐ No   ☐ No need for signing; students do not sign

7. Please indicate if the following services are provided to your deaf high school students by your state VR agency.

YES	NO	
☐	☐	Orientation to staff, students, parents about VR services
☐	☐	Participation in school staffings, parent conferences, etc.
☐	☐	Vocational assessment through performance tests, work samples
☐	☐	Medical assessment or treatment
☐	☐	Individual career/vocational counseling
☐	☐	Personal adjustment or family counseling
☐	☐	Job training
☐	☐	Job placement
☐	☐	Follow-up after job placement to see how individual is doing
☐	☐	Financial assistance for postsecondary education
☐	☐	Referral to appropriate community resources
☐	☐	Other (specify) _____

8. Does your school/program have a **formal WRITTEN** cooperative arrangement with the state office of Vocational Rehabilitation for providing services to deaf high school students in the transition from high school to work or from high school to postsecondary education?

   ☐ Yes   ☐ No

9. Please write on a separate page any comments you wish to make regarding deaf high school students and their transition from high school to work/postsecondary education (e.g., further services that VR could provide to your deaf high school students).

240

G A L L A U D E T G U N I V E R S I T Y

STUDENT QUESTIONNAIRE

SURVEY OF JOB TRAINING
FOR HEARING IMPAIRED YOUTH

March 1987

Dear Student:

Gallaudet University is studying the jobs of deaf students. We want to know the work you are doing now. We want to know how your school or vocational rehabilitation helped you.

Please answer the questions. If you need help, you can ask your mother or father to help you. Your teacher or counselor at school can help you.

When you finish the questions, please give this form to your counselor or teacher at school.

Thank you for your help.

The Gallaudet Research Institute
Gallaudet University

FOR SCHOOL'S USE ONLY:

If this student is not currently enrolled in your program, indicate the manner in which the student left. (You do not need to answer the questions inside.)

☐ Graduated with a diploma
☐ Graduated with a certificate
☐ Left without graduating

GALLAUDET RESEARCH INSTITUTE
CENTER FOR ASSESSMENT AND DEMOGRAPHIC STUDIES
(202) 651-5575 (V/TDD)

KENDALL GREEN
800 FLORIDA AVENUE, N.E.
WASHINGTON, D.C. 20002

CONFIDENTIAL: All information will be kept strictly confidential.

A. EMPLOYMENT:

A1. Do you now work for pay?

☐ Yes (Go to A2.) ☐ No (Go to A7.)

A2. What kind of job do you have? (If you have more than one job, answer the questions for the job you do most of the time.)

_____

(For example, TV repair, sewing machine operator, painter, secretary, cook)

A3. What do you do in this job?

_____

(For example, type, cook food, computer data processing, teach children)

A4. About how many hours do you work each week?

_____ hours each week

A5. How much do you get paid for each hour of work?

$ _____ each hour

A6. How did you get the job you have now?

☐ Yes	☐ No	I got the job myself
☐ Yes	☐ No	High school counselor/teacher helped me get the job
☐ Yes	☐ No	Vocational Rehabilitation (VR) helped me get the job
☐ Yes	☐ No	A job placement agency (not VR) helped me get the job
☐ Yes	☐ No	My college/technical school helped me get the job
☐ Yes	☐ No	My family helped me get the job
☐ Yes	☐ No	My friends helped me get the job
☐ Yes	☐ No	Other (Explain.) _____

A7. Do you get any job training in high school?

☐ Yes ☐ No

A8. Have you ever quit or were you ever fired from a job?

☐ Yes ☐ No ☐ Never had a job

If **YES**, why did you quit or get fired?

☐ Yes	☐ No	Problems with my supervisor
☐ Yes	☐ No	Problems with transportation
☐ Yes	☐ No	Disliked job
☐ Yes	☐ No	Did not want to lose Supplemental Security Income (SSI) payments
☐ Yes	☐ No	Could not do job — too hard
☐ Yes	☐ No	Job was finished
☐ Yes	☐ No	Other (Explain.) _____

A9. Did you have a job during the summer of 1986?

☐ Yes ☐ No

A10. If you are not working now, why?

☐ Yes	☐ No	Still in school
☐ Yes	☐ No	No jobs where I live
☐ Yes	☐ No	No one to help me get a job
☐ Yes	☐ No	No one to help train me for a job
☐ Yes	☐ No	Do not want to give up Supplemental Security Income (SSI)
☐ Yes	☐ No	No transportation
☐ Yes	☐ No	Other (Explain.) _____

B. VOCATIONAL REHABILITATION:

B1. Do you have a state Vocational Rehabilitation (VR) counselor?

☐ Yes ☐ No

B2. Have you met with a state VR counselor in the last 12 months?

☐ Yes ☐ No

B3. Have you **asked** for help from your state VR in the last 12 months?

☐ Yes ☐ No

B4. Did you get help in the last 12 months from a state VR counselor?

☐ Yes, got help
☐ No, didn't get help
☐ Put me on a "waiting list" for help

If **YES**, what kind of help did you get?

☐ Yes ☐ No Trained me for a job
☐ Yes ☐ No Gave me money for school
☐ Yes ☐ No Found a job for me
☐ Yes ☐ No Tested me
☐ Yes ☐ No Sent me·for medical examination (audiological, physical)
☐ Yes ☐ No Other (Explain.) _____

C. OTHER INFORMATION:

C1. In the last 12 months, did you get any money or benefits from any of these programs?

☐ Yes ☐ No Supplemental Security Income (SSI)
☐ Yes ☐ No Medicaid or state supported health care program
☐ Yes ☐ No Aid to Families with Dependent Children (AFDC)
☐ Yes ☐ No Public Assistance or Welfare
☐ Yes ☐ No Food Stamps
☐ Yes ☐ No Unemployment Insurance

C2. What is your home address?

Street _____

City _____ State _____ Zip _____

GALLAUDET UNIVERSITY

COUNSELOR QUESTIONNAIRE
SURVEY OF CAREER TRAINING
FOR HEARING IMPAIRED YOUTH

March 1987

TO: The Vocational/Career Counselor
        of the Student Named on the Label Above

FROM: Thomas Allen, Center Director
        Brenda Rawlings, Project Coordinator

RE: Career Training Survey

The student named on the above label has been selected for a special study being conducted by the Center for Assessment and Demographic Studies. This project will focus on an extremely important area — the transition of hearing impaired students from high school to the work world. The federal government as well as state and local school administrators have identified this topic as one of highest priority.

In our biennial publication, *College & Career Programs for Deaf Students,* we examine the postsecondary opportunities for deaf students. This year's project will look at the work experiences of deaf students, including the relationship of high school programs to the work world and to vocational rehabilitation. We believe the Annual Survey data base will enable us to study this area in depth.

Using the 1985-86 Annual Survey data base, we identified those students in your program who have a severe or profound hearing loss and are between the ages of 16 to 22. We have enclosed 2 sets of questionnaires with preprinted labels containing these students' names. One set of forms, the **Counselor Questionnaires,** are to be completed by you. The other set of forms, the **Student Questionnaires,** are to be completed by the students. There is one form for each student. They may need assistance from you, from other staff, or from their parents. **The students can complete the forms independently or you may want to use the forms as a class exercise** —whatever is most appropriate for those in the study.

GALLAUDET RESEARCH INSTITUTE
CENTER FOR ASSESSMENT AND DEMOGRAPHIC STUDIES
(202) 651-5575 (V/TDD)

KENDALL GREEN
800 FLORIDA AVENUE, N.E.
WASHINGTON, D.C. 20002

To limit your work, we have restricted the number of **Counselor Questionnaires** to be filled out. If your program contains more than 40 students identified for the study, we have randomly selected 40 for whom we are asking you to complete Counselor Questionnaires.

If a named student is no longer enrolled in your program, please complete Section A on the Counselor Questionnaire and the section at the bottom of the front of the Student Questionnaire. **Collect** all the completed forms **(both Student and Counselor Questionnaires)** and return them to us, no later than **April 30th,** in the postage-paid envelope(s) provided.

We would like to emphasize that the information collected is confidential; names of students or individual programs are never identified in our reports. In nineteen years of collecting large amounts of information on hearing impaired children and the schools they attend, we have never had a problem with confidentiality. (If you are more comfortable with deleting the name of the student, simply indicate that on the questionnaire and we will erase the name from the transition study data file. All we need is the CADS unique ID number on the label; we do not need to know names of students.)

We look forward to working on this important topic for deaf youth and their future and want to be sure that your school and students are represented in this national study. Results of the study will be mailed to you.

Thank you for your cooperation. If you have any questions regarding the questionnaires or the study, please do not hesitate to contact our office by mail or by phone at 800-672-6720, ext. 5575.

CONFIDENTIAL: Information which would allow identification of any individual or institution will not be released.

A. CURRENT ENROLLMENT STATUS:

A1. Is the student named on the front label currently enrolled in your program?

☐ Yes (Go to B.) ☐ No (Go to A2.)

A2. Which of the following best describes the manner in which the student left your program? (Check only one.)

☐ Graduated with diploma
☐ Graduated with certificate
☐ Left without graduating

A3. If the student left without graduating from your program, is the student currently enrolled at another secondary program?

☐ Yes (Specify name of program.) _____
☐ No
☐ Do Not Know

If the student is no longer enrolled in your program, stop here and return the form to the survey office.

B. COURSEWORK & TRAINING:

B1. Is the student receiving any kind of vocational training as part of an educational program?

☐ Yes (Go to B2.) ☐ No (Go to C.)

B2. Which of the following best describes the training the student receives? (Check only one.)

☐ Training **ONLY** as part of the official **school** curriculum (Go to B4.)
☐ Training **ONLY** at agencies **outside** of school (Go to B3.)
☐ Training **BOTH** at **school** and through agencies **outside** of school (Go to B3.)

B3. Through what agencies or programs outside of school does the student receive vocational training or assistance?

☐ Yes	☐ No	State Vocational Rehabilitation
☐ Yes	☐ No	Job Training Partnership Act (JTPA)
☐ Yes	☐ No	Private training agency or program
☐ Yes	☐ No	Employer (on-the-job training)
☐ Yes	☐ No	Rehabilitation center or facility
☐ Yes	☐ No	Other (Specify.) _____

Questions B4 through B7 pertain to the training and occupational areas listed below.

B4. Circle T for the vocational areas in which the student is currently receiving **training** either in or out of school.

B5. Circle C for those areas in which the student is receiving actual **coursework** in school.

B6. Circle O for those areas in which the student is receiving some form of **on-the-job** training at a work location either outside of school or in school in some non-course related setting (e.g., school cafeteria, maintenance department, central office.)

B7. Circle I for those areas in which the student is receiving training in an **integrated setting,** one in which the student interacts regularly with hearing students/co-workers in the training setting.

Training	Coursework	On-the-job Training	Integrated Training	
T	C	O	I	Agriculture, including horticulture
T	C	O	I	Auto Mechanics
T	C	O	I	Commercial Arts
T	C	O	I	Computer Programming/Operations
T	C	O	I	Construction Trades (e.g., carpentry, electrical, masonry, plumbing)
T	C	O	I	Cosmetology, Hairdressing, or Barbering
T	C	O	I	Drafting
T	C	O	I	Electronics
T	C	O	I	Home Economics, including dietetics & child care
T	C	O	I	Machine Shop
T	C	O	I	Medical or Dental Assisting
T	C	O	I	Practical Nursing
T	C	O	I	Quantity Food Occupations (e.g., "fast foods")
T	C	O	I	Sales or Merchandising
T	C	O	I	Secretarial, Stenographic, Typing, or Other Office Work
T	C	O	I	Welding
T	C	O	I	Other (Please specify.) _____

B8. Which of the following best describes the mix of academic and vocational training the student receives as part of the educational program? (Check only one.)

☐ All vocational training
☐ Mostly vocational with some academic training
☐ Roughly equal mix of vocational and academic training
☐ Mostly academic with some vocational training
☐ All academic training

C. PLACEMENT AND PLANNING:

C1. Does this student's school offer separate academic and vocational tracks?

☐ Yes (Go to C2.)   ☐ No (Go to C5.)

C2. In which track is the student enrolled? (Check only one.)

☐ Vocational
☐ Academic
☐ Both vocational & academic
☐ Other (Specify.) _____
☐ Student not yet placed in a track (At what grade do you anticipate making a track decision?

Grade: _____ (Go to C5.)

C3. In what grade was the tracking decision made for this student's current placement?

Grade: _____

C4. If the student's tracking placement has changed, in what grade was the original tracking decision made?

Grade: _____   ☐ Student's original track has not changed

C5. Indicate if tests contribute(d) to the tracking and/or course placement decisions for this student. For each type you check YES, please list the tests used. If the tests are self-made, please indicate that.

☐ Yes   ☐ No   Academic Achievement Tests _____

_____

☐ Yes   ☐ No   Vocational Assessment Tests _____

_____

☐ Yes   ☐ No   Social-Emotional Assessment _____

_____

C6. Has the local state rehabilitation agency developed an IWRP (Individual Written Rehabilitation Plan) for this student?

☐ Yes (Go to C7.)   ☐ No (Go to D.)

C7. Do you have a copy of the current IWRP on file with this student's records?

☐ Yes   ☐ No

D. EMPLOYMENT WHILE ENROLLED AT SCHOOL:

D1. Is the student currently employed?

☐ Yes (Go to D2.)   ☐ No (Skip remaining questions & return form.)
☐ Do Not Know (Skip remaining questions and return form.)

D2. How did the student get the job?

☐ Yes   ☐ No   Student's family helped
☐ Yes   ☐ No   Student's friends helped
☐ Yes   ☐ No   Student got the job by himself/herself
☐ Yes   ☐ No   High school counselor/teacher helped
☐ Yes   ☐ No   Vocational Rehabilitation (VR) helped
☐ Yes   ☐ No   A job placement agency helped
☐ Yes   ☐ No   Other (Specify.) _____

D3. Did the student get job training in high school to perform the **current job duties**?

☐ Yes   ☐ No   ☐ Did not receive any job training in high school

Index